PERGAMON INTERNATIONAL LIBRARY
of Science, Technology, Engineering and Social Studies
*The 1000-volume original paperback library in aid of education,
industrial training and the enjoyment of leisure*
Publisher: Robert Maxwell, M.C.

PERGAMON GENERAL PSYCHOLOGY SERIES

Editors: Arnold P. Goldstein, *Syracuse University*
Leonard Krasner, *SUNY, Stony Brook*

Interpersonal Communication

KURT DANZIGER

PGPS-53

—— Publisher's Notice to Educators ——

THE PERGAMON TEXTBOOK
INSPECTION COPY SERVICE

An inspection copy of any book published in the Pergamon International Library
will gladly be sent without obligation for consideration for course adoption or
recommendation. Copies may be retained for a period of 60 days from receipt and
returned if not suitable. When a particular title is adopted or recommended for
adoption for class use and the recommendation results in a sale of 12 or more copies,
the inspection copy may be retained with our compliments. If after examination
the lecturer decides that the book is not suitable for adoption but would like to
retain it for his personal library, then our Educators' Discount of 10% is allowed on
the invoiced price. The Publishers will be pleased to receive suggestions for revised
editions and new titles to be published in this important International Library.

Interpersonal Communication

Kurt Danziger
York University

PERGAMON PRESS INC.

New York · Toronto · Oxford
Sydney · Paris · Braunschweig

U. K.	Pergamon Press Ltd., Headington Hill Hall, Oxford OX3 0BW, England
U. S. A.	Pergamon Press Inc., Maxwell House, Fairview Park, Elmsford, New York 10523, U.S.A.
C A N A D A	Pergamon of Canada Ltd., 207 Queen's Quay West, Toronto 1, Canada
A U S T R A L I A	Pergamon Press (Aust.) Pty. Ltd., 19a Boundary Street, Rushcutters Bay, N.S.W. 2011, Australia
F R A N C E	Pergamon Press SARL, 24 rue des Ecoles, 75240 Paris, Cedex 05, France
WEST GERMANY	Pergamon Press GmbH, D-3300 Braunschweig, Postfach 2923, Burgplatz 1, West Germany

First edition 1976

Library of Congress Cataloging in Publication Data
Danziger, Kurt.
    Interpersonal communication.
    (Pergamon general psychology series; 53)
    Includes bibliographical references.
    1. Communication--Psychological aspects.
I. Title. [DNLM: 1. Communication. 2. Inter-
personal relations. BF637.C45 D199i]
BF637.C45D33   301.14   74-26809
ISBN 0-08-018756-0
ISBN 0-08-018757-9

Printed in Great Britain by A. Wheaton & Co., Exeter

Contents

Preface

While the volume of research in the area of interpersonal communication has increased greatly during the last decade, the material remains scattered in various journals and publications devoted to such diverse fields as social psychology, child development, psychiatry, speech and communication, animal behavior, clinical psychology, sociology, and anthropology. As a result the growing number of students of the area are faced with an enormous task of coordination and integration. It is the purpose of this book to make a contribution to this task and to discuss the general issues that emerge from work in this area.

In the second place the book is intended as a contribution to the literature of social psychology. It is this discipline that should be concerned with the study of the basic processes of interpersonal communication and with a consideration of the most general issues in this area of research. However, the standard social psychological texts tend to pay little attention to these topics. This is due to a preoccupation with the outcomes rather than the processes of social interaction and to the dominance of a social influence model of interpersonal relationships in which the two-way effects of communication are ignored in favor of one-way effects. By way of contrast the present volume emphasizes the importance of reciprocal influence processes in face-to-face interaction.

The selection of material has been governed by its relevance to conceptual and methodological issues shared by several disciplines insofar as their work converges on the area of interpersonal communication. The integration of portions of this material has led to some new conceptual distinctions and tentative generalizations that are intended to stimulate further discussion and research in this area.

An earlier draft of the book has been successfully used in advanced courses in interpersonal communication, and in its present form it should also prove useful in certain interdisciplinary courses. Apart from its use by social psychologists it may well be of interest to those working in neighboring disciplines who require a social psychological treatment of the subject that is more closely related to their concerns than a standard social psychology text.

I wish to take this opportunity of expressing my gratitude to Alan Campbell, Esther Greenglass, Irwin Silverman, and Peter Ziffo whose insights and comments were invaluable in connection with the preparation of various parts of this volume. Dulcis Prendergast and Ursula Wiggins displayed unusual patience and understanding in typing the manuscript. A special word of thanks is due to Gerald Deegan of Pergamon Press whose help and encouragement were always forthcoming when most needed.

KURT DANZIGER

Acknowledgments

Permission to reprint material is gratefully acknowledged from the following: Collins Publishers, London, and McGraw-Hill Book Co., New York for excerpts from *The Jail Diary of Albie Sachs* in Chapter 1; Mr. Z. Stypulkowski and Walker & Co., New York for excerpts from *Invitation to Moscow* in Chapter 1; Alfred A. Knopf, Inc., New York, and McClelland and Stewart Ltd., Canadian publisher for excerpts from *The Big Sell* by P. Berton in Chapter 1; Williams & Wilkins Co., Baltimore and F. E. Inbau and J. E. Reid for excerpts from *Criminal Interrogation and Confessions* © 1967 in Chapter 1; John Wiley & Sons Inc., New York for excerpts from J. H. Flavell, *The Development of Role-Taking Skills in Children* © 1968 in Chapter 8; The Society for Research in Child Development for the figure in Chapter 8; Academic Press Inc., New York and Dr. S. M. Ervin-Tripp for the two figures in Chapter 3 from "Sociolinguistics" by S. M. Ervin-Tripp in *Advances in Experimental Social Psychology*, Vol. 4.

The Author

Kurt Danziger (D. Phil. University of Oxford, England) is Professor of Psychology at York University, Toronto, Canada. He has held university teaching and research appointments in Australia, Indonesia, and South Africa. His primary interests are in methodology and theory related to the study of processes of interpersonal interaction, socialization, and the history of psychology. He has made numerous contributions to scholarly publications and has edited a volume of readings on socialization. He is also the author of a book on socialization which has been translated into several European languages. He is a Fellow of the Canadian Psychological Association and has been a member of working groups of that body and of the Social Science Research Council of Canada concerned with various aspects of research policy.

Introduction

In spite of some notable exceptions the discipline of social psychology continues to suffer from the consequences of a long outmoded set of basic assumptions whose basic perspectives not only reduce the significance of many of its research studies but severely limit the importance of these studies for the understanding of vital areas of human interaction.

Some of these assumptions are a relic of the historical fact that, at least in North America, social psychology has been largely an outgrowth of the study of individual psychology and has been slow to develop its own fundamental perspectives and shed the metatheoretical burdens of its ancestor.

Among these traditional preconceptions, going back to at least the nineteenth century and sometimes beyond, the doctrine of an essentially atomistic, monadic view of the individual plays a special role. It has led to a marked tendency to explain the phenomena of social interaction in essentially intraindividual terms like social motives, attitudes, cognitive balancing mechanisms, personality characteristics, and so on. Viewing social processes in terms of the influence that one set of intraindividual variables has on similar variables in another individual has led to a relative neglect of the process of communication, which constitutes the ongoing interrelationship *between* individuals. The possibility that the relationships among individuals may be immanent in the messages that pass between them has too often been neglected in favor of a reification of purely individual qualities that are supposed to express themselves in these messages (Bateson, 1972).

A closely related preconception is based on an excessively rationalistic or a closely related utilitarian view of man which in social psychology leads to the presupposition that what is exchanged between individuals is information (in a restricted cognitive sense) or reinforcements of essentially intraindividual dispositions. This leads to an elevation of the verbal code to the level of a prototype for all communication (cf. Wiener *et al.*, 1972) and to the conception of changes in the communication process solely in terms of intraindividual learning mechanisms that are not essentially different from the learning that takes place in a nonsocial context.

Such a perspective is indissolubly linked with methodological prescriptions that are based on an essentially linear model of cause and effect relationships, as in classical physics. Instead of attempts to study reciprocal interindividual relationships we get investigations of one-way influences based on a sharp distinction between antecedent and consequent variables. The applicability of studies based on a rigid distinction between sources and recipients of influence to situations where mutual influence prevails must be seriously questioned. Nor is it likely that the role of the wider social context can be effectively dealt with by a mere multiplication of discrete antecedent variables in conventional research designs. The basic limitations of the linear social influence model are that it proceeds as though the cybernetic revolution in science had never happened, as though feedback mechanisms had no place in human interaction, and as though social psychological events could be treated as closed systems rather than open systems which maintain a constant interchange of information and energy across their boundaries.

If we are to escape from the aridities of much of the conventional social psychological literature and develop an alternative perspective, it would be healthy to begin by taking a look at what actually happens in a few real-life situations marked by strenuous attempts at exerting influence in a face-to-face setting. Chapter 1 represents a step in this direction, taking its chief examples from the exercise of salesmanship and from the interrogation of prisoners—criminal, military, and political.

What are some of the more striking features of such situations in the light of our fundamental concerns? The first thing we might notice is that the interchanges between salesman and potential customer or between interrogator and prisoner are essentially concerned with the definition of their interrelationship. On a purely rational level questions of outcome are clearly involved: Is the potential customer going to buy? Is the prisoner going to confess or supply desired information? But the nature of these outcomes is deeply dependent on the interpersonal relationship that develops between the contestants. Every practical guide to salesmen and to interrogators recognizes this most explicitly. If a certain structure can be imposed on the interpersonal relationship the desired outcome can be relied upon, irrespective of purely rational or utilitarian considerations, and the successful resistance of the "target" person depends equally on establishing an alternative definition of the interpersonal relationship.

What does the imposition of a particular definition of the interpersonal relationship mean in practice? It certainly does not mean an explicit verbal agreement but rather the eliciting of the appropriate social *feedback* from the other person whose communications must imply his *implicit* acceptance of the proposed interpersonal relationship. Without such appropriate feedback the influence attempt fails. Typically, the contest between the participants in such situations is not decided at once; in the case of political prisoners it generally develops over a period of many months. But even where the time scale is relatively brief the picture is one of a stepwise development of reciprocal feedback, gradually proceeding in a certain direction. Strictly speaking the communication process is not by any means circular because it never returns to its starting point and because both participants actively throw in new material; a spiral or helix provides a better pictorial model of what takes place (Dance, 1967), although such an image exaggerates the element of progressive development and does not allow for the sudden changes of direction and ups and downs which often characterize these situations.

The process of psychotherapy, which is examined in Chapter 6, provides an illustration of essentially the same principles of interpersonal communication in a practical setting. Traditionally, this process has been analyzed in terms of the intrapersonal dispositions of the participants, the personality structure of the patient, and the skills of the therapist. Such formulations automatically lead to a linear model of the psychotherapeutic process in which influence passes unidirectionally from therapist to client. But a number of studies reviewed in Chapter 6 have shown quite clearly that the client in his turn influences the style of the therapist quite profoundly. Unintended affective expressions and manipulation of the interaction by declining appropriate feedback or providing paradoxical feedback are not the prerogative of the therapist. At the same time, both the verbal and the nonverbal communication of the members of this dyadic system may, over a period of time, show convergencies that are anything but deliberate.

The fact that the study of social skills requires a very different level of analysis from the investigation of individual capacities emerges very clearly from the perspective of individual development, which forms the basis of Chapter 8. Not only must we make a clear distinction between the development of linguistic competence and the development of communication competence, but the relative scarcity of studies with the latter perspective provides cause for reflection on the individual-centered predilections of research traditions in this field. The phenomenon of "private speech," for example, has little bearing on the child's motive to communicate but a great deal of significance for its deficiencies in role-taking capacities, the development of which appears to play a crucial role in the growth of communication competence.

Some further examples of the need to apply a transactional rather than a linear model of social influence are considered in Chapter 10, and this leads to some general considerations about the wider theoretical and methodological implications of these types of model. What the transactional model searches for are not linear chains of cause and effect but nonrandom patterns of interaction sequences unfolding over a period of time. The discovery of order, or redundancy, in interaction sequences provides clues for the constraints that operate on the system. By shifting its focus from questions about *what* influence individuals have on one another to questions about *how* they influence one another, social psychology also shifts its data base from "before and after" measures, that is to say, aggregate data based on the properties of individuals, to process data that are concerned with the mechanisms of interindividual communication as such. Some of the more promising examples of the use of process data are to be found in studies of communication in natural groups, like families, and these are discussed in Chapter 7.

If the study of the processes and mechanisms of interpersonal communication is to be more than a collection of disconnected measures, it must be directed toward the discovery of the contribution of these processes to the establishment and maintenance of a pattern of interpersonal order or structure. The existence of such a structure arises from three kinds of consideration. First, the interaction of individuals takes place in space and time. The way in which space and time are allocated in the process of interaction is not random but shows certain empirical regularities that depend on the exchange of social signals. As shown in Chapter 5, this process can be observed quite clearly in groups of subhuman primates. The distance that members of such groups maintain between themselves and the way in which they place themselves relative to one another show a certain pattern that is a reflection of the social relationships in the group. Similarly, there are regularities in the way in which their interaction is patterned over periods of time. Examples of the use of nonverbal signals to achieve a similar regulation of space and time in human interaction are considered in Chapter 4. Primates do not live in a physical but in a socialized spatiotemporal framework. The construction of such a framework involves the regulatory and monitoring functions of interindividual communication.

Second, certain constraints are imposed on human interaction by the fact that individuals share a similar biological equipment. This fact determines the number and nature of the channels available for the transmission of interpersonal communication and the kinds of messages that can be conveniently transmitted through each channel. But as these channels act simultaneously rather than in turn, messages from several channels interact. The pattern of this interaction must depend in part on the nature of the channels themselves and is therefore also subject to inherent constraints which constitute a further source of nonrandomness, or order, for interpersonal communication. Insofar as the state of current research permits it this aspect receives some attention in Chapter 4.

The extent to which inherent features of the channel determine the content of the messages it transmits is not a question to which a definitive answer is possible at present. However, the fact that current evidence seems to favor the existence of some cross-cultural generality in this respect is discussed in Chapter 9, taking the classical question of the link between facial expression and emotional meaning as an example.

The third aspect of orderliness or structure in interpersonal transactions arises out of the fact that such transactions must involve some selection from the potentially infinite pool of communications that could conceivably pass between the participants. The task or purpose of the transaction, as well as the mood and personal inclinations of the participants, obviously supply some of the criteria that form the basis of such a selection. These factors have received sufficient attention in the past, but what has too often been overlooked is the existence of a further set of criteria that has its source in the nature of the social relationship between the interactants. Whatever their purpose or personal preference individuals modulate their messages by considering the relationship in which they stand to the person or persons being addressed. They simply do not address themselves in the same way to various friends, to different members of their family, to strangers, or to all kinds of people they meet in their work relationships. On one level this is simply a matter of specific social role requirements. But at a higher level of abstraction every one of these relationships involves a limited set of dimensions along which all interpersonal relationships can be shown to vary. These are the dimensions of intimacy, status, and solidarity; and the converging lines of evidence that point to their existence are considered in Chapter 3. It is the operation of such universal parameters that provides the basis for much of the observed regularity in the structure of interpersonal communication.

The referents of interpersonal communication are of three types: They may be matters in the external environment, they may constitute subjectives states of the interactants, or they may involve the relationship among the communicators themselves. Communication about the environment is impersonal in its pure form but in face-to-face communication is always embedded in a personal matrix. Much of what masquerades as communication about the environment carries strong personal overtones and in fact communicates much more personal than objective information. Much "communication" about subjective states is not communication at all but expression whose status as communication involves difficult problems of encoding and decoding, which have been thoroughly discussed by Dittman (1973). The present volume emphasizes the importance of communication about the relationship among the communicators which forms such a large component of face-to-face interaction.

This component assumes proportions because it provides the matrix in which the other components of communication are embedded. It has too often been assumed that the social matrix of interpersonal communication can simply be specified in terms of role definitions externally imposed on the interaction system. This ignores the fact that such definitions are only maintained by a constant flow of signals within the system, a fact that is not only demonstrated by the careful study of group structure in subhuman primates but that emerges clearly in sociolinguistic studies of address systems and language registers to which reference is made in various parts of this book.

Moreover, the limitation of the definition of the relationship among communicators to general social norms overlooks the large area of interpersonal relationships that these norms leave undefined. Except in the marginal case of extremely formal relationships, the precise structure and often the most significant features of the relationship must be negotiated within the relationship process itself. As the practical examples considered earlier have shown, this involves the continuous reciprocal definition and counterdefinition of the relationship that is at the same time a definition of the more specific social identity of the participants. A consideration of the different kinds of feedback mechanisms involved in this process leads to the consideration of possible pathological consequences in the last part of Chapter 7, which is concerned with the special case of interaction in families.

In order to obtain a fundamental understanding of the nature of the type of communication among human communicators that defines their relationship, it is necessary to recognize that its messages are characterized by a special feature that is not found in other types of messages. This feature involves a question of coding, or the relationship between signifier and signified. Under the influence of the prestigious model of information theory and the tendency to take language as the prototype for all communication a certain type of relationship between sign and referent has generally been taken for granted. The sign *represents* the referent in terms of a shared code, and what it communicates about the referent is either true or untrue. But when I choose a certain form of address, tone of voice or position vis-à-vis my partner in a face-to-face transaction I do not represent our relationship, I *present* it. The relationship has no existence outside the relevant messages that pass between us. My message is not an assertion about the *truth* of something that exists independently of our relationship but a claim about the *validity* of my definition of that relationship. The truth of statements is established by an independent checking of the objective facts, the validity of a claim is confirmed by the kind of interpersonal feedback that occurs as part of the relationship. This distinction is further discussed in Chapter 2, and it underlies the selection of material in much of the rest of the book.

The distinction between presentation and representation is not by any means identical with the distinction between verbal and nonverbal channels of communication (or between "digital" and "analog" coding*). Presentation may be verbal, as in address systems, and representation may be nonverbal, as in a picture. One of the most interesting aspects of human interpersonal relationships is that they are not only presented but also represented, usually in words, but occasionally also in diagrams or even in gestures. Like all representations such depictions can be tested for their truth value, that is, for the correctness with which they signify the presentations that they claim to represent. The question of congruence between presentation and representation usually becomes important in disturbances of interpersonal communication, a matter that receives

---

*Digital coding makes use of arbitrary signs, analog coding of "iconic" signs. This distinction is briefly discussed in Chapter 2. For an interesting speculative discussion of the significance of iconic communication see Wilden (1972).

some consideration in parts of Chapters 6 and 7. In this connection it should also be noted that the distinction between presentation and representation is not equivalent to the distinction between communication and metacommunication (e.g. Watzlawick, Beavin, and Jackson, 1967). A metacommunication is simply a communication about a communication, e.g. "this message is not meant seriously," or, "ignore this message." Such metacommunications may constitute presentations (as in forms of address), or they may not. Similarly, communications themselves may be representations, as when they convey impersonal information, or they may be presentations of various aspects of an interpersonal relationship. Disturbed communication may involve paradoxical presentations or lack of congruence between presentations and their representation. Some of the controversy and confusion surrounding the theory of the "double-bind" and related positions may well arise from a failure to achieve clarity about this distinction.

The study of presentations on the nonverbal level is greatly assisted by the fact that interpersonal communication utilizes channels that can be readily distinguished by the fact that they involve different somatic mechanisms, such as gross body movement, facial expression, gaze direction, voice quality, and so on. On the verbal level this is not the case, and this is one of the reasons why the study of interpersonal presentation on this level has not advanced beyond certain tentative beginnings. For a long time global measures of interaction styles, as discussed in Chapter 3, were our only source of quantitative data in this area. But these measures are not designed to yield information about the specific verbal channels through which interpersonal presentations are communicated. More recently the analysis of address systems has demonstrated what can be achieved in this respect. The study of language registers, mentioned in Chapter 9, and the partially related work of Moscovici and his co-workers (1967) has alerted us to another aspect of verbal communication with implications for the presentation of social relationships. Further promising beginnings are to be found in the isolation of the channel of "immediacy" in verbal communication by Wiener and Mehrabian (1968), and in the analysis of conversational structure by Sacks (1972).

The appendix to the present volume presents a practical guide to the analysis of yet another aspect of the verbal presentation of interpersonal relationships, namely, the use of rhetorical codes. Such codes become operative in face-to-face situations whenever it is a matter of resolving an interpersonal conflict by means of verbal exchange. The conflict may involve diverging interpretations of situations or a divergence of interests.

In these cases the participants seek to convince each other of the correctness of their point of view by the use of verbal strategies. On the surface much of the content of the discussion may consist of more or less rational considerations about the situation that has caused the conflict, but the form in which the relevant statements are made always implies claims about the interpersonal relationship among the communicators. Ultimately, the issue is likely to be decided not by purely logical arguments, but by the outcome of the interpersonal maneuvering that takes place. For example, one participant may succeed in establishing himself or herself as an expert while the other is a relative ignoramus, so that the former's interpretation ought to prevail. Alternatively, one participant might seek to establish his or her claim to a status difference that legitimizes his or her right to make demands that the other will obey, or establish a position where his or her subjective preferences or evaluations are to be taken more seriously than those of the other. It is possible to categorize each statement in such an interchange in terms of its functional contribution to various kinds of interpersonal outcome. The coding scheme evolved for this purpose has proved useful in a number of empirical studies and has an in-built flexibility that makes it potentially applicable to a variety of interpersonal situations.

It is necessary to conclude this introductory section on a note of caution concerning the semantics of interpersonal communication. The successful use of artificial communication systems has had effects on our thinking about human communication that have by no means been an unmixed blessing. Artificial systems are based on codes with a fixed number of elements that cannot be added to, moreover, the meaning of each element is arbitrarily fixed and purely denotative, i.e. depends purely on its relationship to its referent and not on its relationship to other elements. Such codes have the function of reducing uncertainty. But the codes used in interpersonal communication are not of this type. Even language in its purely representative function is a constantly changing system in which the stock of words and their meaning is not fixed and in which meaning depends as much on the relationship of words to other words as on their relationship to their referents, i.e. it is connotative as well as denotative. Nor does its use necessarily reduce uncertainty. While artificial languages are closed systems, natural languages are open systems (Parry, 1967).

In communication about interpersonal relationships and particularly in communication by presentation the same considerations hold. We must guard against the temptation to interpret anything that is said about this subject in terms that are not appropriate to open systems. In particular we must constantly bear in mind that the meaning of messages is not fixed once and for all but depends on the social setting in which they occur, on other messages being communicated at the same time, and on the pattern of messages that passes between communicators over a period of time. In this field it is less important to pin one's faith on the mechanisms of uncertainty reduction than to learn to live with ambiguity.

REFERENCES

Bateson, G. (1972). *Steps to an Ecology of Mind.* New York: Ballantine.

Dance, F. E. X. (1967). Toward a theory of human communication. In F. E. X. Dance (Ed.), *Human Communication Theory: Original Essays.* New York: Holt, Rinehart & Winston.

Dittman, A. T. (1973). *Interpersonal Messages of Emotion.* New York: Springer.

Moscovici, S. (1967). Communication processes and the properties of language. In L. Berkowitz (Ed.), *Advances in Experimental Social Psychology.* Vol. 3. New York: Academic Press.

Parry, J. (1967). *The Psychology of Human Communication.* London: University of London Press.

Sacks, H. (1972). An initial investigation of the usability of conversational data for doing sociology. In D. Sudnow (Ed.), *Studies in Social Interaction.* New York: Free Press.

Watzlawick, P., Beavin, J. H., and Jackson, D. D. (1967). *Pragmatics of Human Communication.* New York: Norton.

Wiener, M. and Mehrabian, A. (1968). *Language within Language: Immediacy a Channel in Verbal Communication.* New York: Appleton-Century-Crofts.

Wiener, M., Devoe, S., Rubinow, S., and Geller, J. (1972). Nonverbal behavior and nonverbal communication. *Psychol. Rev.*, **79**, 185–214.

Wilden, A. (1972). *System and Structure: Essays in Communication and Exchange.* London: Tavistock.

CHAPTER 1

The Manipulation of Interpersonal Communication

SALESMANSHIP

The Salesman versus Mrs. Jones

Let us begin with the proverbial vacuum cleaner salesman. The scene is Mrs. Jones' living room and the actors are Mrs. Jones and the salesman who is just closing in for the kill.

> "You like the special action brush then?"
> "Oh yes."
> "And you understand how all these other features (points) will help you?"
> "Sure."
> "You said you appreciated the ease of operation particularly?"
> "That's right."
> "So you're convinced that a Hoover will make your work easier?"
> "Hm hm."
> "And you do admit that buying later won't help you now, don't you?"
> "I guess so."
> "In fact you owe it to your family to get one now, isn't that right?"
> "Yeah."
> "So you have decided to take this model then?"
> "O.K."

The deed is done, the sale is closed, and a proved and tried sales technique has scored another victory.

We have witnessed a little example of face-to-face communication that runs off smoothly in accordance with a script that one of the participants has rehearsed only too well. But what happens when both parties to the interaction follow their own script and the scripts do not agree? Tired of

1

being manipulated, Mrs. Jones has taken some lessons in how to deal with salesmen who are too smart, and the next time one of them comes around the following interchange takes place:

> "You are interested in better nutrition and health for your family if it's possible to get it aren't you, Mrs. Jones?"
> "No."
> "No?"
> "They're too healthy now. They're running me ragged. I'm going to start feeding them less. They've had too many vitamins, that's the trouble. They're going to burn themselves out."
> "But surely you want them to be properly fed?"
> "That's been the problem—too *much* food. I'm cutting them right off milk next week, soon's I use up the box of crystals. Maybe that'll help quieten my husband down nights." (From P. Berton, 1963, p. 237).

Of course the sale doesn't go through. What has happened to Mrs. Jones? In her own small way she has become a student of interpersonal communication; she has become wise to some of the techniques salesmen use to obtain compliance and is using them for her own defense.

Let us see what it is that she has learned. In the first place she has discovered that the salesman's questions are traps—they are attractive invitations that cut off her line of retreat and limit her freedom of movement to the point where her only reasonable alternative is to buy. So she refuses to accept even the most innocent of these invitations and preserves her freedom of maneuver.

But what is the nature of the trap the salesman prepares? What makes the Mrs. Jones' of this world vulnerable to his techniques? Clearly, it has something to do with the impression created by her answers. She will be judged by her replies, and she wants to avoid an adverse judgment. It takes some guts to present oneself as the kind of woman who does not want her family to be properly fed or the kind of person who does not believe in education for his children. So much is obvious, but people are equally reluctant to appear inconsistent without good reason, to accept all the advantages of a course of action and then to refuse to embark on that course. Once the salesman has deprived her of valid excuses Mrs. Jones' resistance crumbles because she does not wish to present herself as an unreasonable person who will be thought stupid, silly, or odd.

Mrs. Jones' newly found sales resistance depends on her realization that her communication with salesmen does not simply deal with vacuum cleaners, health foods or encyclopedias, but that it deals also with personalities, her own in particular. The salesmen of course recognized this all along. That is why they use flattery to link adoption of their product with a favorable self-image that the potential buyer will be reluctant to repudiate: "Our more discriminating customers prefer these. . . . To an experienced person like yourself I don't need to stress that. . . . To someone who puts his children's future first it will be obvious that. . . ." They are equally quick to supply rationalizations to protect the customer's saintly image against the suspicion of selfishness or impulsiveness: "These shoes not only look better, they are also more advisable from a health point of view. . . . You'll have more time for the kids if you can cut down on these chores. . . . After all these sacrifices you deserve a little relaxation."

Becoming sensitized to the interpersonal implications of successful salesmanship will help to fortify Mrs. Jones' resistance up to a point, but if her insight went no further her stance would remain merely defensive. However, her replies on the subject of health foods show her as a real "hard head," and the successful hard head, like the successful salesman is aggressive rather than passive. Instead of meekly accepting the salesman's leads she throws out some of her own, and they are such as to preclude her from buying the product. She has realized, what the salesman knew from the start, that this is a struggle for control. The questions he put to her are just so many ways of controlling the situation and defining it in his terms. Now she takes over and redefines the situation in *her* terms. This disarms him because he is no longer laying down the rules according to which the game is to be played.

Of course, if she had been really determined she might have saved herself some time by taking the initiative at the very beginning of their encounter. Like this perhaps:

> "Good afternoon, madam, I represent the Family Counseling Division of the National Home Service League."
> "Is that a Communist front organization?"
> "Wh-at?"
> "My husband is in a sensitive industry. Have you been cleared for security?"
> "Well, just a minute. My company is one of the largest. . . ."
> "How do I know that? There are spies everywhere."
> "Freedom's arsenal is a vigilant America. Don't you agree?"
> "Why, yes, but. . . ."
> "You bring your security clearance along, properly stamped and countersigned, and we'll talk again."   (P. Berton, 1963, p. 231).

By this time Mrs. Jones has become more bold in the manipulation of interpersonal communication than the salesmen who call on here. She has understood that in interacting with each other, individuals must define their relationship. The salesman wants to define it in a way that casts him in the role of the supremely well-qualified advisor, so she retaliates by proposing a definition that is as remote from this as possible. If she is quick to snatch the initiative she can make her definition prevail and pull the rug from under his feet.

Some Hints for the Successful Salesman

Much more commonly, of course, it is the salesman's definition that wins the day. He arms himself for the encounter by following the manuals that tell him to check his outward appearance, to avoid flashy or sloppy clothing, extreme hair styles, and unbrushed teeth. He tries to assume a confident posture, to simulate a smile, and to control his gaze and facial expression. He knows that people do not communicate by speech alone and that he must present an acceptable first impression if he is to gain any ground for maneuver.

The salesman's appearance and manner are calculated to present him as a reliable sort of person who is not to be lightly suspected of shady dealing. What he tries to do is to project an image of himself that makes it difficult to question his credentials and motives. His speech may be of vacuum cleaners, encyclopedias or health foods, but his appearance and manner are directed at the control of the interpersonal relationship with the potential customer. For his success the latter is actually more important than the former. The mere fact of his presence on the doorstep bears witness that personal confrontation sets up pressures of an altogether different magnitude to those generated by printed information. If people were essentially persuaded by information alone the printed brochure would completely replace the salesman and "personalized" selling would never have been thought of. The very existence of salesmen proves how little we trust the effect of information that is not embedded in an interpersonal setting.

Face-to-face confrontation with another person sets up pressures that are peculiarly difficult to resist. The source of these pressures lies less in the objective information that the other person offers than in the demands made by his personality. If he successfully presents himself as the embodiment of conventional virtues there are quite serious penalties involved in contradicting him. One must accept the risk of being exposed as a slob, a dumb clod who does not know his own interests, a saboteur of accepted values, an egotist, or worse. Far easier to go along with his definition of the situation and end up a few dollars poorer.

The key to successful salesmanship lies in making one's own definition of the situation prevail. This definition involves the enactment of a scenario in which salesman and customer each have their allotted place. No gaps must mar the smooth presentation of one's own part in the scenario. Even fumbling for a pencil or an order blank can create opportunities for a redefinition of the situation by the prospective catch. The successful salesman radiates confidence in his own part in the scenario; he is advised to act so as to take the compliance of the potential customer for granted. Before the customer has explicitly given his consent he is to start wrapping the product or writing the order, ask whether the prospect is paying cash or using the "easy-payment" plan, inquire whether the black model is preferred over models in other colors, determine how the product is to be delivered. All these techniques involve an "implied consent" to the sale, a powerful lever to ensure compliance (Gross, 1959). The successful salesman knows how to avoid arguments and tries not to take objections seriously, otherwise he would be allowing his quarry the right to present a definition of the situation that runs counter to the scenario that the salesman is attempting to impose.

Quite obviously the secret of successful sales resistance lies on one's ability to impose one's own definition of the situation that one is enacting with the salesman. That means boldly presenting an image of oneself or of the salesman that is totally at variance with the scenario the salesman desires to enact. One may present oneself as a slob who cares nothing for conventional values of polite society or one may question the integrity of the salesman in an unanswerable manner. Am I to be sold an encyclopedia? Not if I pour scorn on the value of book learning. Am I to give a hearing to a helpful expert on home appliances? Not if I define him as a security risk. These are humorously exaggerated examples, but they illustrate the point that is at issue between the salesman and his prospect: Whose definition of the interpersonal relationship is to prevail?

Of course this issue is not limited to the interaction between salesmen and their more or less unwilling clients. A husband and wife often show the same concern in their relationship to each other. Perhaps each party would like to present themselves as the blameless victim of the other's oppression, and each attempts to maneuver the other into the role assigned to them in their own private scenario. Or the issue may be about who is to appear as a tower of strength and who as a tower of virtue. Two colleagues may engage in subtle maneuvers to prove to each other who is the real expert and who the relative tyro. Even where there is no real dispute about the nature of the relationship the mutually accepted definition still needs to be **constantly** displayed and confirmed if doubt and anxiety are to be avoided. Superior status is seldom so secure as to dispense with appropriate outward trappings and demands for explicit recognition. Whether desired or accomplished, definitions of interpersonal situations require a flow of *communication* to maintain themselves.

The crucial difference between the definition of an interpersonal relationship that is merely desired and one that has been accomplished is the provision of appropriate feedback by the partner. The salesman would like to cast his prospect in a certain role, but he has not succeeded until the prospect provides the feedback appropriate to that role. To become a buyer, one must say "yes" or sign the order. But these are only the final steps in a process that begins by accepting the salesman's right to be listened to and that progresses through expressions of interest and manifestations of desire. Successful salesmanship involves considerable skill in eliciting the appropriate forms of feedback at each stage.

"Perhaps nothing is more disconcerting to a salesman than to be permitted to go through his demonstration without the prospect's batting an eye.... Seldom will an experienced salesman involve himself in such a fix. He will stop. He will ask for questions. He will bring the prospect into the presentation" (Gross, 1959, p. 345). By contrast, the ineffective salesman tends to rely on what has been called the stimulus–response approach to his craft (Thompson, 1966). He rattles on according to a canned script learned by rote, relying on the power of a series of key stimuli to evoke a favorable response: "This is a real opportunity, a real money-maker.... The market is really ready for these.... You'll really enjoy having one of these in your home." But he does not wait for confirmatory feedback and so misses the crucial point in the interpersonal situation that exists between him and the prospect. People do not react passively and automatically to the content of verbal messages. Their reactions are determined by the definition of the interpersonal relationship they have accepted, and without feedback the salesman has no means of knowing whether his definition is shared by his listener.

Lack of sensitivity to the principles of interpersonal communication has meant frustration and disappointment for many a salesman. Good salesmen are rarely able to generalize effectively about their skills. But certainly they appreciate the fact that they must obtain confirmatory feedback from the prospect to show that he is actively accepting the role in which he is being cast. Conversely, the lack of such feedback causes them to alter their presentation to fit the circumstances. They are alive to the crucial role of two-way communication in any interpersonal confrontation (Crissy and Kaplan, 1969).

The position of the salesman or of his prospect is by no means unique. Effectiveness in interpersonal situations requires considerable sensitivity to the ways in which people communicate their relationship to one another. The selling situation serves as a useful starting point for a consideration of face-to-face confrontation because in this case the purpose of at least one and perhaps both the parties is so explicit and concrete. The significance of various maneuvers and stratagems can therefore be judged in terms of an unambiguous criterion of success. But things are not so very different when the goals of interaction appear less clearly in the consciousness of the participants. As we have seen, husbands and wives as well as friends and professional associates also seek to give certain definitions to their relationships, and in doing this they have to rely on the same basic processes of interpersonal communication as the salesman.

Ordinarily these processes are simply taken for granted and receive little attention. Some individuals are more skillful at handling these processes than others, but they hardly know how they do it. This makes the systematic study of what actually happens in interpersonal communication particularly fascinating. Such systematic study will of course require much careful experimentation and controlled observation. But as a first step it is quite useful to analyze one or two interpersonal situations in which the goals of at least one of the participants are as clear and deliberate as those of the salesman.

THE INTERROGATION OF PRISONERS

Alternatives to Torture

One situation that provides quite exceptional opportunities for the manipulation of interpersonal communication occurs in the interrogation of prisoners. This may take the form of police interrogation of criminal suspects, the interrogation of prisoners of war by intelligence officers, or the pressuring of political prisoners by officials who specialize in this kind of work. The principles of manipulation are much the same in spite of many differences in context. They involve a careful and deliberate psychological assault on the prisoner's resistance in order to produce an outcome desired by the interrogator.

Physical assault and third-degree methods are of course occasionally resorted to by interrogators of prisoners, but are avoided for good reason in the majority of cases. They are apt to lead to unfavorable publicity, they involve infringements of legal regulations or international conventions, they are often incompatible with the interrogator's self-image as the representative of a higher morality, and confessions extracted by physical force are apt to be retracted when this force can no longer be exercized, as in public trials. Above all, physical torture is not an effective technique when it is a matter of securing a broader form of compliance rather than the extraction of highly specific items of information. It is apt to generate deep resistance to the interrogator and the institutions he represents and is therefore inadvisable in situations where the life of the prisoner is not regarded as totally expendable (Biderman, 1957; Farago, 1954). If some value is placed on the prisoner's life, even if this only arises out of his potential usefulness after the period of interrogation or out of a fear of reprisals, it is unwise to resort to physical torture. Only systems that have no further use for the prisoner as a human being have used physical torture systematically; in other cases the physical assault of prisoners is apt to be the sporadic result of the extreme exasperation and frustration of the interrogator. This is often correctly interpreted as a kind of victory by the prisoner. In these instances the assault is apt to strengthen rather than weaken resistance.

Psychological techniques of interrogation, in situations where the systematic use of torture is proscribed, have a very impressive record of success. Police statistics indicate that more than 80% of all criminal cases in the United States are solved by confession (Zimbardo, 1967).

In World War II virtually all American prisoners of war who were interrogated other than perfunctorily divulged information beyond what they had been instructed to give. One German interrogator indicated after the War that he obtained all the information he wanted from all but a handful of the five hundred downed American aviators he had interrogated. German and Japanese prisoners were equally cooperative. Large numbers of them yielded under interrogation to give away crucial information about gun positions, reserve assembly areas, observation post locations, and artillery concentrations. At the end of the War the concensus of experts was that it was virtually impossible for anyone to resist a determined interrogator (Biderman, 1963, pp. 229–231).

These results were of course obtained without any recourse to mysterious techniques of "brainwashing"; in principle the approach of the military interrogator differs little from that of any competent police interrogator. In both cases the aim is to manipulate an individual, so that he will engage in actions that are actually contrary to his real self-interest or the interests of groups with which he is identified. This cannot be accomplished by an impersonal, intellectual discussion. It is necessary to structure the interpersonal relationship between interrogator and prisoner in such a way that the desired compliance of the prisoner arises as a necessary consequence of that relationship. If every man were an island, if his personality and self-image involved only fixed and unalterable components, the task of the interrogator would be an impossible one. However, we are deeply social creatures and our conceptions of appropriate behavior are extremely vulnerable to situational constraints. Given time, skill, power, and determination it is usually possible to maneuver an individual into a position where he will willingly engage in behavior that under different circumstances would seem to him reprehensible or extremely foolish.

The manuals issued to police and other interrogators are quite explicit in their insistence on the fact that the securing of confessions depends on an appropriate manipulation of interpersonal relationships. Just as the salesman seeks to stage a scenario to which the conclusion of the sale forms the natural climax, so the interrogator enacts a scenario that inevitably leads up to the prisoner's confession. The difference is that the interrogator has much greater control over the situation and can therefore expect a higher rate of success. But in both cases the secret of success lies in the imposition of a definition of the situation that allows the victim only one way out. The desired outcome involves a scenario for two actors whose roles are mutually complementary. The manipulator begins by presenting his own role in appropriate terms. If the intended victim resists the implications that this has for his own role the manipulator systematically modifies the interpersonal feedback the victim receives so that only behavior consistent with his intended role is confirmed while all contrary definitions of the situation are disconfirmed (Schein, 1961).

Interrogation as a Fine Art

The key to the effective self-presentation of the interrogator lies in the achievement of a delicate balance between the communication of his overwhelming power and the communication of his interest in the welfare of the prisoner. Let us look at the advice given in a widely used manual of police interrogation techniques (Inbau and Reid, 1967). It insists that "the interrogator must always remain in psychological control of the situation." He should look directly at the subject with an obvious air of confidence in what he says and he should avoid jumping up and down and walking around because these may be interpreted as signs of impatience.

"After the interrogation is under way the interrogator should move his chair in closer, so that, ultimately, one of the subject's knees is just about in between the interrogator's two knees." The reason for this is that "distance or the presence of an obstruction of any sort constitutes a serious psychological barrier and also affords the subject a certain degree of relief and confidence not otherwise attainable" (Inbau and Reid, 1967, p. 27).

The prisoner should be impressed with the full potential power of the law enforcing agencies: "You know what will happen to you if you keep this up, don't you? . . . There'll be a trial, and when it's all over, despite the efforts of your parents and relatives . . . you'll either have to spend the rest of your life in the penitentiary or else sit down on the hot seat and have a lot of electricity shot through your body until your life's snuffed out" (Inbau and Reid, 1967, p. 78).

Other manuals stress the need to emphasize the power of the interrogator in many small ways, telling the prisoner where he may or may not sit, making it necessary for him to ask for permission to smoke, go to the washroom, have a drink of water, use the telephone, or rest.

But if the interrogator limited himself to displays of power he would run the risk of achieving exactly the opposite of what he is after with many prisoners. By these means he may merely confirm the prisoner's definition of the interrogator as the enemy who is to be defied. This is particularly likely to happen if the prisoner is a hardened criminal, an ideologically convinced opponent or a member of the other side in a war. It is therefore necessary to temper displays of strength with displays of sympathy for the prisoner so as to undermine his potential defiance. Sophisticated police manuals advise the officer to sympathize with the subject by telling him that anyone else under similar conditions or circumstances might have done the same thing.

Other ways of feigning sympathy with the prisoner might involve a condemnation of the victim of the presumed offense. For example, in the case of a man suspected of killing his wife "much can be gained by the interrogator's adoption of an emotional (choked-up) feeling about it all as he relates what he knows about the victim's conduct toward the husband" (Inbau and Reid, 1967, pp. 48–49). Another version of this approach involves an expression of sympathy for the suspect who was supposedly led astray by criminally minded associates.

But expressions of sympathy need not necessarily take such specific forms. The important thing is that the interrogator should present himself as a sympathetic person who is worthy of the prisoner's confidence in spite of his official position. "It is surprising how effective a well-timed pat on the shoulder or a grip of the hand can be in obtaining a confession. . . . Gestures of this type produce a very desirable psychological effect. They impart to the subject an attitude of understanding and sympathy far better than any combination of words the interrogator can put together" (Inbau and Reid, 1967, pp. 59–60).

But it is not usually convincing for the same interrogator to present himself simultaneously as the relentless impersonation of the force of law and as the sympathetic friend of the prisoner. He may try to strike the right balance by varying his act, assuming one role during some part of the interrogation and the other role at a later stage. This is a tricky exercise in stagemanship, which requires much skill and experience to bring it off successfully. Therefore, a highly recommended variant is often resorted to. This simply involves the splitting of the roles of bully and of kind friend between two interrogators who take turns at attempting to crack the prisoner. The first interrogator uses standard techniques for instilling fear in the prisoner, then the second interrogator intervenes and expresses disapproval of the first interrogator's unfriendly conduct. The bullying interrogator leaves and hands the prisoner over to his sympathetic "friend" who convinces him that he will protect him from further unpleasantness if he will only cooperate.

"The psychological reason for the effectiveness of the friendly–unfriendly act is the fact that the contrast between the methods used by each interrogator serves to accentuate the friendly, sympathetic attitude of the (one) interrogator and thereby renders this approach more effective," state Inbau and Reid (1967, p. 63).

The successful manipulation of the interrogator's role therefore depends on a two-pronged definition of the prisoner's situation in which he is made to feel helpless in the face of the power of authority but is given sham support from a source that presents compliance with the authority as the only available path out of an extremely distressing situation.

But an interpersonal situation can only be effectively manipulated by providing appropriate definitions of the role to be played by all the participants. Just as the sophisticated salesman tries to undermine those aspects of his prospect's self-presentation that do not fit in with the outcome he has in view, so the skillful interrogator will attempt to maneuver the prisoner into a position where the desired confession is a necessary part of the self the prisoner is trying to present.

The key to this manipulation lies in the systematic control of all interpersonal feedback available to the prisoner. If the interrogator is in a position to do so he may cut the prisoner off from all information that could be used to throw doubt on his guilt. Instead, he may be bombarded with information that appears to decrease the likelihood of his innocence. Depending on the scruples of the interrogator, such information may even be manufactured or appropriately distorted. It is a very common technique to convey to the prisoner that his associates and presumed accomplices have already confessed and left him in the lurch.

In this way the prisoner is presented with a credible model of the kind of role that will be acceptable to the interrogator and also made to feel that further resistance will only increase the antagonism of the authorities. He is also deprived of the motive to present himself in such a way as to retain the respect and support of his former friends and associates.

If the prisoner is to play the role that has been allotted to him in the interrogator's scenario, the interpersonal feedback he receives from the latter must be systematically regulated to disconfirm the prisoner's attempts at self-definition that are at variance with the identity he is expected to adopt. Inbau and Reid advise police officers that "a 'big shot' subject such as the prominent business or professional man should never be allowed to capitalize on his status. One little procedure toward that end is to address such a person by his first name (e.g. Joe) rather than by the appellation Mr. —" (1967, p. 29). Stripped of his protective respectable identity the prisoner is more vulnerable to the suggestion that he is something other than what he seems.

Another way of manipulating the interpersonal feedback received by the prisoner is to tell him that his involuntary actions are giving him away and attesting to his guilt. To do this the interrogator only needs to refer to general indications of tension or anxiety, which most people would be likely to show while being accused and interrogated, and to claim that these indications are clear symptoms of guilt, which of course they are not. In this vein the interrogator may point to the overactivity of the prisoner's Adam's apple, the accelerated pulsation of his carotid artery in the neck, his reluctance to establish eye contact with the interrogator, his restlessness, his fidgeting and fumbling with objects. He may suggest that the prisoner is "giving himself away" by these signs, that an innocent person would have no cause to show signs of nervousness under these circumstances.

Each one of the prisoner's protestations of innocence is met by a wall of confidence in his guilt on the part of the interrogator. To quote the police manual again: "At various times during the interrogation the subject should be reminded that the investigation has established the fact that he committed the offense; that there is no doubt about it; and that, moreover, his general behavior plainly shows that he is not now telling the truth" (Inbau and Reid, 1967, p. 28). Circumstantial details compatible with the prisoner's guilt are to be reiterated by the interrogator who is advised to avoid the issue of whether the prisoner is guilty but to concentrate on the reason why the subject committed the act.

In this connection it becomes important for the interrogator to offer the prisoner an acceptable self-image that is compatible with his commission of a criminal act. Perhaps the biggest obstacle to gaining a confession is the prisoner's reluctance to present himself as a subhuman character capable of indulging in despicable acts. The effective manipulation for removing this obstacle lies in minimizing the moral seriousness of the offense and offering the suspect a relatively acceptable motivation for the crime he is supposed to have committed. Suspected sex offenders are told that many or most people share their inclinations, presumed thieves are told that almost anyone exposed to the temptation would have acted likewise, possible murderers are told that they were obviously provoked beyond endurance, embezzlers and such like are flattered by imputing various altruistic motives to them. In short, the suspect is given a role in which his admission of a criminal action is compatible with the presentation of a relatively favorable self-image.

The success of interrogators of prisoners depends entirely on their skill in manipulating an interpersonal situation so as to push the prisoner into the role in which he has been cast. The key features of this manipulation involve the presentation of the interrogator's own role, the control of the interpersonal feedback that the prisoner receives, and the provision of viable forms of the role the prisoner is to adopt. These same principles apply in the interrogation of civilian, military, or political prisoners and certainly do not involve any mysterious techniques of "brainwashing." The point is that our social selves depend to a very large degree on the kind of interpersonal feedback we receive from those with whom we interact, and the greater the possibilities of deliberately shaping this feedback, the greater the scope of producing crucial changes in social behavior.

The dilemma of the prisoner is that it is really impossible for him *not* to communicate. American prisoners of war in Korea who attempted to meet their interrogators' questions by silence or by a refusal to answer found that their very silence was thrown back at them as an indication of guilt and implication in crimes with which they had not the slightest connection. In sheer self-defense they were obliged to start talking, and once they began an interchange with their interrogators the stage was set for further manipulation of interpersonal feedback. The prisoner who refuses to talk relinquishes to the interrogator the opportunity for defining the meaning of his behavior. Sooner or later these definitions become intolerable and the prisoner attempts to correct them. This of course is already a form of "cooperation"; prisoner and interrogator are engaged in a joint effort to define a mutually acceptable role for the prisoner. Soon the prisoner finds himself actively trying to anticipate the interrogator's demands and requirements. At first the interrogator may appear to accept merely feigned and superficial signs of cooperativeness, but having pushed the prisoner so far he now withdraws his support and pours scorn on these first steps in cooperation. In doing this the interrogator can play on the prisoner's guilt in having cooperated at all and so undermine the prisoner's confidence in the new image he is now trying to present. The prisoner is again deprived of confirmatory interpersonal feedback, and it is made clear to him that this will only be forthcoming if he adopts a more genuinely cooperative role. Having once embarked on this road it is difficult for the prisoner to turn back (Biderman, 1960).

The research studies conducted on returning American prisoners of war all seem to indicate that induced ideological sympathy with the doctrines of the captor had at most only slight effects in producing collaboration (Biderman, 1963, p. 75). The crucial factors in the production of clearly collaborative behavior, such as the signing of propaganda petitions, making propaganda recordings, and signing false confessions lay in the manipulation of interpersonal pressures of the type we have been discussing, including the manipulation of relations among the prisoners. Human experiences in such extreme situations provide an incisive demonstration of the vulnerability of the self-concept to interpersonal feedback. In situations where escape from systematically manipulated interpersonal feedback is impossible the consequences for the victim may be very far reaching.

A Study of the Manipulation of Political Prisoners

Some years ago the present writer had an opportunity of interviewing some twenty political prisoners in South Africa after they had been released from police confinement, which had varied from a few weeks to many months. They were a very heterogeneous group, which included black laborers with four or five years of formal education and a number of black and white professionals. They had all been fairly active opponents of the regime of *apartheid*, or racial domination in its rigid South African form. It is not legal to organize multiracial opposition to this system, and the political police is empowered to hold persons suspected of having knowledge of such activities until they have obtained any relevant information that such persons may possess. In accordance with the usual South African practice in such cases all the persons in the interviewed sample had been kept in solitary confinement during the intervals between their interrogations, although in the end all were released without any formal legal charges being made against them. This study was conducted at a time when the use of physical torture against political prisoners was far less usual than it subsequently became, and in fact none of the persons interviewed was subjected to such treatment. The interrogators of the political police were therefore relying essentially on their exceptional powers to manipulate the interpersonal relationships of their prisoners who were deprived of their rights to consult lawyers, see relatives, communicate with other prisoners, and so on for indefinite periods of time. In many, though not in all, cases these techniques were effective and provided the police with some of the information they were after.

The reports of the prisoners provided many examples of precisely the kinds of interrogation techniques we have already discussed. In the first place prisoners were impressed by the absolute power the authorities had over them and were made to feel completely dependent on their interrogators for all their personal requirements. Cigarettes were sometimes withheld as a punishment for lack of cooperation, prisoners could not control the switching on and off of their cell light, and in at least one case the uncooperative prisoner was for a time consigned to a cell that was so small that he could not stretch out in it. During interrogations the interrogators attempted to dominate the situation by doing most of the talking, threatening the prisoner with indefinite confinement and occasionally tying the prisoner to his chair and in one case forcing him to strip off all his clothes. They tried to give the impression that they had all the time in the world, bragged of their past successes, and lied freely about their current effectiveness with other prisoners.

But these demonstrations by themselves might have produced little but sullen apathy or resentment. The prisoner had to be *actively* involved in the role that had been prepared for him. To this end relatively innocuous questions about personal background, and so on, were ordinarily put first, and potentially more critical questions were kept for later use. The prisoner would see little point in not answering the more innocuous questions and so would help to establish an interaction pattern that recognized the role of the interrogator as interrogator. Then he would be faced with the difficult decision of precisely when to refuse to answer further questions, and any attempt in that direction could easily be interpreted by the interrogator as evidence of a guilty conscience. Moreover, instead of routinely proceeding to the crucial questions, the interrogator would often try to play on the prisoner's natural curiosity about these questions and encourage him to guess what they might be. In this way the prisoner might be induced to play an active role in his own incrimination.

At other times the interrogator would try to avoid appearing as the mere depersonalized representative of an all powerful authoritarian regime so as to be able to play on the prisoner's deeply ingrained habits of interpersonal response. He might expatiate on how he was trying to do his job, which forced him to take certain measures as a matter of duty and not of personal malice. He would display passionate conviction in the political principles of the regime as a matter of deep personal belief, which was worthy of the prisoner's respect. Such displays were often more effective than standard political lectures.

But the most successful forms of the personal approach to the prisoner were undoubtedly provided by the feigning of personal sympathy and understanding. One or two officers had obviously specialized in this technique and would regularly appear on the scene at what was considered to be the appropriate moment. Suddenly the prisoner would be confronted with a strongly supportive fatherly figure who would lament over his undeserved fate to the point of putting a protective arm around him and even producing a discrete tear or two. He would promise to intercede for the prisoner, but somehow a promise of greater cooperation was delicately worked into the act. These were strong pressures to resist for anyone indefinitely isolated from genuine sources of interpersonal support.

It was of course standard practice to make the prisoner doubly vulnerable to the "soft approach" by seeking to undermine his trust in his former friends and associates by repeatedly insinuating to him that he had been left in the lurch, that others had already implicated him, that he had been misled by agitators with ulterior motives or by those favorite scapegoats of racialist regimes, the Jews. At the same time his regular interrogators were often careful to deprive him of anything that might provide social support for his normal sense of identity and self-esteem. He might be subjected to disrespectful terms of address, assaults on his personal space, exposed to the real or manufactured disapproval of relatives, and subjected to countless minor indignities like being made to run rather than to walk to his interrogation sessions. He might even be taunted with not conducting himself like a good rebel or an estimable opponent of the regime.

Small wonder that every one of the prisoners interviewed reported feelings of demoralization and self-doubt. The symptoms of demoralization did not take the same forms in every prisoner. A feeling of passivity, of not being in control of one's own reactions, was a common complaint. Others reported doubts in their own previous political convictions, some even felt that their might be some truth in their interrogators' anti-semitic allegations. After a time many were inclined to agree that they had indeed been left in the lurch by their friends and all were made uncomfortable by the lack of information and social input that would counteract the world built by their interrogators. A few developed more pronounced psychological symptoms of disintegration. Some felt that the past and the future had become unreal and only the present mattered. Others began to doubt their own statements during interrogation and one or two wondered if they were going mad. A few developed violent psychosomatic symptoms such as acute anxiety attacks, nightmares, anorexia, and vomiting.

But in the present context the most interesting reactions of the prisoners were those that related directly to their interpersonal relationships with their captors. Undoubtedly, the most striking feature of these reactions was the surprising lack of proportion between what had been done to these people and the almost total lack of direct and uncomplicated hostility that they expressed toward those who were clearly responsible for their privations and humiliations. Only one of the persons interviewed claimed that his hostility to the regime and its representatives had persisted in untainted and undiminished form during the period of his imprisonment. While none of the others had in any way become converts to the regime, their interpersonal reactions to their captors were full of ambiguities. As one of them put it: "I just couldn't afford to be angry at the police." Another was annoyed with herself when she did express some overt anger against her interrogators. A third worried about his inability to feel much hostility toward his jailers. A fourth reported a great deal of fear of annoying his captors and a gradual decline of antagonism toward them.

In many cases these reactions went much further and led to a number of positive reactions to the jailers. Almost all the exprisoners were aware of a tremendous pressure to communicate with other human beings, and as they were in solitary confinement their only opportunity to satisfy this need lay in their interaction with their interrogators. This led some of them to attempt to joke with their interrogators and others to pathetic attempts to prolong the interrogation sessions. One of them, who subsequently published a detailed account of his experiences, writes: "Though I hate their intrusion into my life yet, once they come, I do not want them to leave. They are the only people to whom I am allowed to talk. It is only with them that I can assert myself, that I can hear my voice arguing for me, that I can articulate some of my thoughts" (Sachs, 1966, p. 36). The fundamental need for *some* form of interpersonal feedback could not be more clearly expressed.

But in most cases this need went far beyond a desire for *any* kind of feedback. It was positive feedback that the prisoner wanted; he wanted signs of approval and esteem, and he wanted to believe that the officials he was dealing with still regarded him as a human personality and that his interaction with them was still governed by some of the rules of ordinary human interaction. That is why some of the prisoners made deliberate attempts to please their interrogators, and one became so zealous in his efforts at cooperation that he fell to worrying about the completeness and acceptability of his statements. Others managed to get by with a show of surface compliance and preserved something of their old identifications in private. Many found it difficult to suspend their normal assumptions about interpersonal communication even though they knew rationally that these assumptions were no longer applicable. Against their better judgment they found themselves believing in the trustworthiness of various claims and promises of the interrogators that were obviously part of the latter's plan of deliberate manipulation. Some reacted with gratitude to little concessions that obviously had an ulterior motive. In particular, they were deeply affected by the behavior of the officer who pretended to be their friend and helper. One was actually reduced to tears by this show of fake sympathy, and another became quite desperate when this officer suddenly dropped his mask and became as harsh as the rest. Even the most resistant prisoners attached great importance to the impression they were making on their interrogators and fell to ruminating about what their enemies really thought about them.

Even when overt outbursts of anger did occur they usually manifested themselves in the context of relatively trivial annoyances, such as being searched or deprived of cigarettes and food sent to them by relatives.

The broad effects of the manipulation of the interpersonal situation by the interrogators are quite clear. By demonstrating to the prisoner his complete dependency on the authorities his hostility is kept in check because few individuals can face the risk of openly antagonizing human figures with that degree of power over them. By cutting the prisoner off from possible sources of support in the outside world he is deprived of the kind of interpersonal feedback that would maintain his previous identity. Eventually, this isolation increases the prisoner's reliance on the only source of interpersonal feedback that is still available to him, and that is the feedback he gets from his interrogators. Increasingly, he looks for some normal tokens of human recognition in his interaction with his interrogators, and this renders him particularly vulnerable to interpersonal manipulations that make collaboration the price he has to pay for phoney demonstrations of respect and sympathy.

Techniques of Countermanipulation

However, there are prisoners who were able to resist these pressures with remarkable success over long periods. How were they able to do this? Fortunately, some of them have provided quite elaborate accounts of their experiences and from these we can piece together the principles on which such successful resistance rests. The primary factor in these cases appears to be a deliberate and consistent attempt to actively redefine the interpersonal situation so that it became embarrassing to the interrogators. For all their show of invincibility and imperviousness interrogators are human too, and few prisoners are so deprived of resources that they are left without the possibility of manipulating the situation so as to emerge as the moral victors in at least some of their encounters with their captors. Of course, such a response on the part of the prisoner requires him to take the initiative at every possible opportunity—the passive prisoner is always at the mercy of his interrogators.

Depending on circumstances, such active interventions by the prisoner may take many forms. Complaints to superior officers generally have no tangible results but they are often useful in terms of their nuisance value to the interrogator and in demonstrating that the prisoner is still an autonomous being with an established right to present his own definition of the situation. In making the complaint the prisoner demonstrates to himself and to his captors that he has not adopted the compliant role provided for him in the official scenario.

Other techniques that prisoners have used to counteract the impressive array of pressures brought to bear on them include various forms of strike, notably hunger strikes and language strikes. One lady who spent several years in Hungarian prisons (Bone, 1957) considerably embarrassed her jailers by refusing to speak Hungarian although this was her mother tongue. Hunger strikes can be used to obtain concessions when the authorities still attach some value to the life of the prisoner. Above all, they serve to demonstrate that the prisoner is still in full control of himself and prefers death to psychological disintegration. Minor forms of the strike weapon may involve refusal to carry out certain duties, like cleaning the cell, or refusal to use approved forms of address to the interrogators. Any of these maneuvers may succeed in causing some demoralization among the interrogators in that they show their attempts at manipulation to have failed, so that their confidence in ultimate success becomes sapped.

The resistant prisoner is careful to preserve whatever outward forms of dignity he is able to insist on. One of the South African prisoners writes: "There is one rule to which I still adhere strictly—just as the British colonial official invariably dresses for dinner, or so they say, so I always dress for interrogation. I don my suit and my white shirt, and put on shoes and socks" (Sachs, 1966, p. 221). The same report comments on the importance of adhering to a self-imposed plan of regular activities, which reassures the prisoner that he is still in control of significant areas of his life and is not merely a passive reactor to external controls.

The key factor in the success of the resistant prisoner lies in his continued ability to define the interrogation situation as an interpersonal contest in which he answers every manipulation of the other side with maneuvers of his own that are calculated to defeat the intended effect of the manipulation. By becoming an active contestant rather than a passive victim he opens up the possibility that the very situation that was meant to withdraw all support from his normal social self may actually become a source of very positive feedback that further fortifies his resistance.

A Polish politician imprisoned in 1945 and accused of anti-Soviet activities refused to sign a confession after over one hundred interrogations. For him the sessions with his interrogator became a personal contest of wills. This is how he describes the critical phase in their encounter: "After the failure of his psychological offensive he could only wait in the hope that my physical resources would give out. But at the same time his own strength dwindled away. He became nervous. Once when he was looking very tired, with dark rings round his eyes, he burst out: 'I know what you are waiting for. You hope you will hold out longer than I. But you are mistaken. I am stronger' . . . a feeling of great joy overcame me as I realized that my opponent had exhausted his ammunition. Our forces became equal. He began to lose faith that he would defeat me and admitted that he was tired. Maybe he was becoming anxious—his career was at stake" (Stypulkowski, 1962, pp. 282–283).

The South African political prisoner, from whose exceptionally insightful account we have already quoted, also came to define his position in terms of an interpersonal contest in which he actively attempted to undermine the other side's self-confidence just as they were trying to undermine his: "I wonder what the security men think privately of me. It is incredible how eager I am to get them to regard me as a man of principle. Yet I feel I am not being entirely naïve in this wish. The more they unconsciously respect me, the harder will it be for them to assert their personalities over mine. If secretly they admire my stand they are partially disarmed before they start interrogating me . . . By grounding myself on principle, I not only impede the progress of their machine, I challenge their very right to hold me. The extreme isolation to which we detainees are subjected can be justified in their terms only on one basis, and that is that it gets results. If it fails to get results then it is exposed for what it is: a refined form of torture." (Sachs, 1966, p. 214).

IMPLICATIONS AND QUESTIONS

What emerges with the greatest possible clarity from the study of deliberate attempts to manipulate human behavior in face-to-face situations is the insight that the individual personality is not an island but exists in an interpersonal context. It has long been recognized that people internalize their orientations to significant models, to reference groups, and to various standards of social comparison. But these are essentially influences that the individual carries around with him—their direct effect was critical at a particular stage in his development but they have achieved a certain degree of internal autonomy, and he is no longer crucially dependent on continued exposure to them. The normal adult has his principles and values, which remain relatively permanent and express themselves spontaneously in his behavior.

A closer look at situations of deliberate interpersonal manipulation reveals however that these internalized components of personal identity and self-esteem are far more vulnerable to face-to-face communication than one might be inclined to assume. Man remains essentially a communicating organism, and the effects of interpersonal communication are not limited to an early formative period. His life remains one of constant confrontation with other individuals who provide him with interpersonal feedback that provides a constant source of challenge or support to his internalized self-image. As long as his social interaction is limited to situations defined by well-established reciprocal role patterns to which everyone adheres we hardly become conscious of the subtle interchange of communications on which the smooth course of such interactions depends. However, even in these cases writers like Erving Goffman (1967, 1971) have done much to draw our attention to the intricate pattern of interpersonal communication on which the pattern of normal "interaction ritual" depends. But when interactions become plainly manipulative, when one side seeks to impose a unilaterally defined outcome on the situation, the importance of techniques of interpersonal communication becomes quite explicit and can no longer be ignored.

Our examples of interpersonal manipulation were purposely chosen from areas where the aims of the manipulation were quite explicit and were pursued with deliberate conscious intent. Under such conditions some of the critical aspects of interpersonal communication have to be carefully programmed for the guidance of the manipulator, and this can provide us with useful hints for the direction that objective research in this area ought to take.

But such highly codified examples of interpersonal manipulation only provide one extreme of a wide range of human situations in which interpersonal communication modifies the relationship in which the interactants stand to one another. These situations vary from those in which the manipulation is deliberate, though its techniques remain largely intuitive, to those in which there is no conscious intent to manipulate the other but in which the effect of the manipulation can nevertheless be extremely effective. Among the former we can mention the relationships between teacher and pupil, between client and therapist, and also many bargaining situations. Among the latter we are particularly reminded of family relationships, involving the interaction of spouses or the interactions of parents and children.

All these situations could benefit from a better understanding of the principles and scope of interpersonal communication. The teacher may learn to improve the monitoring of his own communications so as to enhance the effects he wishes to achieve and minimize undesirable side effects. The therapist's sensitivity to the likely significance of his own and his client's communications could be improved if we possessed adequate systematic knowledge of the fine grain of such communications in this particular interpersonal context. Family members engaged in self-defeating and destructive forms of interpersonal communication could be helped to redefine their relationships if we were able to identify the crucial pathogenic forms of communication and bring them to the conscious attention of the participants.

Certain efforts in these directions are not lacking. But in many cases they amount to little more than a collection of practical wisdom that compares unfavorably with the systematic and detailed instructions that any competent police interrogator has at his disposal. What is now needed is to proceed from this level to a much more systematic and specific study of the precise details of the process of interpersonal communication so that we can learn to identify the source of all this intuitive and often untested wisdom.

Certain areas of investigation stand out as requiring special attention. The whole field of nonverbal communication offers a tremendous challenge to the research worker. It is clear that in interpersonal encounters verbal messages are constantly qualified and even disqualified by a tone of voice, a gesture, a particular posture, an invasion of personal space, or a certain facial expression. These cues frequently provide the clue as to how the verbal message is to be interpreted. Without them verbal statements remain purely intellectual exercises that lack interpersonal reality. It is often only the nonverbal component that gives the verbal message an interpersonal punch. Trained manipulators are well aware of this, yet the ordinary person is probably less consciously aware of this level of discourse than of any other. Perhaps the greatest potential value of interpersonal communication research lies in its promise of increasing our sensitivity and understanding at this level.

Verbal communications must be examined in terms of the *functions* they fulfill in the interpersonal communication process. What is the effect intended by a given statement, and what effect does it in fact have? What patterns are discernible in the sequence of alternating statements, what repeated figures, circles, spirals, parallel, or converging lines will the temporal progression of verbal statements reveal to the systematic investigator? What is the relationship between the form of statements and their interpersonal function? We do not have answers to most of these questions but we are at least ready to try out alternative ways of getting at the answers.

If our study of interpersonal communication is to become more than a compendium of separate investigations we must face the task of developing some general framework within which individual findings find their place. Are there general features or dimensions of interpersonal communication that recur again and again at different levels? What would be the nature of such general features and what abstract principles would they express? Would such principles merely be extensions of known principles of individual psychology or of biology, or would they represent a different level of discourse resistant to the temptations of reductionism?

One thing is clear, and that is that some of the habits of thought and traditional approaches to the problems of individual psychology will not carry us very far into the field of interpersonal communication. For in that field we are less interested in what happens *within* individuals than in what happens *between* individuals. This means that it is at least the dyad and not the isolated individual that becomes our basic unit of analysis. But this has all sorts of implications for the kinds of causal relationships we look for. Instead of restricting ourselves to unidirectional relations between causes and effects we are much more likely to be interested in feedback mechanisms in which people influence each other and each of them function as both cause and effect for the other. We have seen how even in the interrogation of prisoners, where one side seems to hold all the keys to a unilateral control of the situation, the other side is not without resources that can be used to demoralize the interrogator. The target of the salesman is even better equipped in this respect, and in less extreme and less explicitly manipulative situations the dice are much more evenly loaded for most of the participants. So we are never really faced with one-way influence situations but with complex interactions in which cause and effect cannot be as neatly sorted out as in most laboratory studies.

But these somewhat abstract considerations lead us well beyond the scope of a preliminary treatment of the issues and deserve a more detailed examination of their own.

REFERENCES

Berton, P. (1963). *The Big Sell*. Toronto: McClelland and Stewart; New York: Alfred A. Knopf.

Biderman, A. D. (1957). Communist attempts to elicit false confessions from Air Force Prisoners of war. *Bulletin of the New York Academy of Medicine*, **33**, 616–625.

Biderman, A. D. (1960). Social–psychological needs and "involuntary" behavior as illustrated by compliance in interrogation. *Sociometry*, **23**, 120–147.

Biderman, A. D. (1963). *March to Calumny*. New York: Macmillan.

Bone, E. (1957). *Seven Years Solitary*. London: Hamish Hamilton.

Crissy, W. J. E. and Kaplan, R. M. (1969). *Salesmanship: The Personal Force in Marketing*. New York: Wiley.

Farago, L. (1954). *War of Wits. The Anatomy of Espionage and Intelligence.* New York: Funk & Wagnalls.

Goffman, E. (1967). *Interaction Ritual: Essays on Face-to-Face Behavior.* New York: Doubleday.

Goffman, E. (1971). *Relations in Public: Microstudies of the Public Order.* New York: Basic Books.

Gross, A. (1959). *Salesmanship.* New York: Ronald Press.

Inbau, F. E. and Reid, J. E. (1967). *Criminal Interrogation and Confessions.* Baltimore: Williams & Wilkins.

Sachs, E. S. (1966). *The Jail Diary of Albie Sachs.* New York: McGraw-Hill; London: Collins.

Schein, E. H. (1961). *Coercive Persuasion.* New York: Norton.

Stypulkowski, Z. (1962). *Invitation to Moscow.* New York: Walker.

Thompson, J. W. (1966). *Selling: A Behavioral Science Approach.* New York: McGraw-Hill.

Zimbardo, P. G. (1967). The psychology of police confessions. In *Readings in Psychology Today.* Del Mar, Calif.: CRM Books.

CHAPTER 2

The Dual Aspect of Human Communication

THE DISTINCTION BETWEEN PRESENTATION AND REPRESENTATION

There is a rather hoary model of human verbal communication according to which there is always a speaker, a listener, and a referent that is talked about. Presumably the speaker becomes a speaker because he wants to tell his listener something about the referent, the subject of the verbal message. In its most general sense this account is too abstract to be analytically useful, but when a more specific meaning is given to "the referent" the model may become quite misleading. Quite typically, the referent is assumed to be some object or event in the world outside, something or some happening about which the speaker wishes to pass along information to the listener. Thus, in a celebrated example, the speaker proudly informs his listener: "it is raining."

Semantically, this statement undoubtedly refers to the rain, but anyone who has spent some time in the company of human beings will know that this conversation is probably not about rain at all. In many settings in which such statements are likely to occur we will be dealing with polite exchanges about the weather among relative strangers. It would be fatuous to suggest that these exchanges are motivated by a burning desire among the participants to inform each other of the obvious. If the transmission of information is indeed the aim (and this depends on how one chooses to define "information"), it is not the need to pass along metereological information that causes a speaker to break his silence in these situations. Mention of the rain is apt to be prompted by a sense of embarrassment at the silence that is the alternative, and this in turn derives from a knowledge of the rules governing ritual exchanges among strangers and superficial acquaintances.

In other words, many real-life statements about the rain are likely to have very little to do with the weather but a great deal to do with the relationship between speaker and listener.

The same thing applies to human communication in general. It is a great mistake to suppose that people always say what they seem to be saying. The words they exchange may refer to automobiles, elections, personal tastes, or books; but in talking about these matters they confirm or challenge the social relationship that exists between speaker and listener. A verbal message is never merely a neutral transmission of information about the world outside, it is always also a communication about the relationship between the speaker and his audience. Occasionally, the information transmission function of verbal communication predominates; but more usually the semantic reference of individual statements is entirely secondary to the major purpose of the communication, which has to do with the social relationship between speakers and listeners. In face-to-face communication it is quite possible to talk without conveying any real information about the world outside, but it is not possible to talk without saying something about the relationship between the participants in the communication situation.

We must therefore make a distinction between the *semantic* and the *pragmatic* content of messages (Morris, 1955). The former is concerned with the ostensible topics of the conversation, the aspects of the person, or the environment that are being talked about; the latter is concerned with the "hidden agenda" of the exchange, the way in which the participants present themselves to each other. For the present we may merely note for later analysis the special case of the interaction in which semantic and pragmatic content coincide, i.e. groups in which the relationship of the members to each other forms the ostensible topics of conversation. Most of the time, the two domains of content diverge quite sharply and require quite a different sort of analysis.

The presuppositions for an understanding of the semantic and of the pragmatic content of messages are emphatically not the same. In order to understand the semantic of verbal messages we merely need a knowledge of the language in question, but for an understanding of pragmatic contents this is not enough. We also need to know a great deal about the social norms and conventions under which the participants are operating, and for a richer understanding some familiarity with certain of their idiosyncrasies will also be required. In other words, semantic content can be comprehended simply on the basis of a shared linguistic competence, but this is quite inadequate for understanding how language functions in real human situations. The conditions that determine linguistic competence are quite different from those that determine the use to which this competence is put by a performing speaker (Chomsky, 1965).

It is proper to distinguish two kinds of answers that can be given to the question: What is the message about? On the one hand, the message is undoubtedly about such things as cabbages and kings. But on the other hand, it is also about what is going on between two or more individuals who are talking to one another. The referents of linguistic signs exist in an interpersonal space as well as in a geographical space. Much of the time people talk in order to confirm or to challenge the nature of their relationship to one another, and the world to which their messages refer, albeit obliquely, is the world of status and power, love and protection, hostility and politeness.

The distinction between the semantic and the pragmatic content of speech goes further than the distinction between linguistic competence and performance. What is involved is a fundamental difference in the relation between signifier and signified. This difference is expressed in terms of the distinction between arbitrary and iconic signs. In the former case the signifier has a purely arbitrary conventional relationship to that which is signified, as in the relation between word and thing, but in the case of the icon there is some intrinsic similarity between signifier and signified, as with the drawing of an object. But this dimension or resemblance does not exhaust the ways in which different kinds of relationship between signifier and signified can be distinguished (Ekman and Friesen, 1969).

It may be said that both arbitrary signs and icons *represent* their referents, but there are instances where it would be more correct to speak of the *presentation* of the signified by the signifier. When the officer says to the private: "I order you to advance," his verbal statement is hardly a mere symbol of his authority, it is an expression or presentation of that authority. In the appropriate setting such an order clearly signifies something about the relationship between the two men, but the manner of signification is surely different from the signification of a chair by the drawing of a chair. The possibility and likelihood of the issuing of orders is a necessary part of the authority relationship by definition, but chairs are defined quite independently of the representations that may or may not be made of them. Yet the order clearly is not to be equated with the authority relationship, it merely signifies its existence.

The link between relationships of authority and verbal orders constitutes one example of a very general type of link between certain classes of signifiers and that which they signify. The order of human relationship has to manifest itself in certain interchanges among individuals. Such interchanges do not constitute this order, even in their totality, because the existence of an order always implies the possibility of further interchanges that have not yet occurred, yet they do signify such an order and are necessary to its existence. The link between an underlying social relationship and a particular overt expression of it involves the function of signification but not in the sense in which the word "apple" signifies an apple. The interpersonal relationship is *presented* rather than *represented* by means of the signifier. (The term "presentation" is to be preferred to the term "expression" because of the traditional use of the latter in connection with affects and emotions that are not necessarily involved here.)

The relationship between specific commands and underlying relationship of military authority is certainly one of the simplest and most explicit cases of presentation we are likely to encounter. Most of the time social relationships present themselves in a far more subtle and oblique manner. Yet, this does not alter the nature of the basic function involved. Relationships of authority may present themselves in a tone of voice, a choice of words, forms of address, and the kind of content to which verbal messages among the participants are limited. The same holds true for social relationships other than those of authority. To the outsider the meaning of these presentations may be far from obvious, and reading them correctly may become a matter of deciphering a code.

The situation is further complicated by the fact that over vast areas of their interaction people are quite content to present their relationships without representing them as well. The authority relationships that exist in a formal bureaucracy like the army are of course explicitly described in various public rules and regulations, but this is not true for authority relationships in more informal settings like the family. Moreover, attempts by the participants to represent informal relationships as though they were objective events often end in disastrous failure. Without special and prolonged training most people do not find it easy to give a correct *representation* of their relationships to one another. Yet they *present* these relationships all the time. The analysis of these presentations is therefore our main source of evidence for judging the nature of their interpersonal relationships.

THE COMMUNICATION OF SOCIAL DEMANDS

The distinction between "presentation" and "representation" has much in common with the distinction between the "report" and the "command" aspects of language introduced by Ruesch and Bateson (1951). These writers pointed out that when people communicate they usually do two things simultaneously. On the one hand, they convey information to each other about the state of the world, they "report" on what they have seen heard or thought; on the other hand, they also seek to impose some behavior on each other with every act of communication. Every communicative act carries at least an implicit "command" to enter into some kind of relationship with the communicator.

For a number of reasons the Ruesch–Bateson nomenclature is not suitable in the present context. The term "command," for example, is ill chosen to refer to something that may manifest itself in extreme subtleties, implications, and innuendos. More important is the fact that "reports" and "commands" really describe messages rather than people. A "command" never stands alone but is embedded in a matrix of interpersonal communication. In the "command" aspects of communication the individual implies that he is the right and proper person to make such demands, and he therefore presents himself as such a person. He lays claim to a certain social identity and seeks to confer a complementary identity on the person at whom the "command" is directed. In other words, he seeks to define the social situation in a certain way. The "command" character of messages is important only when they are seen in terms of a self-presentation by individuals in particular situations.

Another reason for the distinction between representation and presentation lies in their diverse logical status. Representations can be true or false, if I say the earth is flat, my statement can be checked for its truth value. But it makes no sense to ask whether the command aspect of my communication is true or false. My demand that someone listen to me has no truth value; however, it may have *validity*. Just as we can check reports for their truth, so we can check for their validity. One way of doing this is to test them against social or institutional norms and rules. If the lieutenant issues an order to his captain that is an invalid command, but the same order addressed by the captain to the lieutenant will be judged to be valid. In other words, the validity of commands depends on the institutional or normative framework within which they are issued (Austin, 1965).

But human institutions ultimately depend on human agreement. If people fail to honor institutional norms, those norms cease to have any effective existence. The validity of individual presentations therefore depends on recognition of the legitimacy of normative frameworks. But few institutions spell out their rules as explicitly as the army. In many cases the norms governing a particular relationship are implicit, and so there is much more room for debate about what the rules are. Also, in many cases people are free to make their own rules within very broad limits. A married couple or a parent–child pair can define many of the norms that are to govern the relationship for themselves. All it needs is the tacit agreement of both partners and the norm is established. This tacit agreement occurs every time someone accepts the partner's attempt to define the relationship in a certain way. Every time a wife obeys her husband's command without protest she helps to establish the validity of his commands, or, in other words, she helps to establish a norm governing their relationship. The command aspects of interpersonal communication are therefore validated by carrying out the command, by honoring the definition of the relationship that the command implies.

THE STAGE MODEL OF PRESENTATIONS

One influential writer who has been very much concerned with the analysis of social presentations is Erving Goffman (1959). He has emphasized the importance of *impression management* in social interaction and likened behavior in face-to-face situations to a performance on a stage. Participants in social encounters are like actors who attempt to play certain characters that they wish the audience to accept. Individuals assume a certain social status vis-à-vis others and attempt to give a credible presentation of the character that is supposed to go with that status, acting out courage, modesty, sagacity or what have you, as the occasion demands. Such "presentations of the self" are always somewhat idealized, but they are meant to be taken seriously. If the role cannot be maintained there is general embarrassment, and all concerned take steps to repair the temporarily tarnished image. But most of the time we manage to project a pretty credible image of ourselves in our various roles, using such techniques as the modulation of our voice, the control of facial expression, and the monitoring of our statements to censor discrepant and discreditable information.

Most of the time the player and his audience collaborate in maintaining the fiction of his presented self. In fact, in ordinary face-to-face situations, player and audience have to change places all the time. Taking each other's performance seriously is therefore a matter of reciprocity, and the effectiveness of each performance depends on a tacit protective collaboration among the participants. However, at times this collaboration is abandoned and the encounter becomes a contest in which at least one of the participants attempts to score points off the others (Goffman, 1967). This possibility makes it clear that every performance in a social role involves a *claim* to have one's presented role-appropriate character taken seriously, a claim that may or may not be honored by one's audience. The honoring of such claims is based on reciprocity, which is perhaps the source of the anxiety that arises when a really bad performance is put up. For if one's partner's performance is so bad that it cannot be taken seriously one has lost the assurance that one's own performance will be taken seriously simply by way of reciprocity. A single bad performance is therefore an implied threat to the integrity of all those involved. Perhaps this is the reason why the awkward social performance of many psychotics makes others treat them as a threat.

Goffman refuses to be tied down on the question of whether his analysis of social encounters involves deliberate or unconscious playacting. He rightly emphasizes the fluidity of the transition from the one to the other and the frequent occurrence of performances that are partly spontaneous and partly a matter of deliberate manipulation. Probably the best performances of everyday life are those in which the actor is not conscious of himself as an actor, where the appropriate gestures and bearing have been acquired in the course of socialization and are not deliberately constructed for the occasion. But in any case, the degree of artifice involved in a performance does not alter the fact that a role, as Sartre (1956) says, can only be *realized* by being acted.

The danger of the metaphor of life as a stage lies in the temptation to attribute to the players a degree of artifice and planning that they do not possess, and Goffman frequently gives the impression of having been seduced by this temptation. What is true about his account of social interaction is the concept of a *steered* performance that underlies it. To say that people act their parts implies, first, that their behavior in a given situation follows certain prescriptions, that there is a "script," second, that the parts of the script fit together into a coherent whole, a "play," and third, that the purpose of the exercise is the creation of an impression.

At a somewhat higher level of abstraction this leads to a useful paradigm for social interaction. The immediately visible part of such interaction can only be understood by regarding it as an attempt at making a presentation. Such a presentation involves the translation of a script into a performance. The script ensures the existence of prescribed, coherent relations among the players, but it is rather schematic and leaves much to individual interpretation. It corresponds to the underlying social relationship among the participants. The performance is concerned with impressions among an audience, always remembering that the players may be their own audience. It expresses the fact that social actors are motivated by the images that others have of them. We act to confirm or to change the roles we play in the lives of others. (The analogy of the play breaks down when we change these roles so much as to change the script.)

The play analogy also wears thin when we consider the *translation* of the script into the individual acts of the performance. In performing a play the actors are consciously aware of the script and deliberately give their interpretation of it. This is decidedly not the case in the everyday *presentation* of interpersonal relationship. While people do indulge in more or less deliberate playacting at certain times, the constant feature of all social interaction is the spontaneous and unreflecting signification of the interpersonal relationship by means of a stream of verbal and nonverbal signs. Differences of status and various degrees of intimacy, for example, constantly codetermine the flow of communication between individuals without the slightest hint of a deliberate performance. In fact, in the usual case the participants are unable to give a coherent account of the whole performance without a great deal of probing and reflection; even then they may remain unaware of large parts of their performance.

We must return to the distinction between *presentation* and *representation*. Both represent a relationship between a signifier and something that is signified, but in a very different mode. Propositions constitute an explicit representation of their semantic content, but at the same time, when uttered in a particular interpersonal context, they present claims whose reference is the relationship between the communicating individuals. They may imply claims to expert knowledge or to a certain level of intimacy, for example. People do not commonly establish such claims by means of explicit verbal statements, like, "I am an expert and you are not," or, "We two can talk freely"; but rather convey such messages by implication, by a tone of voice, by the form of their statements, and by what is and what is not said openly. Here is a set of signs that certainly conveys meaning, but these meanings are not to be found in any dictionary.

Like all communications these presentations mediate between a source and a target, a speaker and a listener, a performer and an audience. We may express the fact of such mediation by saying that the communications have a *function*—in an ongoing interaction they tend to establish congruency between the interpretations of the social situation among the participants. In this they may meet with varying degrees of success. The presentation of the situation by a speaker or "performer" is only a claim to have his interpretation of the interpersonal situation accepted. My demeanor may imply a claim to superior status, to be regarded as an expert or to be accepted as a confidant, but it depends on the addressee whether the claim is partially or wholly accepted or perhaps totally rejected. A successful claim establishes congruency between the images that the participants have of their relationship; such a relationship is likely to continue. Unsuccessful claims are associated with interpersonal conflict and the possible redefinition of the situation on the part of one or more participants. At times the relationship may be terminated because the participants cannot agree about the basis on which it is to continue.

The concept of *function* avoids the subjective overtones of Goffman's theatrical analogy. The social claim involved in a given presentation has a detectable function in the context of an interpersonal relationship, irrespective of the deliberateness of the performance and the level of awareness of the participants. If presentations are to be empirically investigated this must be done in terms of their objective functions. It will not do to ask "actors" about their "performance" because there is general agreement about their frequent inability to give a coherent account of what is essentially a spontaneous, unreflective production. Instead, we have to analyze the elements of the production in terms of their likely effect or function in the given social context. While this may not be easy in the case of highly idiosyncratic performances, there remains a large territory of acts whose functions are unambiguously determined by well-known social rules and conventions. In these cases the function of each element of the performance is likely to be far more transparent to the objective observer than to the participant immersed in a spontaneous presentation.

A further advantage of the functional approach to the analysis of presentations lies in its avoidance of a confusion that may be introduced by the distinction between performers and audience. Such a distinction is useful as a metaphor, but in ordinary social interaction the roles of performer and audience are of course simultaneously played by all the participants. We are all performers *and* audience for one another, and even while we are listening and not talking there are nonverbal performing aspects to our behavior. It is most unusual to act solely as an audience or solely as a performer. The distinction has its analytic uses in that it enables us to focus on various performers in turn, but beyond this it contributes little to the empirical analysis of social interaction. The acts of all participants in a social interaction must be analyzed in terms of the functional attributes of their performance. The existence of a communication situation simply provides the necessary and sufficient conditions for the occurrence of presentations, i.e. the presence of a potential audience.

Among the specific features of Goffman's account of the "presentation of self" there is one that must be explicitly repudiated in a more generalized functional analysis of interpersonal behavior. Goffman's actors are always assumed to aim at presenting a "creditable" picture of themselves. While this is true for many situations, it is not true for others. Where interaction becomes a matter of scoring points off one another or where there is a deliberate attempt at creating a good impression the actors may be preoccupied with presenting an admirable performance. But in most everyday situations the presentation process is far too automatic and routinized to allow much room for such considerations. Indeed, at the other extreme, some of the interpersonal situations that most frequently claim the attention of psychologists are those in which at least one of the participants presents himself or herself as the incompetent, ignorant, or culpable partner. Such a presentation may be pursued with as much determination and skill as one that allows the performer to appear in an entirely favorable light. The desire to present the most creditable image is far from being a universal function of all social performances, and the implication that it greatly restricts the range of social situations to which one's model may be validly applied. At this stage the existence and nature of universal functions in social presentations remain an open question.

CONCLUSION

We have introduced a distinction between two fundamentally different functions of human communication—the functions of "representation" and of "presentation." The former is concerned with conveying information about the world in which the communicators live, the latter conveys something about the relationship between the communicators themselves. This distinction is similar to the analytic division between the "semantic" and the "pragmatic" aspects of messages, the former being concerned with the meaning of statements in terms of external referents, the latter involving influence on the target of communication. It is the "pragmatic" or "presentational" aspects of interpersonal communication that are of primary interest to the social psychologist. The distinction between the two aspects of human communication involved is a fundamentally different relationship between signifier and significate. In the one case the referent remains quite unaffected by its symbolic representation in communication—a house does not change its nature simply because the word "house" or the word "maison" occurs in conversation. In the other case the message is itself part of what it signifies, so that changes in its expression involve a change in the referent. A change in the pattern of gaze direction or the establishment of interpersonal distance indicates a change in the relationship between the communicators because such nonverbal signals are essentially an expression of the underlying relationship. Furthermore, while the semantic relationship between signal and referent remains stable and unambiguous, the "pragmatic" or "presentational" aspect of communication usually carries an ambiguous message whose meaning depends on the social context. This aspect of communication represents claims to define social relationships in certain ways. If these claims are successful the message has *validity*, whereas the "semantic" or "report" aspects of communication have *truth value*. In the one case messages are tested against the responses of other parties in a social relationship, in the other case they are tested against the relevant referents in the objective world outside the expressed relationship among the communicators.

The difference between *representational* and the *presentational* function of messages can be summarized as follows: The former involves the informative function of reporting about the external world, the latter involves the overt expression of the relationship that exists among the communicators. Such forms of behavior as the establishing of interpersonal space or of a certain level of eye contact do not represent some external referent, in the sense that the word "apple" represents a real apple, rather do they exist as part of a *"presentation"* in which each individual expresses his claim to define any given social relationship in a certain manner.

REFERENCES

Austin, J. L. (1965). *How to do Things with Words*. New York: Oxford University Press.
Chomsky, N. (1965). *Aspects of the Theory of Syntax*. Cambridge, Mass.: M.I.T. Press.
Ekman, P. and Friesen, W. V. (1969). The repertoire of nonverbal behavior: Categories, origin, usage, and coding. *Semiotica*, 1, 49–98.

Goffman, E. (1959). *The Presentation of Self In Every-day Life.* New York: Doubleday Anchor.

Goffman, E. (1967). *Interaction Ritual.* New York: Doubleday Anchor.

Morris, C. (1955). *Signs, Language and Behavior.* New York: Braziller.

Ruesch, J. and Bateson, G. (1951). *Communication: The Social Matrix of Psychiatry.* New York: Norton.

Sartre, J. P. (1956). *Being and Nothingness.* New York: Philosophical Library.

CHAPTER 3

Dimensions of Social Interaction

THE ANALYSIS OF ADDRESS SYSTEMS

It is not too difficult to think of concrete examples of the presentation of interpersonal relationships from everyday life. Literature also provides an almost inexhaustible source of sensitive and penetrating portrayals of such presentations. The scientific study of presentations, however, must limit itself to the analysis of general features in order to establish regularities that go beyond the individual case. Examples of such systematic analysis of presentations are relatively rare. At the present time the analysis of the rules of personal address probably constitutes the most developed part of this field of study.

All societies have forms of address that are generally understood. The use of forms like *Mr.* or *Mrs.* and of familiar and polite forms of pronouns, like *tu* and *vous* in French or *Du* and *Sie* in German is precisely regulated by the relationship of the interactants. My use of a person's first name rather than *Mr. Smith* will constitute a presentation of a certain degree of familiarity in our relationship. My choice between these two forms does not involve the representational function of language because both first and second name represent the same individual. The difference between the two forms arises out of the manner in which I *present* our relationship.

The distinction between the two forms of signification is quite clear here. The referent is unchanged by my representational use of *John* or *Mr. Smith*, but the use of one or other of these forms makes an immediate difference to my relationship to this individual. As a *presentation* the use of different forms of address expresses something that exists between

38

myself and the addressee—it is part of our relationship in a way that a name is never part of the thing it represents. Strictly speaking, my use of a certain form of address is of course a *claim* that our relationship is of a certain kind. But it is a claim that the addressee has to come to terms with—he can accept it or reject it, but it is never a matter of indifference to our relationship. His reply constitutes a counterclaim that may or may not be congruent with my original ploy. In any case, our exchange of certain forms of address rather than others will signify something important about our relationship.

The universal existence of rules about appropriate form of address in all societies suggests that some very general features of social relationship are being expressed here. However, one must be careful not to jump to hasty conclusions because language communities all have different rules about forms of address. For example, the degree of familiarity signified by the use of first names is not the same in Europe and in North America, and the line of distinction between *tu* and *vous* is not quite the same as that between *Du* and *Sie*. The same degree of familiarity among colleagues that is expressed by the use of first names in North America may require the use of titles in Europe, and a German child may use *Du* to a relative where a French child may use *vous*. In French Canada there are in fact social class differences in forms of address, with working-class parents expecting to receive the nonreciprocal *vous* from their children and middle-class parents more likely to favor the use of reciprocal *tu* (Lambert, 1967).

However, one would hardly be justified in concluding from such observations that North American colleagues are on more familiar terms than their European counterparts, that German children are closer to their relatives than French children, or that parental status is respected more in French Canadian working-class than in middle-class families. Such a conclusion would require the assumption of a precise equivalence in the meaning of given forms of address in different language communities. This assumption is of course quite false, because in terms of the presentation of social relationships *Mr. Smith* does not signify precisely the same thing as *Herr Schmidt*, and *vous* does not signify precisely what *Sie* signifies. The precise rules governing the use of forms of address in different communities have to be explored before any conclusion can be reached about the significance of any particular form.

The discipline of *sociolinguistics* has accomplished a great deal in explicating differences in the rules of address in various language communities. Such rules can be represented as a system of choices about the nature of the social relationship that is to be presented in the form of address. The speaker acts as though he were applying a set of *alternation rules* that involve an ordered series of (generally binary) choices about the nature of the relationship.

As a simple example let us take the choice faced by children in a language community where either a familiar (T) form or a nonfamiliar (V) form of address might be used. In one reported case (Ervin-Tripp 1969) this choice depended on only three considerations—age, kinship, and intimacy. Depending on the mixture of these three elements in the relationship either the T or the V form is used, as represented in Fig. 1.

The chart should be read from left to right. The first decision to be made is whether the relationship to the person addressed is one of kinship or not. If the answer is positive the approximate age relationship must be established; if the other individual is not more than about fifteen years older the familiar (T) form may be used. However, if the age difference is more than this a decision about the intimacy of the relationship is necessary—the familiar form may only be used with a much older kin if the relationship is an intimate one. Similarly, if no kinship relationship is present and the relation to the addressee is not an intimate one the nonfamiliar (V) form must be used, while with an intimate nonkin addressee the decision about the correct form depends on the additional consideration of age.

This example illustrates how an apparently simple distinction between only two forms of address is in fact used to present several facets of a social relationship simultaneously. In the representational code it is common to have a one-to-one relationship between the sign and the referent; particular words unambiguously stand for a certain category of things, actions, etc. Representation is generally *unconditional*; words like "table" and "chair" signify tables and chairs, no matter what their relationship to each other or to the speaker. This is what makes the

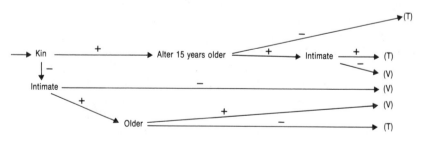

Fig. 1 A child's address system.

construction of dictionaries possible. But presentational codes do not function in the same way. An element in such a code, such as the familiar form of address, may signify any number of combinations of different aspects of a social relationship. In our example the use of the familiar form may signify a relationship between nonkin intimates of the same age or a relationship between nonintimate kin without a major age difference. We do not know which relationship is involved unless we have additional information, for example, about the existence of a kinship relation.

Thus to decipher a message in a presentational code it is generally necessary to have all kinds of extra information that does not form part of the particular message. Where we are dealing with messages governed by generally known social rules, as in the case of forms of address, we can construct a list of the various aspects of the relationship that enter into the decision as to which form to use, and we can arrange these aspects in form may signify a relationship between nonkin intimates of the same Fig. 1. In a sense such a schema functions as the equivalent of a dictionary; it tells us what information we need in order to come to an unambiguous conclusion about the meaning of a given element in a presentational code. At the present time the adequate construction of such partial "dictionaries" has been limited in the main to the case of such highly stereotyped and extremely simple elements of the presentational code as forms of address. The more idiosyncratic and complex the act of presentation, the more difficult it is to develop rules for unambiguously decoding its meaning.

Even in the case of forms of address the aspects of the social relationship that enter into the situation quickly become more complex when we enter the everyday world of adults. By using the same principles of representation as in the previous figure we can construct a diagram to illustrate the rules of a common North American address system (Fig. 2).

This system is more complex than the previous one because there is a larger set of alternative outputs, and because more aspects of the social relationship have to be taken into consideration. Among these aspects we should particularly note marital and sex status as well as "dispensation," that is, the option possessed by a senior addressee of dispensing the speaker from the use of title plus last name, and "identity set," or the list of occupational or courtesy titles due to people of certain status (Professor or Doctor).

The use of marital, sex, and occupational status illustrates the very important fact that the speaker's recognition of the addressee's social

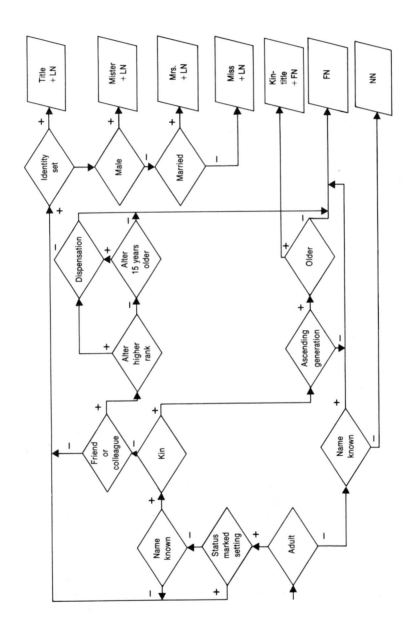

LN = last name; FN = first name; NN = no name

Fig. 2 A North American address system (Ervin-Tripp, 1969).

42

status is a vital part of their relationship. One of the commonest ways of varying the presentation of a social relationship is by discriminating among the other's social statuses to which one chooses to give explicit recognition. For example, the failure to accord an occupational or courtesy title may be intended or received as an insult or as a claim that the occupational status is irrelevant in this relationship. In any case, the manner in which I recognize or fail to recognize the various social statuses of another becomes an important part of my relationship to him.

The introduction of the "dispensation" category illustrates the fact that the meaning of a given presentation cannot often be unambiguously established by taking the contribution of only one of the partners to an interchange into account. Thus the use of a first name form of address to one of higher rank will have a completely different significance when a dispensation from the use of title plus last name has been obtained and when it has not been obtained. If the dispensation was not forthcoming the use of the first name may constitute the presentation of a claim to a degree of familiarity that is not reciprocated, or it may constitute a repudiation of the difference in rank. These implications do not exist where the first name form has been preceded by a dispensation. On the other hand, the dispensation may be given and ignored. In that case we may be dealing with a case of excessive formality, a desire to keep the other person at a distance, an inability to become familiar with one of higher rank, or even a resentment of the presumption implied in the giving of the dispensation.

In any case, the dispensation mechanism is only one example of the operation of a historical dimension in personal relationships. In very many cases the significance of a particular presentation can only be assessed by reference to certain events in the history of the relationship, a fact that does not simplify the task of decoding the meaning of presentations.

The North American address system depicted in Fig. 2 contains one further determinant that is of great significance. Near the point of entry on the left of the diagram there is reference to "status marked setting." If the speaker decides that he is in such a setting he has to proceed immediately to decisions about titles coupled with the addressee's last name; if the setting is not status marked, other decisions about the relationship between speaker and listener have to be made and the speaker may end up using first or last names, depending on circumstances. In other words, the manifest content of the final message depends not only on the relationship of the interactants but also on the setting in which the interaction takes place. It is possible that the same persons will address each other differently in a formal committee meeting and at a cocktail party.

The setting of the interaction modifies not only forms of address but other aspects of linguistic expression as well. The most common instance involves the switch between familiar or colloquial forms of speech used in informal situations and more elaborate or ceremonial forms of speech used in formal situations. Colloquial or familiar speech involves more abbreviation, ellipsis, metaphor, and slang than formal speech. Colloquially, ellipsis may involve the omission of the subject or object, leading to sentences that are incomplete and in fact inadmissible in terms of formal syntax. Such switches from formal to informal speech as a result of the redefinition of the setting can often be observed when a formal lecture is succeeded by a question period or a formal meeting is followed by a social get-together.

Labov (1966) found that speakers would use a more formal style in interview settings. Switches to more casual speech also involved a consistent complex of changes in tempo, pitch range, rate of breathing, etc. as well as syntactic and semantic changes. He therefore postulated the existence of a single dimension of "self-monitoring," which underlies the switch from less to more formal styles of speech as determined by the setting.

What makes it difficult to analyze the meaning of such stylistic differences is the fact that the same characteristics of speech may indicate either a more informal setting or a higher level of intimacy among the interactants. Similarly, more formal speech may indicate the nature of the setting or the status differential among the interactants or both. When styles of speech are analyzed as forms of presentation of social relationships it is necessary to decide whether the presented relationship is of a relatively permanent character or whether it is essentially a product of a particular setting.

Presentations are subject to a principle of contemporaneity. Their manifest content is determined by whatever social relationship exists momentarily. However, that relationship is partly determined by the setting and partly by more abiding features of the interaction between the participants. For example, the presentation of familiarity based on an informal setting may be hard to distinguish from the presentation of familiarity based on long acquaintance. There are probably some differences, but they may be too subtle for our present methods of systematic analysis. That being the case a knowledge of the prevailing conventions regarding definitions of social settings becomes necessary for interpreting the deeper significance of many linguistic presentations of social relationships.

THE STRUCTURE OF SOCIAL SPACE

European languages which, unlike English, have maintained a distinction between different pronouns of address, like *vous* and *tu* or *du* and *Sie*, seem to regulate their use by reference to two fundamental aspects of social relationship: status and solidarity (Brown and Gilman, 1960). These aspects operate independently of temporary changes in social settings and give us an insight into the more abiding structure of social relationships.

Where there is a choice between a polite and a familiar form of the pronoun of address the inferior person generally uses the polite form to his superior and in turn receives the familiar form. In medieval Europe the master used the familiar form to the servant as did the nobility to commoners and parents to children; in return they expected to receive the polite form. But equals would use the same form to each other, and this might be either the polite or the familiar form. Thus the asymmetrical use of pronouns of address would be used to present the existence of a status differential in the relationship.

Individuals equal in status still have the choice of the symmetrical use of either the polite or the familiar form. This is decided by considerations of "solidarity," with the familiar form presenting the existence of this aspect of the relationship and the polite form its absence. Thus the familiar form would be used among brothers and sisters, spouses, friends, and comrades; but the symmetrical polite form would be used among strangers and superficial acquaintances.

Because the aspects of solidarity and status vary independently it is quite possible to get relationships that involve both solidarity and a status differential. The relationships of parent and child or employer and employee would exemplify this state of affairs where there is a potential conflict between considerations of status and considerations of solidarity. Should the polite or the familiar form be used? To solve this problem societies use rules that prescribe which consideration takes precedence under different conditions. For example, the situation might be resolved by prescribing symmetrical use of the polite form between employer and employee and symmetrical use of the familiar form between parent and child. This is in fact what has happened. Brown and Gilman (1960) produce convincing evidence that the trend of historical change in Europe after the French Revolution has favored considerations of solidarity over those of status where doubtful cases had to be decided.

At a more abstract level relationships of status and solidarity are expressions of the fundamental *dimensions* of social relationships. Quite apart from their qualitative peculiarity, social relationships exist in a social space whose coordinates can be used for a description of those properties that all of them share. To speak of a relationship implies the use of a frame of reference to which the constituents of the relationship are referred. The metaphor of a social space gives expression to the existence of such a frame of reference. The very widespread tendency to use spatial terms like "close" and "distant," "high" and "low," in reference to social relationships is more than a manner of speaking. It expresses the fact that these relationships can only be represented in terms of a frame of reference, and it uses the spatial frame as the one that suggests itself most readily to human thought.

But the spatial representation of social relationships is not simply a convenience of thought, it arises out of some very concrete problems. Individuals who enter into social relationships are also physical bodies that necessarily assume positions in physical space relative to other individuals. The facts of proxemics and personal space discussed in Chapter 4 make it clear that this positioning is not left to chance but expresses the social relationships among the individuals concerned. Degrees of horizontal proximity commonly express degrees of intimacy, and positioning "above" or "in front" commonly expresses claims to superior status. Individuals think of social relationships in spatial terms because they have to make decisions about where to place their bodies relative to the bodies of other individuals. "Social space" is more than an analogy, it has a very concrete existence.

Considerations of status refer to the ordering of individuals, either symmetrically (relationships of equality) or asymmetrically (status differential). In spatial terms individuals on the same status level are placed next to each other on the same horizontal line, while individuals who differ in status are arranged along the vertical dimension. Horizontal distances would represent degrees of solidarity, while vertical distances would represent degrees of status differentiation. Any relationship could be presented in terms of these two coordinates.

The analysis of common usage of European pronouns of address leads to a clear distinction between only two dimensions of social space. However, if the analysis is extended to a further component of address systems, the use of *names* and *greetings*, a third dimension appears to emerge. Names and greetings commonly have a familiar and a polite form, just like pronouns of address. The difference between an individual's full first name and a diminutive form like "Bobby" or "Bill" or a nickname has many parallels to the difference between the familiar and polite form of pronouns of address. This is especially true in American English where the difference in solidarity implied by the transition from last name to first name usage is quite small. The distinction between "Hi" and "Good morning" reflects the same thing. Brown and Ford (1961) found that while "Good morning" is used with superiors and distant acquantances, "Hi" is more common to intimates and subordinates. The combination of "Good morning" with first name seems to imply a combination of some solidarity with little intimacy.

In languages that have retained the distinction between familiar and polite pronouns of address the combination of the familiar pronoun with a title may also express a certain disjunction between intimacy and solidarity, as in addressing God or a worldly master. A subject addressing his lord might well stress his solidarity without implying intimacy by using a formulation like "Du mein Herr' in German. Other languages, like Korean (Ervin-Tripp, 1969), may have specific address forms to signal intimacy or its absence in solidary dyads.

In the North American address system special significance may be attached to the use of *multiple naming*, when several versions of the person's proper name are used, including one or more nicknames with phonetic variations. Brown and Ford (1961) found that the use of multiple names was directly related to the degree of self-disclosure to the person so addressed, with self-disclosure constituting a direct measure of intimacy. The use of reciprocal first name forms indicates solidarity but not necessarily intimacy, while the reciprocal use of last names and titles apparently indicates the absence of both solidarity and intimacy.

The point is that solidarity may be based either on mutual participation in a common status system or on personal intimacy. There may be solidarity with some persons who differ from one in status but not with others. Examples of this may be derived from members of the same institution, the army, the church, a university, when contrasted with persons who differ in status but lack a common loyalty. Solidarity implies shared loyalties but it does not necessarily imply intimacy. In fact intimacy with solidary colleagues may be actively avoided. In some institutional environments such solidarity without intimacy may be expressed by reciprocal last name usage.

The extension of the analysis of address systems beyond the use of pronouns indicates that the two-dimensional scheme may be too simple to account for all the subtleties of interaction. At the very least, a distinction between solidarity and intimacy seems to be required, giving a three-dimensional scheme with status as the third component. In terms of the spatial analogy the vertical and horizontal dimensions of status and solidarity will need to be supplemented by a "depth" dimension expressing degrees of intimacy. Thus one arrives at a set of coordinates that can be used to locate certain common features of all dyadic interaction. The relationship between military superior or subordinate, for example, may be marked by high status differential, high solidarity, and low intimacy. The relationship between some spouses, on the other hand, may involve high intimacy and solidarity with little status differential. The relationship between parents and children may be high on all three dimensions, and that between strangers low on all dimensions.

GENERAL DIMENSIONS OF SOCIAL INTERACTION

The conception of the universal parameters of social relations in terms of the dimensions of a social space leads to a useful taxonomy, which is however limited by its static quality. The underlying relationships among individuals imply more than the taking of positions, they involve an active give-and-take among the participants. Relative positions in social space are simply indications of the kinds of interaction that are likely to take place among the occupants of those positions. Status differential along the vertical dimension implies asymmetrical acts of control and assertion on the one hand and obedience and submission on the other; intimacy along the depth dimension implies acts of self-disclosure, and solidarity along the horizontal dimension implies acts of support.

A number of studies have approached the problem of the deep structure of interpersonal behavior from the point of view of an analysis of acts rather than an analysis of positions. They have begun with complex examples of social interaction and attempted to find a parsimonious explanation of the intercorrelation among a variety of such interactions. The existence of convergencies between this approach and the structural analysis of address systems would increase our confidence in the underlying dimensions revealed by each type of analysis.

Among the types of data that have been used in the dimensional analysis of interpersonal behavior, those based on the observation of small task groups have proved particularly interesting. An early attempt to analyze small group behavior along these lines was undertaken by

Carter (1954) who concluded that the behavior of individuals working in these groups could be categorized into three dimensions: (A) Individual prominence and achievement, (B) aiding attainment by the group, and (C) sociability, efforts to establish and maintain cordial and socially satisfying relations with other group members. The first of these factors clearly relates to the vertical dimension of status differential, the second is a social solidarity factor, and the third is closely akin to the dimension of intimacy. The convergence between the triadic dimensions suggested by structural and by functional types of analysis appears to be substantial.

Somewhat similar dimensions have emerged in the work of Schutz (1958) and of Bass (1967), which is also concerned with data from small task groups. Schutz's FIRO system involves a distinction between the three factors of Control, Inclusion, and Affection, which appear to run parallel to the status, solidarity, and intimacy dimensions of the structural analysis. Bass and Dunteman (1960) have distinguished between self-orientation (enhancing one's own status), task orientation (helping the group to accomplish its task) and interaction orientation (concern with achieving satisfying social relationships). Again, there is considerable overlap with the definition of the three dimensions derived from an analysis of address systems. The well-known analysis of Bales (1956), which is also based on small group data, allows us to detect a similar convergence. His distinction between task behavior and social–emotional behavior corresponds to Bass' distinction between task orientation and interaction orientation and parallels the distinction previously made between solidarity and intimacy. Status differential is empirically related to Bales' third factor of overall social participation.

There is thus an impressive degree of overlap in the nature and number of underlying dimensions that have emerged from various studies of social interaction. One of these dimensions involves factors of relative social status and differences in the degree of prominence, control, influence, and activity that go with it. While a structural analysis naturally tends to stress status as such, functional analysis tends to focus on its behavioral correlates. The second dimension involves the factor of solidarity, pulling together to achieve a common goal or maintain a common commitment. Again, the structural analysis is more concerned with the abiding, relatively static features and the functional analysis of behavior in groups brings out the active, behavioral aspect. Finally, the commonly recognized third dimension has to do with person-to-person social–emotional satisfaction, which involves relative closeness or intimacy rather than distance and impersonality.

These three dimensions of interaction express the fact that individuals must simultaneously relate to one another as sources of power and influence, as sources of resources that need to be shared, and as sources of personal satisfaction. It is these fundamental aspects of their relationship to one another that they present in their concrete interaction, in forms of address, in types of participation in groups, and in other ways.

The interaction of mothers and children has provided another source of data for the discovery of basic dimensions of interpersonal behavior. Focusing on reports of maternal behavior from a number of studies, Schaefer (1959) developed a two-dimensional structure whose axes were labeled Love–Hostility and Control–Autonomy, respectively. Various types of maternal behavior could be categorized in terms of these dimensions. Thus the authoritarian mother would be high on control and hostility and the democratic mother would be high on love and autonomy. Subsequent reanalysis of some of Schaefer's data together with a consideration of other studies indicates that a three-dimensional solution fits the observed correlations in this area much better than Schaefer's two-dimensional solution (Becker, 1964). The control–autonomy dimension divides into two other dimensions: restrictiveness versus permissiveness and anxious–emotional involvement versus calm detachment. This makes it possible to make some very necessary distinctions. For example, both the democratic parent and the indulgent parent are high on the dimensions of warmth and permissiveness, but the indulgent parent is high on emotionality while the democratic parent falls near the calm end of this dimension.

It is not difficult to recognize the congruence between the restrictiveness factor, which is defined by an abundance of demands, and the previously distinguished dimension of status and control. Nor does the overlap between maternal warmth and the generalized dimension of intimacy present major problems. The relationship between parental calmness and the solidarity dimension is not so obvious. It must be remembered that solidarity has been defined in terms of a shared orientation to a common task or commitment. Given the generally highly involving task commitment of mothers it is possible that in this context the analysis of individual differences leads to a displacement of the definition of the underlying scale in the direction of overcommitment. This is hardly likely to happen in the case of temporary work groups that have formed the basis for analyses that emerge with a dimension of task-orientation. In the case of mothers there is probably a wholesale shift toward one pole of this dimension, leading to a redefinition of the scale as a whole.

Several analyses of the underlying dimensions of interpersonal behavior have used a two-dimensional rather than a three-dimensional
framework. Leary (1957) uses two orthogonal axes,
Dominance–Submission and Hostility–Affection, to account for correlations among inventory items about interpersonal behavior. Foa (1961)
uses this work and that of Schaefer as a basis for his own analysis. Straus
(1964) sees evidence for a two-dimensional structure of family interaction, the two axes being Power and Support. It is therefore appropriate to
enquire into the conditions that will favor either a two-dimensional or a
three-dimensional analysis of social interaction.

A study by Longabaugh (1966) throws some interesting light on this
question. The data consisted of coded observations of the social behavior
of children in six cultures located in Mexico, Kenya, India, Okinawa,
Philippines, and New England (Whiting *et al.*, 1966). Twelve coding
categories were used for scoring social behavior:

Gives help.
Suggests responsibility.
Reprimands.
Attempts to dominate.
Acts sociable.
Calls attention to self.
Gives support or approval.
Physically contacts.
Is succorant.
Assaults sociably.
Assaults physically.
Symbolic aggression.

Two frequency measures were derived for each category: the frequency of occurrence of the behavior was divided by the amount of time
the child was observed to obtain a behavioral *rate*, and divided by the
total amount of interpersonal activity initiated by the child to obtain a
proportion score. Twelve correlation matrices were calculated, one for
each measure in each culture. For each type of measure a significant
number of correlations were found to be cross-culturally significant.
Factor analysis of a matrix of average correlations based on all the
cultures yielded a different solution for the rate data and the proportion
data.

Behavioral *rate* data could best be described in terms of three factors.
The first of these represents activities that aid group attainment, like
suggesting responsibility, reprimanding, and approving. The second

factor represents individual domination as expressed in sociable but not physical assault, symbolic aggression, and attempts at domination. The third factor involves the categories of succorance and acting sociably. The fit between these factors and other three-factor analyses of social interaction, like those of Carter, Bass, Bales, and Schutz is reasonably close. In all cases we seem to get the factors of task or group attainment, individual dominance or prominence, and sociability of intimacy.

However, the factor analysis of Longabough's data based on *proportion* scores yielded not a three-factor but a two-factor solution. The first of these bipolar factors is defined at one end by the variables of sociable assault and symbolic aggression and at the opposite pole by the variables of succorance and sociability. The second factor is defined by giving help, support, and approval at one pole and sociability and symbolic aggression at the other. This pattern shows resemblance to traditional two-factor solutions, like that of Leary (1957), with a distinction between an affiliation and a control axis.

The real point of interest in the comparison of the three-factor and the two-factor solution, however, is the disappearance of the task attainment factor in the latter. The answer lies in the high correlation of this factor with overall rate of social activity or participation (0.71 in Longabaugh's study), which means that when the analysis is based on proportion scores rather than on actual behavioral rates this factor drops out of sight. Typically, studies of small groups that are the usual source of three-factor solutions have taken social participation rates into account explicitly, while studies based on ratings of personality (Leary) and of maternal behavior (Schaefer) have not been concerned with the measurement of rates and have emerged with two-factor solutions. The third factor in maternal behavior was defined by Becker (1964) in terms of an involvement–detachment continuum (with emotional overtones) and this is clearly a factor closely related to participation rate, as would be expected in terms of our analysis.

The most reasonable conclusion on the basis of all the available evidence is that there appears to be considerable convergence in analyses of the dimensions of social interaction based on different types of data. If participation rates are neglected, as frequently happens in personality and family studies, a control–power factor and a support–affiliation factor are likely to dominate the scene. If interaction data based on rates are used a third factor defined in terms of social task attainment is likely to emerge. These three factors appear to be related to the dimensions of status, intimacy, and solidarity, which can be derived from an analysis of address systems. In all cases the first factor can be thought of as supplying the vertical dimension of social space, the second factor as contributing the depth dimension, and the third factor as constituting the horizontal dimension. Social interaction is conveniently analyzed in terms of the three components of *influence*, *intimacy*, and *integration*.

These three components define the underlying structure of social relationships at the most general level. It is this structure that social acts present overtly, in addition to the special content of particular relationships. Every social act presents at the same time an influence relationship, a level of intimacy, and a mode of integration; although the relevance of any particular act is not the same for each component. Overt social acts always say something about these features of the underlying relationship, although sometimes the code may be complex and subtle.

While three dimensions may be adequate for analyzing the most general features of social presentations, an additional consideration becomes relevant as soon as we introduce the temporal element that is always present in social interaction. The data on which analyses of the dimensions of social space are based consist either of overall ratings of long behavior sequences, or of coded individual acts. In either case there has been an abstraction from the actual sequencing of acts in time. The introduction of the temporal dimension forces us to raise questions about the relationship of any social act to preceding and succeeding acts emanating from the interaction partner. Speech acts typically form an alternative sequence of contributions by at least two partners. Quite apart from the features of the social relationship that such acts present, there remains the additional problem of how successive acts are related to each other. This type of question supplies a fourth dimension in the analysis of social interaction.

At the most general level the answer to the question involves a distinction between the initiating and the reactive properties of social acts. Every act embedded in an interaction sequence is both a reaction to a preceding part of the interaction and a stimulus that initiates succeeding acts. This forms a dimension of responsivity on which acts could be located in terms of the relative weight contributed by the reactive component. Acts might vary from those that are entirely determined by antecedent acts to those that ignore preceding parts of the sequence and play a purely initiatory role.

The need for such a temporal component becomes apparent when one tries to approach the structure of social interaction via an analysis of the meaning of interpersonal verbs. Osgood (1970) collected 198 of these, including verbs like "promise," "impress," "resist," "challenge," and showed that they could be distinguished from one another in terms of judgments about their position on each of ten dimensions. Three of these dimensions involved the affective scales of valuation, potency, and activity, which appear to have a very general role in the definition of semantic spaces. Three other dimensions were necessary because Osgood wished to relate his data to the meaning of *intentions*. The remaining four dimensions are concerned with the structure of interpersonal behavior. Three of them are readily identifiable with the dimensions of social space that generally emerge from an analysis of interaction; they are concerned with status differential, affective relations, and the achievement of effects in ego or alter.

But the effective discrimination of interpersonal verbs requires a further dimension, concerned with the question of whether the speaker intends to elicit some response from the addressee or whether he wishes to respond to some prior behavior of the other person. In the first case the intent is said to be *initiating*, in the second case it is *reacting*. Examples of initiating interpersonal verbs are "convert," "arouse," "inspire," "guide," "pursue," "provoke," "compel"; while verbs like "answer," "follow," "pardon," "accept," "refute," and "rebuke" are reactive. Compared to the analysis of address systems the analysis of interpersonal verbs is still in its infancy. However, it has already proved useful in introducing a temporal perspective into the set of dimensions that describe the most general features of interpersonal relationships.

CONCLUSION

The study of forms of social address provides interesting examples of how the presentational function of communication expresses itself through a linguistic medium. Whether an individual is addressed by his title, his first name, or by the polite form of the appropriate personal pronoun, depends on a series of considerations about the relative age of the speaker and the person addressed, about the degree of intimacy or of status differentiation between them, about kinship relationships, and so on. It also depends on the situational context, which is, as we have noted, a common feature of presentational messages.

Having isolated the function of communication as presentation the next step is to ask whether there is any generality about the categories of social relationships that individuals present to each other when they interact. In most cases there will be strong idiosyncratic overtones that arise out of the qualitative nuances inherent in almost all social relationships. On the other hand, as we have seen in the analysis of address systems, the general features of social relationships that are presented in interpersonal communication are often simply an expression of age, sex, and kinship roles. The question arises, however, whether one can distinguish general dimensions of interpersonal behavior to which social presentations are reliably linked. Such dimensions would provide a set of coordinates for the location of any social presentation in a kind of interpersonal space.

Empirical studies of social interaction in various contexts have emerged with a characterization of the fundamental coordinates of interpersonal space that show a considerable degree of convergence from one study to another. Most of these investigations have emerged with three general components in terms of which interpersonal communication can be adequately described. Although different investigators have used a varying nomenclature it is not difficult to recognize an underlying convergence in their results. These suggest that social interaction can conveniently be analyzed in terms of three components that we may call *influence*, *intimacy*, and *integration*. The first component involves factors of social status and the associated social power, the second component is self-explanatory, and the third involves solidarity and a common commitment. These components can be used as the coordinates of an interpersonal space in which any given presentation can be located.

The fact that any extended act of interpersonal communication presents, at the same time, an influence relationship, a level of intimacy, and a mode of integration is merely an illustration of the fact that individuals must simultaneously relate to one another as sources of power and influence, as sources of personal satisfaction, and as sources of resources that need to be shared.

REFERENCES

Bales, R. F. (1956). Task status and likeability as a function of talking and listening in decision-making groups. In L. D. White (Ed.), *The State of the Social Sciences*. Chicago: University of Chicago Press.

Bass, B. M. (1967). Social behavior and the orientation inventory: a review. *Psychol. Bull.*, **68**, 260–292.

Bass, B. M. and Dunteman, G. (1960). Behavior in groups as a function of self, interaction, and task orientation. *J. abnorm. & soc. Psychol.*, **66**, 419–428.

Becker, W. C. (1964). Consequences of different kinds of parental discipline. In M. L. Hoffman and L. W. Hoffman (Eds.), *Review of Child Development Research*. Vol. I. New York: Russell Sage Foundation.

Brown, R. and Ford, M. (1961). Address in American English. *J. abnorm. & soc. Psychol.*, **62**, 375–385.

Brown, R. and Gilman, A. (1960). The pronouns of power and solidarity. In T. Sebeok (Ed.), *Style in Language*. New York: Wiley.

Carter, L. F. (1954). Evaluating the performance of individuals in small groups. *Personnel Psychol.*, **7**, 477–484.

Ervin-Tripp, S. M. (1969). Sociolinguistics. In L. Berkowitz (Ed.), *Advances in Experimental Social Psychology*. Vol. 4. New York: Academic Press.

Foa, U. G. (1961). Convergences in the analysis of the structure of interpersonal behavior. *Psychol. Rev.*, **68**, 341–353.

Labov, W. (1966). *The Social Stratification of English in New York City*. Washington, D.C.: Center for Applied Linguistics.

Lambert, W. E. (1967). The use of *tu* and *vous* as forms of address in French Canada: A pilot study. *J. verb. Learning and verb. Behavior*, **6**, 614–617.

Leary, T. (1957). *Interpersonal Diagnosis of Personality*. New York: Ronald Press.

Longabaugh, R. (1966). The structure of interpersonal behavior. *Sociometry*, **29**, 441–460.

Osgood, C. E. (1970). Speculation on the structure of interpersonal intentions. *Behavioral Science*, **15**, 237–254.

Schaefer, E. S. (1959). A circumplex model for maternal behavior. *J. abnorm. & soc. Psychol.*, **59**, 226–235.

Schutz, W. C. (1958). *FIRO: A Three-Dimensional Theory of Interpersonal Behavior*. New York: Holt, Rinehart & Winston.

Straus, M. A. (1964). Power and support structure of the family in relation to socialization. *J. Marriage and the Family*, **26**, 318–326.

Whiting, J. W. M., Child, I. L., and Lambert, W. W. (1966). *Field Guide for a Study of Socialization: Six Culture Series, Vol. 1.* New York: Wiley.

CHAPTER 4

Nonverbal Communication

INTRODUCTION

If we are to be serious about studying interpersonal communication as a process we cannot ignore its mechanisms. As long as we are content to treat interpersonal communication simply in terms of inputs and outputs in the form of individual characteristics of the participants we need not concern ourselves with what actually happens when people communicate. We can, for example, measure individual attitudes before and after a discussion, or individual adjustment before and after psychotherapy, without inquiring *how* discussion changes attitudes or psychotherapy changes adjustment. But then we are not really studying interpersonal communication, we are only studying its effects. If we want to find out anything about the process itself we have to study the actual mechanism of communication.

By mechanism we do not mean the physical process of voice production or the process of speech perception but only such aspects as are relevant to an understanding of those unique features of interpersonal communication that we are interested in. Among these aspects the concepts of channel and code are of central importance. Like all communication the process of interpersonal communication involves the use of channels for the transmission of messages and of codes that carry the message. Without channels and codes there is no communication.

A channel involves some physical apparatus that transmits messages coded in a particular manner. The human voice and hearing constitute one such channel, or rather two, because it is possible for messages flowing through this apparatus to be coded in two different ways. One way of coding involves words, the other involves nonverbal signals like sighs groans, laughter, and cries. Because of the different coding principles involved we speak of two channels, although they share the same physical apparatus. The nonverbal channel that utilizes the speech apparatus also involves variations in voice quality during speech. Quite apart from the verbal content of what a person says, variation in the loudness, pitch, tempo, stress, etc. of his speech can communicate something of his feelings. He may talk in an excited, animated way at times, and at other times his speech may become halting and hesitant. Such changes communicate information to the sensitive listener and therefore constitute a true communication channel. The nonverbal aspects of speech are often referred to as *paralanguage*—they accompany linguistic expression but are not themselves part of language. In written language the paralinguistic channel is almost completely excluded, except for such practices as the use of dashes to indicate hesitation or the use of italics to indicate emphasis.

The existence of paralanguage should alert us to the fact that human communication is not exclusively verbal. There is a strong tendency to think of human communication solely in terms of language, because the verbal component is what we are most aware of when we communicate. But apart from paralanguage there are numerous other nonverbal channels that all contribute to the total pattern of human communication. The person who sits tensely on the edge of his chair is communicating something, and so is the person who lolls back in his chair with his feet on the table. People communicate with their eyes too, they exchange "killing" or "fetching" looks, they glare at one another or coyly avert their gaze. Facial expressions obviously have a role to play in what we call face-to-face communication, and gestures and movements also take their place in the repertoire of communicative acts. The speech mechanism is far from being the only apparatus used in human communication, and if we want to study the communication process seriously we shall have to pay attention to the multiplicity of channels that it utilizes.

PROXEMICS

Human individuals are not limited to the verbal channel in presenting their social relationships, as in forms of address. On the contrary, nonverbal channels have lost little of the importance they have in the interaction of subhuman primates. For example, men continue to attach considerable significance to the way they position themselves relative to one another. The systematic study of these spatial features of social presentation is commonly referred to as *proxemics* (Hall, 1959).

The simplest proxemic problem, and the one that has been most extensively investigated, refers to the *interpersonal distance* that individuals maintain when they interact with one another. When we talk to someone the distance that is maintained between ourselves and our partner varies surprisingly little. The usual nose-to-nose distance in ordinary conversation is four to five feet and variations of more than some inches either way soon lead to feelings of discomfort. This obviously has little or nothing to do with the carrying capacity of the human voice; it depends on the existence of well-defined norms for such interactions. Space that is simultaneously inhabited by several individuals becomes socialized, and the way in which individuals place themselves relative to one another is an expression of social rather than physical requirements.

If an ordinary acquaintance violated the unwritten rules of interpersonal distance and placed himself within two feet or within ten feet of one's face when talking to us, we would feel uncomfortable and move ourselves away from him or toward him until the "appropriate" interpersonal distance had been reestablished. Why should this be? Clearly, the amount of space that people leave between themselves is not a matter of indifference but communicates something. If we were engaged in an intimate exchange with a loved one a distance of two feet might not prove at all uncomfortable, in fact we may try to reduce it further. So acceptable interpersonal distances vary with the quality of the relationship between the participants. What the amount of space left between them communicates is something about the nature of their relationship. A person who comes too close for comfort is making a claim that we do not wish to meet; so we step back and "put him in his place."

It is not difficult to appreciate that the narrowing of interpersonal distance indicates a claim to a higher degree of intimacy. Under normal conditions there is no dispute about the level of intimacy that exists between two interactants, and they collaborate to maintain a constant interpersonal distance at which they both feel comfortable. The level of this constant is as much a presentation of a feature of their social relationship as is their use of an appropriate form of address.

When experimental subjects were asked to place cardboard representations of human figures at appropriate distances from one another it was found that this distance was a function of the degree of prior acquaintance attributed to the figures (Little, 1965). Conversely, subjects watching silent films of a series of individuals entering a person's office had no difficulty in deducing their level of acquaintance from the way in which they positioned themselves relative to one another (Burns, 1964). The communicative function of social space emerges quite clearly in these studies.

However, in interpreting the meaning of different levels of interpersonal distance the status differential among the participants must also be taken into account. People of equal status tend to sit closer together than people of unequal status (Lott and Sommer, 1967). Where a status differential exists there is lack of reciprocity in the permissible closeness of approach to the other person. The lower-status individual may allow the higher-status individual to approach quite closely but not dare to approach such a high-status person to the same degree of closeness. In one experiment student subjects allowed white-coated experimenters to approach them significantly more closely than they would themselves approach these experimenters (Hartnett, Bailey, and Gibson, 1970).

The level of interpersonal distance achieved between two individuals apparently involves a balance between their respective approach and retreat tendencies. It is not a static parameter but a product of a dynamic equilibrium between tendencies to move closer and tendencies to move further away. At any moment the relative strength of these tendencies is determined by the level of intimacy and the status differential between the interactants as well as the interpersonal distance reached at that time. Among equal status individuals there will be reciprocity of approach and retreat tendencies so that the same balance is reached whether A approaches B or B approaches A. The precise level of interpersonal distance at which this balance is reached will depend on the degree of intimacy that exists among the interactants. Where there are status inequalities there is lack of reciprocity between the approach and retreat tendencies of the interactants. The individual of higher status will be permitted to approach more closely than the individual of lower status. However, it should be emphasized that while these generalizations appear plausible on the basis of the existing evidence they await more extensive confirmation.

The *setting* of the interaction is at least as important in the case of the choice of an appropriate interpersonal distance as it is in the case of the choice of titles in address systems. Typically, interpersonal distances for conversation are somewhat less in the street than they might be in a private home. This suggests that the crucial parameter may be a product of interpersonal distance and the extensiveness of the physical boundaries within which interaction takes place. Social space always includes a boundary as well as the interacting individuals, and their positioning relative to one another is not independent of their positioning in relation to the boundary.

Just as the rules for appropriate forms of address vary from one language community to another, so the rules for appropriate levels of interpersonal distance vary from culture to culture. One study reported more closeness among Arabs than Americans (Watson and Graves, 1966). Another study showed that white middle-class children in New York habitually stand much further apart than poor black or Puerto Rican children of the same age (Aiello and Jones, 1971). Moreover, there was a distinct sex difference in the white group but not in the other groups, with girls maintaining less interpersonal distance than boys. The fact that the children in this study were only six to eight years old indicates that the relevant culturally determined rules are learned quite early in life.

It is obvious that the existence of such differences in norms entails a strong possibility of misunderstanding when members of different cultures interact in face-to-face situations. The American middle-class person used to relatively large interpersonal distances may easily misinterpret the closer distances that are the rule in many other cultures (Hall, 1966). Actual body contact or touching is of course the limiting case of interpersonal distance. By and large, those cultures that rule in favor of relatively high levels of interpersonal distance also seem to discourage touching. Jourard (1966) counted the frequency of contact of couples in cafés in cities in different countries and reports the following contacts per hour: San Juan 180, Paris 110, Gainsville 2, London 0.

Apart from interpersonal distance the physical positioning of interactants to one another is another proxemic factor that may have significance for the presentation of social relationships. Individuals who claim higher status in an interaction, such as a chairman, position themselves so that they face as many other participants as possible (Sommer, 1967). In some cultures it is important to address a high-status person from a lower position, and this may entail kneeling or squatting down. The bow expresses the same relationship of submission along a vertical axis. Among peers the nature of the task-related interaction determines seating patterns. Cooperating pairs tend to sit next to each other and competing pairs place themselves across from one another (Sommer, 1965). Thus, whereas interpersonal distance is clearly related to the dimension of intimacy, positioning in space is more likely to be involved in the presentation of status and task relationships.

POSTURE

Apart from adopting different spatial positions relative to one another the participants in an interaction also have the choice among a large number of possible arrangements of the parts of their bodies. They may turn or tilt head and shoulders at various angles, adopt a variety of positions for arms and legs, and generally hold themselves at different levels of tension and relaxation. These aspects of posture may become so many different ways of presenting a social relationship.

However, before we can analyze posture as a form of communication we must be careful to distinguish the communicative function of nonverbal behavior from its indicative or expressive function (Ekman, 1965). A relaxed posture or a tilted head may indicate something about an individual's attitude or emotional state, but unless it can be demonstrated that others can correctly interpret this indication we have no evidence that any communicative purpose has been served. In other words, the nonverbal behavior must be readable as a code before any communicational significance can be claimed for it. For this purpose it is not always necessary that people are able to translate the nonverbal into a verbal code, it is enough that they respond appropriately to the meaning of the nonverbal code. For example, one may accept the higher-status position that an individual's manner assigns to one without being able to verbalize this fact, let alone analyze the relevant components of the other's nonverbal behavior. Nevertheless, many studies of nonverbal behavior are irrelevant from the point of view of social psychology because they only investigate the indicative functions of such behavior without raising questions about its functions as a medium of communication.

Turning first to the tension–relaxation aspect of posture we find that lack of reciprocity on this dimension tends to occur under conditions of unequal status interaction. When a high-status individual is interacting with a low-status individual the former will probably be more relaxed than the latter (Goffman, 1961). Various measures of limb relaxation as well as sideways tilt indicate more relaxation when addressing a low-status than a high-status person (Mehrabian, 1969). While these experiments show that individuals can *encode* the nonverbal presentation of status differences, the confirmation that they can also *decode* the status aspect of relative relaxation is still tentative.

In regard to body orientation a more direct orientation of the shoulders seems to occur with a high-status than with a low-status addressee (Mehrabian, 1968). In general, a less direct orientation seems to be interpreted as an indicator of a less positive attitude to the addressee (Mehrabian, 1967).

One aspect of body orientation is more related to social distance than to status. If a communicator leans forward, toward the addressee, he will be seen as expressing a more positive attitude than when he leans backward, away from the addressee (Mehrabian, 1968).

Some fairly consistent sex differences in postural communication have been reported. In one study females assumed a more open arrangement of the arms while communicating to liked than to disliked male addressees, but the corresponding difference was not observed for males or for females communicating to other females (Mehrabian, 1968). Moreover, when subjects were asked to interpret the difference between more or less open arm positions they related this difference to different degrees of liking for the addressee with female but not with male communicators. This suggests that this aspect of the postural code may well have a genuine communicative and not merely an indicative function. Such sex differences in the meaning of nonverbal signals demonstrate that the social identity of the communicator must be considered in decoding nonverbal messages.

GAZE DIRECTION

The fact that people communicate by means of a language of the eyes has been apparent since ancient times. Belief in the evil eye is expressed in the literature of ancient Egypt, Babylonia, Greece, and Rome. Francis Bacon felt that love and envy affect the eye with particular ease and so communicate themselves to their object. Yet, although innumerable literary and poetic allusions to the eye as a medium of communication can be found, systematic psychological research of this phenomenon is of quite recent origin.

In the first place we have to establish the fact that variations in eye gaze indeed carry a message for others and are not merely subjective expressions of attitudes and affects that cannot normally be decoded. This is the distinction between the indicative and the communicative function of nonverbal behavior that we already had occasion to make in the case of posture. People may be more inclined to gaze at liked than at disliked others but it is necessary to confirm that this kind of difference is successfully interpreted by individuals without special training.

One striking feature of human gaze behavior that has attracted a great deal of attention among experimental social psychologists is the phenomenon of *eye contact* that occurs when two individuals look directly at each other's eyes. In conversation, a certain proportion of time is spent in this kind of contact, while the rest of the time is taken up by nonreciprocated looking at the other or even by mutual gaze avoidance. Does the relative amount of eye contact in face-to-face interaction have anything to do with the relationship among the interactants and do people use such cues in making judgments about interpersonal relationships?

It has been found that in an interview situation the induction of positive affect toward the interviewer leads to significantly more eye contact on the part of the interviewee, and the induction of negative affect leads to significantly less eye contact when compared to a neutral condition (Exline and Winters, 1965). In other interviews those subjects who were asked embarrassing questions looked significantly less at the interviewer than those who were asked innocuous questions (Exline, Gray, and Schuette, 1965).

The question of how observers interpret such differences in eye contact was addressed in an experiment in which subjects were shown silent films of interviews in which eye contact occurred 80% of the time or only 15% of the time (Kleck and Nuessle, 1968). It was found that the observers interpreted the high eye contact interviews as involving significantly higher degrees of attraction and of tension among the participants. Thus the degree of eye contact appears to have a communicative as well as an indicative function, although this is a finding that needs to be confirmed by data from the actual participants in the interaction.

What is involved in the maintenance of eye contact? Clearly, a person who is being looked at has the choice of either looking back or looking away, i.e. avoiding the gaze of the other. The more strongly the tendency to look back predominates over the tendency to look away for both participants, the longer will be the period of eye contact. We have seen that positive affect for the other increases eye contact and embarrassment decreases eye contact. Thus in dyads where there is strong mutual attraction there will be a great deal of eye contact and in dyads where there is embarrassment there will be relatively little eye contact. The major cause of embarrassment is an invasion of privacy, a revelation of things that are not meant for the gaze of the other. Conversely, a high level of mutual eye contact is indicative of a high tolerance for mutual closeness or intimacy. We have already noted the existence of similar relationships in the case of physical proximity between individuals, with greater physical closeness indicating higher levels of intimacy. It is therefore possible to think of the act of looking at another as a form of moving closer, to him and the act of gaze avoidance as an act of moving away. High levels of eye contact are therefore equivalent to high levels of physical proximity.

There is strong evidence that this equivalence of eye contact and physical proximity is more than an analogy that exists only in the mind of the observer. Interacting individuals seem to behave as though eye contact and physical proximity were alternative channels for the presentation of the same aspects of their relationship. The relationship between these two channels of expression is additive, so that the combination of close physical proximity with high levels of eye contact expresses higher levels of intimacy than either one without the other. This means that when distance in one of these channels is artificially reduced, individuals react by a compensatory increase of distance in the other channel. In crowded places like elevators or public transport eye contact is distinctly reduced as though to make up for the suggestion of intimacy produced by close physical proximity.

In an experimental demonstration of this effect Argyle and Dean (1965) had subjects sit at distances of two, six, or ten feet from an experimenter who gazed at them continuously and engaged them in conversation. It was found that there was significantly less eye contact as interpersonal distance increased. Also, the average length of glances was greater the larger the interpersonal distance. Subjects therefore compensated for variations in physical distance by varying the amount of eye contact so that the two channels in combination always presented about the same level of intimacy that was felt to be appropriate in this particular relationship. In terms of this analysis the content of the conversation can be thought of as yet another channel for expressing different levels of intimacy, and the decreased eye contact that occurs when topics become embarrassingly intimate can be interpreted as another instance of compensatory reduction in the overall level of intimacy presented by the relationship.

In taking the degree of eye contact as an indication of intimacy we must be careful to remind ourselves that eye contact is itself a product of more elementary acts that may individually have a very different significance. The level of eye contact will vary with (a) the duration of the looks each interactant gives the other, (b) the frequency with which each interactant directs his look at the other, and (c) the frequency with which each interactant breaks contact. Only if there is a reasonably high degree of reciprocity in regard to (a) and (b) and if (c) is at a relatively low level for both interactants can really high levels of eye contact be maintained. A reduction in eye contact could be the result of a significant variation in any one of these variables for either of the interactants. High levels of eye contact therefore indicate, first, a preponderance of looking at over looking away, and second, a reciprocity between the interactants.

Where we have lack of reciprocity between the interactants one may spend more time than his partner in looking at the other, or he may look at the other more frequently, or he may break contact more frequently. Such lack of reciprocity is obviously related to other aspects of the relationship than the level of intimacy. Thus where one partner maintains a steady gaze while the other frequently breaks contact and looks away we would be inclined to infer a relationship of dominance and submission. Strongman and Champness (1968) were able to demonstrate the existence of a hierarchy of frequency of glance aversion for ten subjects who interacted with one another in all possible dyadic combinations. These subjects could be arranged in a hierarchy according to the likelihood that they would be the first to break eye contact while the other was still looking at them. This is suggestive of a dominance hierarchy in which the interactants gaze at each other until the less dominant partner looks away.

The dominating qualities of the human look are certainly attested by the widespread belief in the evil eye and by frequent literary references to the "imperious glance" of charismatic individuals. How are these observations to be reconciled with the notion that eye contact expresses affiliative tendencies?

Perhaps the most useful interpretation of the human look directed at another is to regard it as a form of address. To look at another is to address him, to take him into account. The response to this address will depend on the social identity of both the source of the address and the addressee. It will also depend on the verbal and nonverbal content of the message that is sent to the addressee. Looking at the other may be thought of as another way of calling him. It informs him that he is at the focus of the looker's attention. The person being looked at will interpret this information in the light of other aspects of the relationship. If the source of the look is a stranger it will be interpreted as an invitation to assume a relationship, an invitation that may cause interest, embarrassment or revulsion, depending on the circumstances. At other times the look may have the quality of a confrontation that may be accepted by attempting to outstare the other, or rejected, by looking away. But the look of the other may also indicate his interest in oneself or one's actions, and if this interest is mutual a high level of eye contact may result. The person who looks will generally communicate the purpose of the address through other channels, by his posture, gestures, statements and so on, and the social setting will convey further information about the way the address is to be interpreted.

The address contained in the look may or may not be reciprocated. If it is not reciprocated no interaction results. If it is reciprocated there are three possibilities. First, the recipient of the look may look back to an extent that amounts to escalation of the relationship either toward higher levels of intimacy or toward an antagonistic encounter. Second, he may adopt a pattern of looking back briefly and then looking away, in this way signaling an ambivalent posture where the source of the look is at the focus of attention but arouses avoidance tendencies. Depending on the context, this may indicate the acceptance of a dominance relationship or embarrassment. Finally, the recipient of the look may simply restrict his visual response to the minimum required by the need to regulate the rest of the exchange, which may be a conversational encounter. In this case the addressee is adopting a matter of fact, task-oriented definition of the relationship; his pattern of looking signals that the interaction is dominated not so much by the personal relationship of the interactants to each other as by a common task focus.

This *regulatory* function of the look has been studied by Kendon (1967) who finds that in conversation speakers typically look away at the beginning of longer statement and look at the listener as they reach the end of the statement. During the time they are holding the floor speakers characteristically look at their listener at the end of phrases. The pattern of gaze direction therefore serves to regulate interchanges between speaker and listener during a conversation. It is characteristic of human conversation that the roles of speaker and listener have to alternate. The apportioning of speaking and listening roles therefore has to be regulated. The pattern of gaze direction has an important function in this regulation. Looking away at the beginning of a long utterance or during pauses denies the listener the floor and signals the speaker's intention to go on with his statement. Looking up at the end of the statement may be a way of offering the listener the floor.

In addition to these regulatory functions looks during social interaction also have a *monitoring* function, i.e. they provide the speaker with feedback about how his message is being received. Thus in looking at the listener at the end of his statement the speaker may be looking for signs that the listener wishes to change roles and take the floor himself. In looking at the listener at the end of a phrase the speaker may be checking that he still has the attention of the listener and generally informing himself about the effect that his message is having on the listener. Argyle, Lalljee, and Cook (1968) showed that when subjects had to interact with persons who were either partially hidden by dark glasses or a mask or were wholly hidden by a one-way screen they experienced considerable discomfort. This discomfort was maximized when they were on the wrong side of the one-way vision screen, so that they could be observed without being able to see the other. When the other person was invisible, subjects preferred the symmetrical condition of being invisible themselves. Individuals clearly use visual feedback to inform themselves of the effect of their social performance on others and perhaps modify their performance in the light of the information so received. The person who has access to this channel of information while the other has not is apparently regarded as being at an advantage. This may be linked to the asymmetry of looking and gaze aversion in dominance relationships.

It is likely that what individuals chiefly seek to monitor in looking for their effect on others are signs of approval or disapproval. This makes it possible for them to modify their social performance so as to maximize approving feedback. If there is more than one addressee to whom their performance is directed they may achieve a maximization of approving feedback by looking preferentially at the person who is expected to be the most approving of their performance (Efran and Broughton, 1966). The higher the status of the addressee the more valuable his approval becomes. Efran (1968) found that freshmen looked more at individuals toward whom they had developed higher expectancies for approval when these individuals were thought to be seniors than when they were thought to be freshmen.

Some studies in this area have reported large and consistent sex differences with women engaging in more eye contact than men and apparently relying more heavily on visual feedback in social interaction; they are also looked at more than men. However, these differences have not always been observed and any generalization based on them must be treated with care (Kendon and Cook, 1969). One way of accounting for most of the observed sex differences is to suppose that women's visual behavior in social interaction is more influenced by the tendency to increase visual feedback from preferred or important sources while men's behavior is more influenced by the tendency to avoid visual feedback from less preferred or stress inducing sources. Needless to say, no cross-cultural generality could be claimed for this hypothesis.

In summarizing the complex role of the human gaze in social interaction we must start from the fact that the look is a truly interpersonal event that has simultaneous effects on both its sender and its receiver. At one and the same time it establishes a channel through which the sender can receive feedback from its target and it also addresses a signal to the target. Both the feedback received by the sender and the signal received by the target have repercussions. By means of visual feedback the sender is able to monitor his own effect on the target and thus to modify any aspects of his behavior that lead to a less desired type of feedback.

In addressing a target by means of his gaze the sender is able to send messages whose effect will depend on the context of the interaction. The effect may be purely regulatory in terms of coordinating the behavior of two participants in a joint activity such as a conversation. But the effect may also involve the establishment of more or less stable features of the relationship between the interactants, especially their level of intimacy or relative dominance. The structuring of the relationship in terms of these features involves a pattern of reciprocity in the gaze direction of the interactants. Where such reciprocity is not achieved the relationship is likely to prove unstable and to be marked by poor coordination of activities and by conflict over acceptable levels of intimacy and dominance.

PARALANGUAGE

Among the nonverbal aspects of communication it is important to include those features of speech that are concerned with *how* something is said rather than with what is said. Here we include the rise and fall in the pitch, stress and loudness of speech as well as its tempo and the hesitations that interrupt it. The same verbal content can be expressed in a variety of ways, and each time a different message will be received. It is even possible to contradict the verbal content paralinguistically and to say "no" in such a way that one obviously means "yes."

Unfortunately, studies of paralanguage have more often concentrated on its indicative than on its communicative aspects. In the present context we are however not concerned with what these aspects of speech express but rather with what they actually communicate in social interaction. That paralanguage is a potential vehicle for communication appears from a number of studies which show that judges can reliably distinguish speech qualities like pitch, loudness and tempo (Duncan, 1969). Other studies indicate that variations in these qualities are used to make judgments about the emotional state of the communicator (Davitz, 1964). However, these judgments are quite gross and relate mainly to distinguishing so-called "active" emotions like anger and joy from quieter ones. These active emotions are inferred from the existence of a fast rate of speech, loudness, high pitch, and blaring timbre, but the different active emotions are frequently confused with one another when only these cues are available. More subtle aspects of speech, like changes in rhythm, inflection, and enunciation are presumably involved in making judgments about other aspects of the emotional state of the speaker but systematic studies of this area are only beginning (Scherer, 1974).

The significance of the "activity" dimension of paralanguage, which includes speech rate and volume as well as intonation, has been further explored by Mehrabian (1970) who considers that this dimension communicates responsiveness to the addressee. This conclusion is arrived at on the basis of experiments in which subjects were required to present messages with varying degrees of persuasiveness (Mehrabian and Williams, 1969). The perceived persuasiveness of a message varied with paralinguistic signs of degree of activity as expressed in speech rate and volume, the unhalting quality of speech and intonation.

It seems clear that certain paralinguistic signs reliably increase the impact of a verbal message. Intonation is of course also used to regulate the alternation of listening and speaking in conversation. But beyond this the role of nonverbal speech qualities in social interaction remains largely a matter of everyday impressions and speculation.

MOVEMENT

People do not keep still when they interact. Apart from gross differences in posture they use their hands in gestures, shuffle their feet, nod their heads, and assume different facial expressions. It is unlikely that these motions play no role in the interaction, though it is not easy to discover just what their role is. At the very least they probably help to keep the other's attention and in conversation they may serve to reduce the ambiguity of what is being said. In addition, they provide the speaker with feedback that he is being received. Certain movements seem to play a definite role in the setting up and maintenance of basic features of the relationship between interactants. Among these, the frequency of head nods, pleasantness of facial expression, and frequency of hand and arm gestures function as indicators of affiliation or solidarity, as we have termed it to distinguish it from the dimension of intimacy. Persons trying to bring about higher levels of affiliation or solidarity with their partners will utilize such movements in addition to verbal and paralinguistic techniques (Mehrabian, 1971). But in addition certain movements play a role in the ongoing regulation of verbal interaction.

This becomes apparent when natural units of speech rhythm are examined. Such a unit is the phonemic clause, which consists of a string of words, averaging five in length, in which there is a single primary stress and which is termined by a juncture, a barely perceptible slowing of speech, often with slight intonation changes at the very end. Body movements, especially of the hands, occur more frequently at the start of such clauses than at other positions (Dittman and Llewellyn, 1969). However, this is true only for clauses that run off smoothly. If the clause is nonfluent, movements tend to follow hesitations closely. One explanation of this observation assumes that speech encoding involves a certain amount of stress, and in some cases this stress spills over into the motor sphere.

Certain types of movements, particularly head nods, help to regulate the speaker–listener relationship. Listeners insert brief responses of the "mm-hmm" or "I see" variety almost exclusively at the ends of rhythmical units in the talker's speech; head nods tend to be associated with such responses (Dittman and Llewellyn, 1968). The combination of head nods with such vocalization appears to serve two interpersonal functions in conversation: (a) a wish of the listener to interject a comment or question, and (b) a response by the listener to some need in the speaker for feedback.

Another function of speech tied movements is to "underline" what is being said by appropriate gestures, thereby reducing the chances that the meaning of the verbal message will be misunderstood. A detailed examination of this aspect of gestures has been undertaken by Birdwhistell (1970) who distinguishes various types of "kinesic markers." For instance, in an address or reference the head, a finger, or the hand may be moved so that a distal extension of the movement can be interpreted as leading toward the object or person referred to. Such movements are often found in association with pronouns like "he," "they," "there," and "any"; while proximal movement of the same parts of the body occur in association with "I," "this," and "now." The future tense may be indicated by accompanying the verb with a distal movement toward the front of the body, while the past tense may involve a similar movement toward the rear of the body. In this way certain parts of the verbal message may be emphasized and the intent of the speaker may become clearer than it might be if the same message were communicated in written form. However, we are not justified in concluding that gestural language will have cross-cultural generality. Gestures are extremely abbreviated and therefore highly ambiguous analogic models and as such their correct interpretation requires a knowledge of cultural conventions.

Not all gestures have the function of emphasizing what is being said. It is possible to distinguish *motor-primacy* movements and *speech-primacy* movements (Freedman, 1972). The latter are subservient to speech, the former to some extent replace speech. Gestures may either accompany a spoken message, and merely punctuate and emphasize it, or they may take over some of the content of the message that remains partly unarticulated in verbal form. A shrug of the shoulders may replace the verbal message or merely emphasize it. In the one case it is the gesture that is used as the primary vehicle for making contact with the listener, in the other case it is speech. It is possible that the relative predominance of speech-primacy over movement-primacy gestures increases with the psychological distance between speaker and listener.

Both types of gesture are related to the intent to communicate, but there are other gestures that do not arise out of such an intention (Freedman, 1972). These movements are focused on the communicator's own body and involve such activities as scratching, stroking, rubbing, and the manipulation of clothing and accessories. They cannot be related to the content and flow of overt communication, and it is possible that they express content that remains completely unverbalized because it is repressed or suppressed.

In a conversation both the speaker and the listener show movement. The latter's movement must be of a different type from the speech accompanying movement of the speaker. It cannot have the function of supplementing the spoken message. There is evidence that much of the listener's movement is speech-preparatory in nature (Kendon, 1972). The head, the limb, or sometimes the whole body is brought to a new position, and this gives an indication that the listener wishes to exchange roles with the speaker. These movements therefore serve as markers that signal transition stages in the interaction process.

Scheflen (1964) described the behavior of a therapist who would keep her head slightly lowered while listening to the patient but when about to make an interpretation she would raise her head and hold it erect. At the end of her remark she would lower her head and return to the listening position. The boundaries of longer interaction sequences, which Scheflen calls *positions*, would be marked by grosser movements, such as leaning forward during a phase of active interpretation and leaning back during a phase of free association by the patient. Such movement markers serve to break the interaction into manageable units and allow the interactants to communicate to each other what phase of the interaction they consider themselves to be in.

Markers of transition points in the interaction sequence are not limited to the behavior of the listener. The speaker also contributes such signals, as when he looks up at the listener near the end of a long statement. The opportionment of the "floor" requires a constant flow of signals from both parties. Some of these indicate a desire to exchange roles and others indicate a confirmation of the current distribution of roles. The speaker may look away to indicate that he has not finished, and the listener may signal his continuing attention by means of special gestures. Head nods, for example, tend to occur at certain pauses in speech where an exchange of roles might be a possibility (Dittman and Llewellyn, 1968). The characteristic role alternation that constitutes a conversation requires each partner to emit and receive a constant stream of signals that regulate both the maintenance of the current phase and its smooth transition to the next phase.

But the attuning of the partners to each other involves more than the function of role distribution. There is evidence that people respond to the rhythm of speech acts as well as to their verbal content, a fact that may assist the process of communication. This leads to a mutual coordination of movements, which Condon and Ogston (1966) refer to as *interactional synchrony*. When sound film records of people in interaction are studied frame by frame the movement of each body part can be followed with great precision. It is found that points of change in the flow of speech occur at the same time as points of change in body movement. Moreover, the boundaries of the movement waves of speaker and listener tend to coincide. This is generally true for small segments of speech, up to the word level, but less so for larger segments. It is as though speaker and listener were using their movements to beat time together like the members of a band. This has led investigators like Scheflen (1973) to suggest that interaction should be studied in terms of its supraindividual programming. Such a program would function much like a musical score known to both interactants.

Kendon (1970) has demonstrated that a third person present during an interaction in which he is not directly addressed may show similar shifts in position precisely at the boundary points in the speaker's speech flow. For example, he describes a filmed interaction between two men in the presence of a smoking girl who leans over to tap the ash off her cigarette and leans back again exactly in time to the speech rhythm of one of the men. Interactional synchrony can be shown to occur even when individuals are not looking at each other but where the flow of speech of one of them is audible. This suggests that the auditory channel is strongly involved in the establishment of movement synchrony.

The detailed analysis of films of social gatherings reveals that several different mechanisms are involved in the establishment of interactional synchrony. In one case we get an immediate following or tracking of the speaker's movements by the listener, in another case the movements of two individuals may be synchronized not by their attention to each other but by their common attention to a single focus, perhaps a third member of the gathering. Another type of synchrony is involved in the *reciprocal coordination* of actions that occurs, for example, when one person lights a cigarette for another. A specially close form of synchrony is established when one person *mirrors* the movements of another—as *A* leans back in his chair *B* leans back too, as *A* moves his right arm to the right *B* moves his left arm to the left, as *A* cocks his head to the right *B* cocks his head to the left, and so on. This type of synchrony has only been observed when *B* is directly addressed by *A*. By mirroring the movements of the speaker the listener emphasizes the bond between them.

In gatherings of several people the level of joint involvement may be gauged by an examination of the degree of interaction synchrony among the members. In this case one must also look for synchrony at the boundary points of longer interaction sequences, such as speaker shifts. These points often provide the occasion for a general shifting of posture and engaging in subinvolvements like smoking or drinking. Some gatherings are tightly organized around a single focus while others may be multifocal and involve many shifts of focus.

In any case it is clear that in face-to-face interaction people do more than exchange verbal messages. At times the coordination of their movements becomes so close as to remind the observer of a dance. However, the systematic choreography of this dance has barely begun.

INCONSISTENCY AMONG CHANNELS

There is an artificiality in considering the effects of various channels of nonverbal communication one by one. In real life, messages in several of these channels are sent simultaneously, and above all, they are usually accompanied by verbal messages that may or may not be consistent with them. Where different types of messages are consistent with one another there is simply redundancy in the overall message, and no great problem arises, but when different message components are inconsistent the question of their relative weight must be faced. Particularly in the case where verbal and nonverbal messages are inconsistent the outcome cannot be predicted without research specifically directed at assessing their relative roles.

With adult subjects exposed to two-channel communication the evidence indicates that the facial channel contributes more than the vocal channel to the decoding of the total message (Zaidel and Mehrabian, 1969). But when a consideration of verbal content is added the picture becomes more complex. In these cases the nonverbal components of the message seem to outweigh the verbal content in determining the meaning of the total message (Mehrabian and Wiener, 1967).

The relative weight of verbal and nonverbal components of messages is based on the fact that, whereas the latter are used to establish and maintain interpersonal relationships, the former are used to communicate about matters of interest to one or both of the interacting individuals. Judgments about the features of the interpersonal relationship therefore rely more heavily on nonverbal cues (Mehrabian, 1970b). This is confirmed by a British study (Argyle *et al*., 1970), which finds nonverbal cues to carry far greater weight than verbal cues in making ratings of the quality of interpersonal relationships.

These findings are all based on studies using adult subjects. They leave open the question of whether the preeminence of nonverbal cues in making judgments of relationship is a spontaneous trend that is already apparent in young children, or whether it involves a process of learning that extends through childhood and is only completed among older children or young adults. This question is directly addressed by studies carried out by Daphne Bugental and her collaborators (1970a, 1970b). These studies suggest that children must learn to discount the verbal components of the message and pay more attention to visual components. In judging the overall positive or negative meaning of a message children pay less attention to verbal content and more attention to facial components as they get older. This is particularly true for the combination of negative verbal content, negative voice quality, and positive facial expression. Adults give such messages a far more positive overall significance than children, apparently because they classify it as a type of joking.

This suggests that the various components of messages do not add linearly but combine to form overall impressions that are qualitatively distinct. Young children (aged five to eight) combine the same message components into different overall impressions than adults and only learn the adult rules of combination as they get older. This becomes particularly striking when the sex of the sender of the message is considered. The reversal in the significance of the facial component is far more striking when the source of the message is a female than when it is a male. It is when a woman's smile is the only friendly component of a message that it has far stronger positive connotations for adults than for children. On the other hand, a man's negative facial expression is given little weight in the assessment of the total message by both adults and children, perhaps because it can be more readily interpreted as representing determination or concentration. The most salient component of positive visual input is the smile, and it may be that young children early learn that a woman's smile represents a socially approved facade and are therefore inclined to discount it. As they get older they learn that it may be part of a joking pattern and are therefore inclined to give it more weight in assessing the overall significance of the message. The salience of different message components therefore depends on the range of qualitatively distinctive message types that the receiver of the message has learned to discriminate.

The assessment of the salience of various components of inconsistent messages is therefore not a matter of linear addition but must take into account the socially defined categories of message types to which the receiver of the total message has become sensitized. It is these categories that will define the weight to be given to various components of the total message.

The various nonverbal channels of communication can readily be distinguished by the fact that they utilize different effector organs to encode the message that is transmitted. But the verbal channel shares its effector organs with other channels, as we have seen, and its distinction from other channels depends on a difference in the coding process rather than on a difference in the physical transmission apparatus. It is unique in that it is based on an entirely different coding principle from that which is used in all nonverbal channels. This makes it difficult to translate verbal messages into a nonverbal form and vice versa. At best the translation is incomplete and involves quite serious loss of information. It is obvious that we cannot very well convey the content of let us say, a scientific book nonverbally. But the opposite is also true. If we try to give a verbal description of the quality of the looks exchanged between two people, or the quality of their tone of voice, we achieve at best an approximation that hints at the nature of the relationship implied by the nonverbal messages but does not express the quality of the relationship as adequately as the nonverbal messages themselves.

Nonverbal communication is very poor at expressing the logical relationships between events because it has nothing equivalent to the logical syntax of language. You cannot express relationships like "either–or" and "if–then" in a nonlinguistic code, nor, for that matter, can you express the negation of a proposition in anything but a linguistic form. Nonverbal messages always assert something positive and can imply a negation only by asserting the opposite. To say "neither–nor," to indicate that neither an assertion nor its alternative is true we need language.

But on the other hand, language is a cumbersome vehicle for expressing the quality of human relationships or the intensity of our involvement in different social situations. To use language effectively for such a purpose requires exceptional talent—only a minority of us are poets and writers, yet we all know how to express quite complex qualities of social relationship nonverbally and do it all the time.

The reason for these differences between verbal and nonverbal channels lies in the fact that they use different coding principles. Nonverbal messages are based on *analogic* coding, verbal messages use *digital* coding. The difference is similar to the difference between a slide rule and an electrical calculating machine. The former represents quantities on a continuous scale of distance, the latter works with discrete entities called digits. Such digits can be combined in various ways and counted. Similarly, verbal messages depend on the combination of discrete elements, phonemes, letters, or their combinations that constitute words.

Digital coding is quite arbitrary—there is no resemblance between the coded message and its referent. For instance, in coding behavior in the laboratory I can feed my calculator the digit "1" to represent the occurrence of a particular response and the digit "0" to represent the nonoccurrence of that response. But the digits have no intrinsic resemblance to what they represent. This is also what happens when I let a particular combination of phonemic digits represent an object or event in the real world; the combination of digits c-h-a-i-r in no way resembles a real chair. But the rise of the mercury in a thermometer has some *analogic* resemblance to the increase in the heat of its surroundings.

Similarly, nonverbal coding in human communication is analogic because the coded signal has some resemblance to that which it represents. So a rise in affect is represented by a rising tone of voice and the closeness of a relationship is represented by long and frequent "eye contact."

In human interaction the two levels of communication, verbal and nonverbal, are used simultaneously, and much of the complexity of human face-to-face communication stems from this fact. At times nonverbal communications may emphasize what is expressed on the verbal level, but at other times a flow of highly meaningful nonverbal communication may accompany talk that is quite trivial and seems to serve only as an excuse for continued nonverbal interaction. Think of a mild flirtation where the verbal content has little or no relation to the play of looks, postures, and movements that seems to express the genuine substance of the interaction. There are times when nonverbal messages may go so far as to contradict the accompanying verbal message. The boy who says: "Who's scared?" while his movements, and facial expression proclaim his fear loud and clear demonstrates this independence of channels as forcefully as the individual who assures us of his peaceful intentions in a voice that is full of threat.

This kind of ambiguity is a human peculiarity. Animals do not have a verbal channel at their disposal, although some of them, notably other primates, engage in an almost continuous flow of communication through nonverbal channels. Because of the general human tendency to overemphasize the role of the verbal channel in face-to-face communication it is instructive to examine some aspects of social interaction among monkeys and apes in order to get an appreciation of the scope of nonverbal communication in creatures with a primate brain. This is the subject to which the next chapter is devoted.

CONCLUSION

In spite of their possession of speech, human beings make extensive use of nonverbal channels in face-to-face communication. These channels include: the regulation of interpersonal distance, gaze direction, posture, movements and gestures, and paralanguage—those aspects of speech that are concerned with how something is said rather than with what is said.

The fundamental question to ask about nonverbal communication is one of *function*—what role does it play in interpersonal communication, what is it that is communicated by means of nonverbal channels? But before we can attempt to answer this question, we must make sure that in any specific case, nonverbal communication has actually occurred. This is because the nonverbal aspects of behavior not only have a communicative but also an expressive function—movements, gestures, postures, and so on express intraindividual affects and attitudes, and unless the other partner in an interaction can decode the meaning of these acts, no communication has in fact taken place. Having assured ourselves on this point we can proceed with the analysis of the communicative functions of nonverbal acts.

The first of these functions is the *presentation* of interpersonal relationships like closeness or intimacy and status differentials. Individuals who are close to each other psychologically also stand or sit closer to each other physically, look at each other more consistently, and probably synchronize their movements and gestures more effectively. Similarly, differences in status express themselves in terms of nonverbal confrontation by means of posture, seating arrangements, direct looks, and so on. In other words, nonverbal behavior helps to define human interaction in terms of certain fundamental properties of social relationships.

Another way of putting this is to regard the salient characteristics of nonverbal communication as constituting different forms of *address*. When individuals interact they must indicate for whom a particular message is intended, and this is frequently done by the use of nonverbal channels of communication. But an address is seldom neutral, it is generally given a specific form, which defines the relationship between addresser and addressee. People are not in the habit of addressing each other as social ciphers, rather they face each other as intimates or strangers, as superior and inferior, and so on. The act of address must be made in a certain mode that defines the fundamental features of the relationship in which the individuals stand to each other. In other words, the forms of address confer particular social identities on the interactants.

Because a nonverbal presentation or address involves events that exist in a physical world characterized by space and time coordinates it confers a particular spatial or temporal structure on the world in which social interaction takes place. This world lacks the homogeneity of physical space and time but is organized around special spatial perspectives and quasi-rhythmic temporal qualities. In other words, nonverbal interaction involves *socialized* as well as physical space and time.

The nonverbal definition of social relationships introduces an element of *ambiguity*, real or potential, into the organization of social interaction. First of all, the interactants may not agree on how the relationship is to be defined, so that there is a lack of reciprocity in their interaction. Second, each individual may be of two minds about the nature of the relationship.

In that case the multiplicity of available channels may be used to convey two different interpretations of the interaction.

Apart from their role in the presentation or definition of social relationships, nonverbal messages have the function of providing much of the *feedback* that is necessary in any ongoing interaction. They provide information about how each of the interactants is defining the situation at any particular time. This applies not only to the broad and relatively persistent qualities of the relationship but also to such elementary matters as the allocation of the roles of speaker and listener in verbal exchanges. If an interaction is not to become chaotic but to continue in a relatively structured form, each participant must constantly monitor the effect his actions have on other participants. It is only on the basis of such information that each individual is able to regulate his own performance so as to maintain the kind of reciprocity on which successful human interaction is based. If this reciprocity is lacking, the interaction will quickly break up, or at least will not be renewed.

In sum, much nonverbal communication defines the social context in which messages are transmitted and received, thus making their interpretation possible. It is nonverbal communication that establishes an essential difference between human interaction and the interaction that takes place when two computers talk to each other.

REFERENCES

Aiello, J. R. and Jones, S. E. (1971). Field study of the proxemic behavior of young school children in three subcultural groups. *J. Personal. & soc. Psychol.*, **19**, 351–356.

Argyle, M. and Dean, J. (1965). Eye contact, distance and affiliation. *Sociometry*, **28**, 289–304.

Argyle, M., Lalljee, M., and Cook, M. (1968). The effects of visibility on interaction in a dyad. *Hum. Relat.*, **21**, 3–17.

Argyle, M., Salter, V., Nicholson, H., Williams, M., and Burgess, P. (1970). The communication of inferior and superior attitudes by verbal and nonverbal signals. *Brit. J. soc. & clin. Psychol.*, **9**, 222–231.

Birdwhistell, R. L. (1970). *Kinesis and Context*. Philadelphia: University of Pennsylvania Press.

Bugental, D., Kaswan, J. W., and Love, L. R. (1970a). Perception of contradictory meanings conveyed by verbal and nonverbal channels. *J. Personal. & soc. Psychol.*, **16**, 647–655.

Bugental, D., Kaswan, J. W., Love, L. R., and Fox, M. N. (1970b). Child versus adult perception of evaluative messages in verbal, vocal, and visual channels. *Developmental Psychol.*, **2**, 367–375.

Burns, T. (1964). Nonverbal communication. *Discovery*, **25**, 30–37.

Condon, W. S. and Ogston, W. D. (1966). Sound film analysis of normal and pathological behavior patterns. *J. nerv. ment. Dis.*, **143**, 338–347.

Davitz, J. R. (1964). *The Communication of Emotional Meaning.* New York: McGraw-Hill.

Dittman, A. T. and Llewellyn, L. G. (1968). Relationship between vocalizations and head nods as listener responses. *J. Personal. & soc. Psychol.*, **9**, 79–84.

Dittman, A. T. and Llewellyn, L. G. (1969). Body movement and speech rhythm in social conversation. *J. Personal. & soc. Psychol.*, **11**, 198–206.

Duncan, S. (1969). Nonverbal communication. *Psychol. Bull.*, **72**, 118–137.

Efran, J. S. (1968). Looking for approval: Effects on visual behavior of approbation from persons differing in importance. *J. Personal. & soc. Psychol.*, **10**, 21–25.

Efran, J. S. and Broughton, A. (1966). Effect of expectancies for social approval on visual behavior. *J. Personal. & soc. Psychol.*, **4**, 103–107.

Ekman, P. (1965). Communication through nonverbal behavior: A source of information about an interpersonal relationship. In S. S. Tomkins and C. E. Izard (Eds.), *Affect, Cognition and Personality.* New York: Springer.

Exline, R. V. and Winters, L. C. (1965). Affective relations and mutual glances in dyads. In S. S. Tomkins and C. E. Izard (Eds.), *Affect, Cognition and Personality.* New York: Springer.

Exline, R. V., Gray, D., and Schuette, D. (1965). Visual behavior in a dyad as affected by interview content and sex of respondent. *J. Personal. & soc. Psychol.*, **1**, 201–209.

Freedman, N. (1972). The analysis of movement behavior during the clinical interview. In A. W. Siegman and B. Pope (Eds.), *Studies in Dyadic Communication.* New York: Pergamon Press.

Goffman, E. (1961). *Encounters.* Indianapolis: Bobbs-Merrill.

Hall, E. T. (1959). *The Silent Language.* New York: Fawcett.

Hall, E. T. (1966). *The Hidden Dimension.* New York: Doubleday.

Hartnett, J. J., Bailey, K. G., and Gibson, F. W. (1970). Personal space as influenced by sex and type of movement. *J. Psychol.*, **76**, 139–144.

Jourard, S. M. (1966). An exploratory study of body-accessibility. *Brit. J. soc. & clin. Psychol.*, **5**, 221–231.

Kendon, A. (1967). Some functions of gaze direction in social interaction. *Acta Psychol.*, **26**, 22–63.

Kendon, A. (1970). Movement coordination in social interaction: some examples described. *Acta Psychol.*, **32**, 100–125.

Kendon, A. (1972). Some relationships between body motion and speech. An analysis of an example. In A. W. Siegman and B. Pope (Eds.), *Studies in Dyadic Communication.* New York: Pergamon Press.

Kendon, A. and Cook, M. (1969). The consistency of gaze patterns in social interaction. *Brit. J. Psychol.*, **60**, 481–494.

Kleck, R. E. and Nuessle, W. (1968). Congruence between the indicative and communicative functions of eye contact in interpersonal relations. *Brit. J. social. & clin. Psychol.*, **7**, 241–246.

Little, K. B. (1965). Personal space. *J. exper. social Psychol.*, **1**, 237–247.

Lott, D. F. and Sommer, R. (1967). Seating arrangements and status. *J. Personal. & soc. Psychol.*, **7**, 90–95.

Mehrabian, A. (1967). Orientation behaviors and nonverbal attitude communication. *J. Communic.*, **17**, 324–332.

Mehrabian, A. (1968). Inference of attitudes from the posture, orientation and distance of a communicator. *J. consult. & clin. Psychol.*, **32**, 296–308.

Mehrabian, A. (1969). Significance of posture and position in the communication of attitude and status relationships. *Psychol. Bull.*, **71**, 359–372.

Mehrabian, A. (1970a). A semantic space for nonverbal behavior. *J. consult. & clin. Psychol.*, **35**, 248–257.

Mehrabian, A. (1970b). When are feelings communicated inconsistently? *J. of Experimental Research in Personality*, **4**, 198–212.

Mehrabian, A. and Wiener, M. (1967). Decoding of inconsistent communications. *J. Personal. & soc. Psychol.*, **6**, 109–114.

Mehrabian, A. and Williams, M. (1969). Nonverbal concomitants of perceived and intended persuasiveness. *J. Personal. & soc. Psychol.*, **13**, 37–58.

Scheflen, A. E. (1964). The significance of posture in communication systems. *Psychiatry*, **27**, 316–331.

Scheflen, A. E. (1973). *How Behavior Means.* New York: Gordon and Breach.

Scherer, K. R. (1974). Acoustic concomitants of emotional dimensions: Judging affect from synthesized tone sequences. In S. Weitz (Ed.), *Nonverbal Communication.* New York: Oxford University Press.

Sommer, R. (1965). Further studies in small group ecology. *Sociometry*, **28**, 337–348.

Sommer, R. (1967). Small group ecology. *Psychol. Bull.*, **67**, 145–152.

Stongman, K. T. and Champness, B. G. (1968). Dominance hierarchies and conflict in eye contact. *Acta Psychol.*, **28**, 376–386.

Watson, O. M. and Graves, T. D. (1966). Quantitative research in proxemic behavior. *Amer. Anthropologist*, **68**, 971–985.

Zaidel, S. F. and Mehrabian, A. (1969). The ability to communicate and infer positive and negative attitudes facially and vocally. *J. of Experimental Research in Personality*, **3**, 233–241.

CHAPTER 5

Social Interaction in
Subhuman Primates

Because of his possession of language the distance that separates man from the nonhuman primates appears particularly pronounced in the field of face-to-face communication. Most human face-to-face interaction involves speech and is therefore decisively different from the interaction of other primates. Nevertheless, because human communication also involves more than speech some points of contact with animal communication can be established.

The analysis of the social behavior of monkeys and apes can be pursued on three levels. In the first place, we can raise questions about the effect of social stimuli on the individual and expect to get answers in terms of the processes of learning and motivation. On this level we may be concerned with such questions as the effect of social stimuli on the arousal level of the individual or the nature of the cognitive capacity involved in various types of social learning. The second level of analysis involves groups rather than individuals and will be concerned with such questions as the size and composition of primate groups in relation to ecological factors.

But there is a third level of analysis that is not covered by the first two. In any primate group there exist certain interindividual phenomena, which are usually left out of account both by the individual and by the group level of analysis. These phenomena involve the manner in which individuals relate to one another in the group. Such relations involve the exchange of signals, the social distribution of space and time, and the development of characteristic patterns of interaction. The study of these relationships obviously impinges on both individual and group processes

83

but it nevertheless forms a distinct level of analysis with its own units and problems.

Each level of analysis involves a different set of relationships. At the group level we are interested in relationships between group properties and ecologically relevant features of the environment like the nature and constancy of the food supply, the pressure from predators, and the nature of the country (e.g. forest or savannah). At the individual level we are interested in relationships between the stimulation provided by social settings and intraindividual processes like arousal level and discrimination learning. Typically, these intraindividual processes are of equal importance in mediating the organism's responses to the nonsocial and to the social environment.

The relationships we are interested in at the third level of analysis are those between social agents. Both terms in such a relationship involve individuals, but only in their function as social interactants or communicators. This function involves processes that are interindividual rather than intraindividual. It is possible, for example, to study the properties of signaling systems or the structure of dominance relationships without raising questions about the mechanisms of perception or the influence of hormones. Such questions are of course perfectly legitimate but they do not relieve us of the task of describing the regularities and structures of interindividual events. It is this task that is the peculiar province of the third, social psychological, level of analysis. Our treatment of the social behavior of primates will be restricted to this level, with only passing references to implications for intraindividual or socioecological processes.

ELEMENTS OF PRIMATE COMMUNICATION

Primates use many channels in communicating with one another, and the choice of channels is generally determined by ecological factors. For example, loud vocalizations are commonly used for intergroup communication among primates living in dense forests. On the other hand, terrestrial and semi-terrestrial primates rely much more on visual communication by means of gestures, facial expressions and looks. Each species has a limited repertoire of vocalizations and gestures but it is rare for any of these to be used separately. The clearest generalization that emerges from a study of close-range communication among members of the same primate group is that composite signals, involving visual, auditory, and often tactile, channels, are the rule. The co-occurrence of verbal and nonverbal communication in humans has its counterpart in the use of several channels for message transmission in nonhuman primates.

Because primate communication relies heavily on the distance receptors of the eye and the ear it makes possible the coordination of activities among the members of a dispersed group who may not be in close contact with one another.

The signals exchanged among primates have a fixed meaning that is shared among all members of the species. There are alarm calls, food cells, threat gestures, submissive gestures, and so on, which are immediately understood by members of a primate group. However, monkeys and apes appear unable to add to their repertoire of signals voluntarily, under natural conditions. Human language makes it possible to produce new signals ad infinitum. Successful attempts to communicate with a chimpanzee by means of sign language (Gardner and Gardner, 1971) indicate some unused capacity in this direction in a subhuman primate.

Even though primate communication depends on a fixed stock of signals with definite meanings it does not mean that this meaning can be established irrespective of context. On the contrary, the same signal will be interpreted differently, depending on its source and on the situation (Altmann, 1967). A threat gesture emanating from an infant will usually not be responded to as a threat, but if the source of the threat is older it will be taken seriously. Similarly, an aggressive vocalization that accompanies a submissive gesture such as presenting will be ignored if the source is a less dominant animal. The meaning assigned to a given element in primate communication therefore depends on the existence of a set of ongoing relationships among the communicators. These relationships are based on age, sex, kinship, dominance–submission hierarchies, group membership, etc. It is not possible to make sense out of primate communication without taking such relationships into account. They constitute a matrix from which individual communicative acts derive part of their meaning. At the same time the exchange of signals maintains these relationships and gives them much of their peculiar quality. The nature of the social relationship between male and female, young and old, dominant and submissive, in-group and out-group member is constantly defined and confirmed by the exchange of signals of a certain type. Gestures of threat and of submission, for example, gain their significance from the existence of relationships of dominance and submission, but at the same time they perpetuate and maintain these relationships.

Another significant feature of primate communication lies in the fact that it is generally *addressed*, that is to say, there is a component of the message that indicates who the signal is meant for. Undirected messages do occur, as in the case of predator-alarm calls or group cohesion calls, but most primate communications are directed at a target. Facing and looking at the addressee is the commonest means of addressing a message. Even when females present their posterior to a male there is often visual contact or facing. Conversely, the avoidance of visual contact is a way of avoiding interaction and usually occurs in the subordinate member of a pair, while direct staring is a form of threat in this context. The main point to note in this context is that the address is itself part of the message. As such it is an example of *metacommunication*, a communication about communication; it indicates whom the communication is meant for.

One way in which the communication of subhuman primates differs from the human use of language is that there is a direct relationship between the intensity of a signal and the intensity of the response to it. This can be observed in threat gestures or in alarm calls. Intense threats evoke an intense response, and loud, rapid alarm calls evoke a more intense response than faint and infrequent calls. Linguistic symbols, on the other hand, are completely arbitrary; the response they evoke need have no relationship to their intensity.

The relationship between the intensity of signals and responses among subhuman primates derives from the fact that the animal's signal is frequently an incomplete part of a more extended reaction. A threat gesture is a truncated part of completed fighting activity and a female's presenting gesture is part of the completed sexual response. The part gesture evokes the same kind of response in the animal to whom it is addressed as the completed action. The more closely the part gesture approximates to the completed action the more closely will the response to the part resemble the response to the whole. If the completed action evokes the most intense response, that intensity will drop off the less the part gesture resembles the whole action. This form of communication therefore involves a *continuous* relationship between the signal and that which it represents. It is an *iconic* signal and the form of representation is *analogical*. That is to say, the signal has preserved some of the pattern of what it stands for.

By contrast, verbal communication involves *digital* coding in which the individual signals are discrete and indicate merely the presence or absence of something represented. A word is an arbitrary way of indicating the existence of a certain state of affairs, it does not indicate levels of intensity. Interestingly enough, humans have recourse to analogical communication to indicate this aspect of events. For example, they make use of *paralanguage*, nonlinguistic features of speechlike variations in loudness, tempo and pitch, to indicate the intensity of the reaction that they wish to communicate. They also use their bodies, in gesture, posture, and gross movement to convey this type of information.

It would be a great mistake to regard language as an evolutionary displacement of analogic communication. So far from having undergone decay, the intricacies of human communication by means of facial expression and vocal intonation exceed anything to be found at the subhuman level. At the same time this type of communication has been elaborated into complex forms of art, music, ballet, and poetry. This suggests that nonverbal, iconic communication may have functions for which verbal signals are not suitable. Digital symbols are excellent for representing relationships among events in the environment, they are less adequate for representing the individual's relationship to these events. It is here that analogic communication comes into its own because it involves a representation of individual reactions by means of a part reaction that symbolizes the whole.

Graded signals have great value in communicating subtle changes in mood or attitude. Compared to birds and more primitive mammals primates have developed very complex signal patterns expressing subtle changes in such relationships as submission, reassurance, threat, and affiliation. In a complex enduring social system in which individuals are obliged to make a continuous series of adjustments and accommodations to one another, it is important to be able to express variations in the intensity of a relationship and to combine different aspects of a relationship into a composite signal (Lancaster, 1968).

The study of primate communication is therefore potentially relevant to that part of human communication that is concerned with the communicator's relationship to the object of the message. In such communication the subject of any predicate does not need to be identified because it is always the emitter of the signal (Bateson, 1967). The communicator is himself engaged in the relationship he communicates about. Such communication makes it easier to predict his future actions in the context of this relationship. The signals he emits are in fact a part of the ongoing relationship in the sense that a threat gesture, for example, is part of an ongoing antagonistic relationship. The relationship consists largely of an exchange of signals among those involved in it. These signals are patterned in time, with regular sequences recurring again and again. This means that the occurrence of any particular signal tells us something about the probability of occurrence of future signals exchanged in that relationship. In the language of information theory such signals have a certain degree of *redundancy*. If some of them are removed from the sequence we can guess at what they are with better than random success. This is equivalent to saying that individual signals are part of a *patterned* sequence of signals spread out in time.

The nonrandom patterns of events within which primate signals are embedded constitute the social relationships in which the individual primate participates. Most primates are members of groups, and most of their communication takes place with other members of the group. Such communication is not random but follows relatively predictable paths. Primate groups have a certain *structure*, a set of regular interactions among the members. The significance of individual communications can only be understood in the context of this structure. Communication in primates rarely occurs among strangers but rather between animals that have known each other for some time and evolved stable social relations. It is the social structure that selects one out of a large number of possible communicative acts at a particular time and place, and the structure is in turn maintained by the sum total of interactions.

This structuring of interactions has considerable biological utility. It makes possible the ecological adaptation of primate populations to their environment (Crook, 1970). Such adaptation demands a regulation of such things as the population density in the available territory, the relative dispersion or coherence of groups and the composition of the reproductive unit. The optimum levels of these variables depend on the relative constancy and abundance of the available food supply, the presence of predators and of cover against them. For example, the proportion of males in primate reproductive units goes down under conditions of low and unreliable food availability due to harsh seasonal climates or overcrowding; population density is high in forest habitats with a plentiful food supply; group coherence is greatest in areas with high predation pressure, and so on. Such exigencies determine the kinds of social interactions that are necessary to maintain the ecological position of the group. The need for protection against ever-present predators imposes certain constraints on the social structure of the primate group, and the need to preserve the sex ratio in reproductive units imposes other constraints. It is necessary to keep these considerations in mind when exploring the nature of social communication among primates.

SOME GENERAL FEATURES OF SOCIAL INTERACTION AMONG PRIMATES

(1) The Socializing of Space

Physical space inhabited by primates assumes a social significance. The distribution of individuals over the available space is never random but expresses the various relationships that exist between them. In some species there is a clear definition of the territory of a particular band, but in other species there is considerable overlap in these territories or constant fluctuation of boundaries. Generalizations about the distribution of space among individuals within bands are much more clearly supported by existing field studies than generalizations about the division of space among bands.

The relative proximity maintained by animals within the group expresses their social relationship to one another (Carpenter, 1942). Infants stay close to their mothers and females stay close to their male consorts. In many heterosexual groups nondominant males avoid the company of females while the dominant male is in sight. In addition, individuals display certain preferences, sexual or purely affiliative, for the company of selected others.

The whole band maintains a certain cohesion, moving about as a group. Distances between individuals are not allowed to increase beyond a certain point. One of the functions of primate communication is the maintenance of patterns of spatial distribution. It is possible to distinguish four categories of communication signals that help to maintain a characteristic pattern of spatial dispersion (Marler, 1968):

(a) Distance-increasing signals.   Infraction of minimum distances between two animals provokes threat gestures like staring, chasing, slapping, and characteristic facial expressions that generally produce a withdrawal of the approaching animal.

(b) Distance-maintaining signals.   In several species characteristic distances among animals of different status are maintained by status indicators like a particular gait and tail position as well as a pattern of looking that includes glaring by the animal of higher status and gaze aversion by the lower-status animal.

(c) Distance-reducing signals.   A reduction in the customary interindividual distance is often achieved by means of special signals like touching, "lip smacking," and other invitations to participate in grooming. Sexual presenting is also used to reduce distance without necessarily resulting in copulation.

(d) Proximity-maintaining signals.   These include activities like sexual mounting and grooming, as well as greeting gestures.

Much of the communication exchanged among primates is therefore intimately related to the pattern of interindividual space distribution.

(2) Reciprocity or the Socializing of Time

Statistically, the social responses of primates to social stimuli are highly predictable. Every social action has its "correct," that is, overwhelmingly most frequent response. A friendly gesture usually receives a friendly response, a threat is responded to by avoiding, an attempt to mount by standing to be mounted, and so on. Where counting has been attempted it has been found that only about 15% of all responses do not fall into the appropriate category (Rowell, 1966).

This means that it always takes the collaboration of at least two animals to establish a predictable, structured relationship. Any social action is a kind of invitation to give the "correct" response. If this invitation is not followed with a high degree of reliability no stable relationship can result. Such relationships as dominance, for example, do not depend simply on the internal characteristics of the dominant animal. If anything, it is the lower-ranking animals that are most active in maintaining rank distinctions (Rowell, 1966). Unless they respond to an assertion of potential dominance by the appropriate submissive response no actual dominance relationship can result.

Perhaps the most closely studied example of reciprocal interaction among primates is the mother–infant relationship. This relationship is marked by a characteristic time course that involves a gradual decrease of direct body contact and an increase in the time the infant spends at some distance from the mother. This development is clearly a product of the reciprocal interaction of both participants. At first the infant shows little or no tendency to leave the mother but in due course it becomes more venturesome and begins to explore the environment.

There is every indication that this development depends as much on the reactions of the mother as on the maturation of the infant. As the infant gets older the mother shows less tendency to retrieve it and carry it actively and an increasing tendency to move away actively after the infant has climbed off her (Jensen and Bobbitt, 1965). She also becomes more and more inclined to punish the infant while it is on her by hitting it, biting it and vigorously pushing it away. At the same time she reduces her active initiation of nipple contact with the infant and instead rejects the infant's attempts at establishing such contact (Hinde, 1971). The active role of the mother in facilitating the independence of the infant is presumably responsible for the finding that laboratory infants raised on cloth-covered, inanimate mothers reduce their contacts with the mother more slowly than infants raised by live mothers (Hansen, 1966).

It is likely that the changes in the mother's behavior are themselves partly produced by an increase in the infant's activity while he is in contact with the mother. As the infant matures he becomes much more active both on the mother and away from the mother. He may climb all over her head, swing from her ears and generally make a nuisance of himself instead of nursing quietly. Close observation shows that the mother is much more likely to punish and much less likely to retain an active infant than a quiet one (Jensen and Bobbitt, 1965). But the infant's greater activity is itself partly a response to the fact that the mother cradles him more loosely while he is on her, tight cradling having an inactivating effect on him (Jensen, Bobbitt, and Gordon, 1967).

In the present context it is interesting to note that from the beginning of life male and female infant rhesus monkeys receive different treatment from their mothers (Jensen, Bobbitt, and Gordon, 1968). At the earliest stages the closest forms of mother–infant contact occur somewhat more frequently with male infants, but after three or four weeks the pattern changes and from then on it is the female infants who remain closer to their mothers and the males who are retained less and spend more time at a distance. However, in the first few weeks the mothers not only hold their male infants more closely, they also handle them more violently and punitively. The quicker achievement of independence by the male infant is probably a reaction to this pattern of early stimulation on the part of the mother. In turn, the difference in the mother's treatment of the infant may be due to the roughness of his play on the mother or his relative interest in the environment. In any case, it is clear that such interactive patterns can only be studied by performing a sequence analysis. If the time dimension is ignored and only summed observations are reported the crucial differences are lost.

The relationship of mother and infant provides a beautiful example of an interactive sequence in which changes in the behavior of each partner are a product of the behavior of the other partner. The final outcome, independence of the infant, is a product of an interaction chain in which the contributions of both partners are closely intertwined. Primate social behavior is generally of this type. The behavior of the individual forms part of an interpersonal sequence and must be studied as such if it is to be properly understood. An element of primate social behavior is generally more than a cause or an effect of the behavior of others. It is also part of an interaction sequence with a definite history and structure. A reaction studied in isolation is simply different from the same reaction as part of an interpersonal sequence. At some stage the study of primate social behavior therefore has to acquire a historical dimension.

(3) Triadic Interaction

It is extremely rare for social interaction among primates to involve only two partners. Typically, third parties are involved in communication among primates and social situations are seldom purely dyadic. Even the interaction of mothers and infants is subject to triadic interference. In most species infants are objects of interest to females other than the mother and in some species to adult males as well. Depending on the species the mother may react to this interest by possessively defending her sole right of interaction with her offspring or by allowing others access to it to the point of using them as "baby-sitters." But in any case she has to come to terms with the reactions of others to her infant.

The presence of third parties has definite effects on the interaction of mother and infant. When isolated mother–infant pairs are compared with pairs living in groups the former manifest more maternal rejection and consequently the infants spend more time off their mothers (Hinde and Spencer-Booth, 1967a). The greater possessiveness of group-living rhesus mothers appears to be a reaction to the unwelcome attentions of other females. On the other hand, the infant in the isolated pair has no peer companions to turn to and so maintains greater proximity to her when he is not clinging to her. It is clear that the quality of mother–infant interaction depends partly on tripartite relationships.

Similarly, the mating of a male and a female generally involves more than a purely dyadic relationship. Others are likely to be interested in each of the partners and must be taken into account. Kummer (1967) reports the following mating pattern among nondominant males and young females in the Hanadryas baboon: "At intervals, both would run to a place where they could see the group leader and there the male sometimes embraced the female with repeated grasps on her flank, grimacing at the group leader; or he carried her on his back to the group leader's place."

The manner in which these triangular relationships are handled varies greatly from species to species but there is a common core in these situations that involves the simultaneous interaction of three individuals such that each of them aims its behavior at both the other partners to the interaction. In primate groups it is very common for sexual behavior to be aimed as much at a rival in a triangular situation as at the immediate partner. When a female presents to a male this is frequently the outcome of a competition among females for the attention and protection of the male; similarly, when a male mounts a female this may be a message directed at other males.

Apart from mother–infant and sexual relations dominance relationships provide a third major context for social interaction among primates. Here too the typical unit of interaction is triadic rather than dyadic. Whether a certain individual dominates over another individual depends much less on their respective aggressiveness or fighting ability than it does on their respective relations to third parties. The dominant monkey frequently achieves this position by establishing an alliance with a subordinate individual, a pattern that raises his status in the group (Varley and Symmes, 1966). Once established as the most dominant animal in the group a monkey will frequently interfere in fights among subordinates (Bernstein and Sharpe, 1965). In such a group an antagonistic encounter among two individuals is rarely a matter that involves only a particular dyad, it usually becomes a triangular relationship in which the most dominant individual in the group is implicated. This animal will react to the altercation by chasing or attacking one of the instigators, and all group members learn to anticipate this reaction. As a consequence their behavior becomes directed simultaneously at the group "leader" as well as the immediate target in the antagonistic encounter.

When individual animals are removed from or introduced into a group the whole pattern of relationships is temporarily disturbed and then restored in a modified form (Hall and Mayer, 1967). The relationships of one individual to the other members of the group do not simply add on to the sum total of relationships in the group but modify the entire set of relationships. "Again and again, in observing a group of monkeys, whether in the field or in captivity, one is impressed by the more or less continual awareness of each member of the behavior, the distance, and the situation of the others" (Hall, 1968a).

A common form of tripartite antagonistic encounter is the "protected threat," in which one subordinate individual threatens another one while in the safe protection of a dominant individual. In the hamadryas baboon dominant males will direct their aggression at the less close of two individuals engaged in antagonistic behavior near him. Youngsters soon learn to compete for the position closest to the dominant male, in this way enlisting his powerful support (Kummer, 1967). They will try to threaten their opponent away from the dominant male, maintaining a position between the two and thus preventing the opponent from moving closer. In this position a threat by the opponent automatically becomes a threat in the direction of the dominant male and is likely to provoke immediate retaliation. The female version of protected threat behavior may involve a simultaneous presenting to the dominant male while threatening another female.

Primate social behavior involves the capacity to integrate complex information from several simultaneous sources. Social reactions are not limited by a single focus of attention but involve the coordination of responses to multiple stimuli. It is no accident that these complex forms of social interaction have become particularly highly developed in animals characterized by a large cerebral cortex that promotes flexibility of adaptive patterns, control of simple impulsive reactions, and the integration and discrimination of complex stimulus patterns. Under natural conditions primates do not appear to make full use of their cerebral capacity in connection with their search for nourishment, which remains on a level comparable to that of animals with a less highly developed brain. It is mostly in their social life that they exploit the possibilities of their larger brains on other than an occasional basis (Chance and Mead, 1953).

(4) Cognitive Control of Social Interaction

The heavy involvement of the highly developed primate cerebral cortex gives a crucial place to cognition in the organization of social behavior. One consequence of this is the important role that observational learning or imitation begins to play in the social life of primates. The individual animal does not have to rely entirely on its own experience but can benefit from the experience of others. In this way limited "traditions" may be formed. For example, when potatoes were put on the beach near a colony of Japanese monkeys one of the animals discovered that the sand could be most effectively removed prior to eating by washing the potatoes in water (Kawai, 1965). This habit gradually spread throughout the colony by imitation, until a considerable proportion of the members were engaging in the new activity.

A somewhat different type of observational learning has been reported in laboratory studies where only one monkey can see a food reward or an avoidance stimulus but another monkey has to operate the machinery that delivers the food or makes the avoidance response effective (Mason and Hollis, 1962; Miller, Banks, and Ogawa, 1962). Pairs of animals can learn to cooperate effectively in these settings, which means that the first monkey must communicate the crucial information to the second.

Under natural conditions the spread of items of behavior by observation is not indiscriminate but depends on the status of the model and the potential followers. In the Japanese study of potato washing the discoverer of the technique was a young female; five years later nearly 80% of the younger monkeys had acquired the behavior but only 18% of the older adults, and all of the latter were females. One may speculate that the mature adult males might have found it easier to overcome their conservatism if the new fad had originated among them rather than among juvenile females. By contrast to the slow spread of potato washing the new habit of wheat eating spread to an entire troop within four hours (Yamada, 1957). But in this case the habit was introduced by the leader of the troop. Transmission from an animal that has an appropriate dominance status to a subordinate animal occurs much more readily than transmission in the opposite direction.

The question arises whether observation of others may not inhibit rather than facilitate various forms of behavior under certain circumstances. There is overwhelming evidence that this is in fact what happens and the setting for such social inhibition is generally provided by dominance relationships. In fact, a description of dominance relationships in primate groups becomes equivalent to a description of social inhibitions. They arise whenever there is a division of functions within the primate group. Ecologically, the advantages of group life are largely based on such specialization. For example, it is highly functional to have a "control animal" in a group who interposes himself between an attacked member of the group and the source of the disturbance. Such control reduces wasteful fighting and injury but its effect would be negated if other animals were not inhibited from usurping the functions of the control animal. Similarly, the locomotion of the group would be uncoordinated and might leave it vulnerable to predators if its direction of movement were not determined by one animal. Again, the function can only be effectively carried out if other individuals do not attempt to substitute themselves for the leading animal as a matter of course.

Unfortunately, discussions of dominance have not been helped by an initial tendency to confuse privileged access to resources with social roles that involve functions of control, direction, and protection (Zuckerman, 1932). There is no necessary relationship between the two in most species. The leading animals do not necessarily get privileged access to food resources or to sexual partners, nor are these two aspects of resource access inevitably correlated with each other. There is enormous inter-species variability here and no safe generalizations are available (Hall, 1968a).

All primate groups are based on some division of functions among the members. These functions are grouped in sets that are characteristic of certain roles within the group, but the way in which the functions are distributed over different roles will vary from one species to another. Often, quite closely related functions are distributed over several individuals. In a group of hamadryas baboons the animal that *proposed* the direction of group foraging for the day was not the same animal that *decided* the final direction of movement (Kummer, 1971). The animal that controls fighting among males is often different from the animal that controls fighting among females, and both control animals depend on the support of individuals in secondary control roles.

Primate societies are very far from being organized around a single dominance hierarchy. Instead, they constitute a system of roles that incorporate different sets of functions. Such a role system can only be effective if all the members of the group collaborate in maintaining it. This means that they must constantly orientate their behavior to one another and inhibit tendencies to usurp alien roles.

Characteristically, the reactions of individuals to one another are based on the *anticipation* of certain outcomes; it is relatively rare for potential sequences of interaction to run their full course. This is particularly true of dominance relationships. Among baboons and macaques, where dominance relationships are marked, they are maintained by noisy "threat displays" rather than by actual fighting. "Even changes in dominance rank amongst the males are reported to occur as a consequence of perisitent harrying rather than by fighting," (Hall, 1968b).

This degree of cognitive control involves a constant regulation of individual behavior by the coordination of complex social stimuli.

In this coordination the direction of attention plays a crucial role (Chance and Jolly, 1970). In an interaction involving several animals the attention of any one of them is not directed equally at all the others. Certain individuals are able to claim a larger share than others of the total attention of the group. This means that the demands they make will become prepotent and will determine the activity of the rest of the group to a large extent. It is this ability to place themselves at the center of attention that makes it possible for certain individuals to assume leadership roles. By claiming more attention than others their social influence is increased. In a group of baboons, for example, the attention of the females is very much focused on the dominant male, and this means that they orientate their movements with respect to his. He therefore comes to determine the direction of movement and the cohesion of the group. Similarly, the attention of infants is focused on their mothers, and they do not allow the distance between themselves and her to increase beyond a certain amount.

One function of aggressive behavior is that it causes a shift in the direction of attention. However, more usually, an animal will maintain himself as a focus of attention by means of threat behavior or by means of affiliative overtures. The signs that produce focusing of attention are generally the same as those that increase or decrease social distance and have already been discussed. In fact, these signs function as regulators of social distance because of their attention claiming quality. There is an intimate relationship between social attention and social distance in primates. Attention has a binding quality in social situations, and its fluctuations are reflected in variations in interindividual distance.

(5) Role of Learning

The complex adjustments of primate social interaction depend heavily on the effects of learning. While there are some fixed communicative gestures their combination into an ongoing interaction requires the adaptive capacity of the primate brain. Individuals that have been deprived of the opportunity for social learning are very severely handicapped in their subsequent social life. Monkeys raised under conditions of social isolation do not show normal sexual, maternal, and affiliative behavior (Harlow and Harlow, 1965). Their social interaction is marked by indifference and hyperaggressiveness. Deficiencies in affectionate behavior and hyperaggressiveness are also found in monkeys raised by their own mothers but deprived of access to peers (Harlow and Harlow, 1969).

Exposing animals to conditions of social deprivation is one way of demonstrating the role of learning in primate social adjustment. Another way of illustrating the same point is by introducing animals to a group of another species with different social patterns. For example, among hamadryas baboons the female is permanently associated with a particular male, while among anubis baboons the association is looser, less exclusive and limited to the period of oestrus. When an anubis female is transplanted to a hamadryas troop she very quickly learns to adapt to the new social conditions and adopts the life style of the host society (Kummer, 1971). This adaptation includes such components as learning to respond to a male threat by approach rather than avoidance and following one male exclusively, yet the situation was mastered in a matter of hours. Hamadryas females showed the converse set of adaptations when transferred to an anubis troop. The primate brain appears to be particularly well adapted to rapid social learning.

Under natural conditions the social position of an individual primate depends on what it learns from its past social experience. This experience is itself determined by the fact that the individual is born into an already existing nexus of social relationships. Thus the state of an individual can be shown to depend at least in part on the status of the mother. In a troop of Japanese macaques the offspring of dominant females became dominant themselves (Imanishi, 1957). They were more likely to adopt leadership roles in adult life. Among baboons the infants of low-ranking mothers who get involved in disputes more often than high-ranking mothers are more clinging and less independent (Hall and DeVore, 1965). This makes them less fitted for certain roles in later life. Rhesus mothers allow females of lower status to handle their infants but adopt a protective stance toward females of higher status (Hinde and Spencer-Booth, 1967b). High-status females are also more likely to act aggressively toward infants not their own. Therefore, the nature of the early experience of tripartite encounters among infants will vary with the position of the mother in relation to other females. This is likely to have consequences for their reaction to such situations in later life.

Social interaction among primates is the outcome of a long sequence of learned adaptations on the part of each individual. As such it provides the strongest possible contrast to the social life of insects and birds, which depends very strongly on fixed action patterns.

CONCLUSION

The social life of primates is characterized by the emergence of a set of interindividual processes that exist at a level between individual behavior and the socio-ecological adaptation of the group. These processes involve signals with certain properties that make it possible for them to be exchanged in structured sequences. Such structures take the form of regular relationships among individuals that can be studies in their own right.

Primate communication relies heavily on complex multimodal signs that are only interpreted in terms of their social context. This context and special forms like the use of address set messages in a matrix of metacommunication, i.e. communication about communication. Primate communication is well suited to the transmission of messages that convey information about subtle variations in moods, attitudes, and social relationships but of little use in the transmission of information about the environment. The communication of subhuman primates is almost entirely limited to matters of social interaction.

Social communication among primates is continuous rather than episodic. There is a constant flow of signals within a primate group, and these signals fall into regular patterns that give the group its structure. One expression of this structure is found in the spatial arrangement of the members. The structure involves relatively stable relationships among individuals playing different roles. The fate of such relationships depends on reciprocal contributions by each partner. But the partners are seldom isolated. Their interaction is usually influenced by others, so that the natural unit for most primate interaction is the triad rather than the dyad. In this situation successful adaptation depends heavily on learning and on the cognitive control of behavior with observational learning and the selective distribution of attention providing particularly important mechanisms.

REFERENCES

Altmann, S. A. (1967). The structure of primate social communication. In S. A. Altmann (Ed.), *Social Communication Among Primates*. Chicago: University of Chicago Press.

Bateson, G. (1967). Redundancy and coding. In T. A. Sebeok (Ed.), *Animal Communication*. Bloomington: Indiana University Press.

Bernstein, I. S. and Sharpe, L. G. (1965). Social roles in a rhesus monkey group. *Behavior*, **26**, 91–104.

Carpenter, C. R. (1942). Societies of monkeys and apes. *Biol. Symp.*, **8**, 177–204.

Chance, M. R. A. and Jolly, C. J. (1970). *Social Groups of Monkeys, Apes and Men*. London: Jonathan Cape.

Chance, M. R. A. and Mead, A. P. (1953). Social behavior and primate evolution. *Symp. soc. exp. Biol.*, **7**, 395–439.

Crook, J. H. (1970). The socio-ecology of primates. In J. H. Crook (Ed.), *Social Behavior in Birds and Mammals*. New York: Academic Press.

Gardner, B. T. and Gardner, R. A. (1971). Two-way communication with an infant chimpanzee. In A. M. Schrier and F. Stollnitz (Eds.), *Behavior of Nonhuman Primates*. Vol. III. New York: Academic Press.

Hall, K. R. L. (1968a). Social organization of the old-world monkeys and apes. In P. C. Jay (Ed.), *Primates*. New York: Holt, Rinehart & Winston.

Hall, K. R. L. (1968b). Aggression in monkey and ape societies. In P. C. Jay (Ed.), *Primates*. New York: Holt, Rinehart & Winston.

Hall, K. R. L. and DeVore, I. (1965). Baboon social behavior. In I. DeVore (Ed.), *Primate Behavior: Field Studies of Monkeys and Apes*. New York: Holt, Rinehart & Winston.

Hall, K. R. L. and Mayer, B. (1967). Social interactions in a group of captive patas monkeys. *Folia Primat.* **5**, 213–236.

Hansen, E. W. (1966). The development of maternal and infant behavior in the rhesus monkey. *Behavior*, **27**, 107–149.

Harlow, H. F. and Harlow, M. K. (1965). The affectional systems. In A. M. Schrier, H. F. Harlow, and F. Stollnitz (Eds.), *Behavior of Nonhuman Primates*. Vol. II. New York: Academic Press.

Harlow, H. F. and Harlow, M. K. (1969). Effects of various mother–infant relationships on rhesus monkey behaviors. In B. M. Foss (Ed.), *Determinants of Infant Behaviour*. Vol. IV. London: Methuen.

Hinde, R. A. (1971). Development of social behavior. In A. M. Schrier and F. Stollnitz (Eds.), *Behavior of Nonhuman Primates*. Vol. III. New York: Academic Press.

Hinde, R. A. and Spencer-Booth, Y. (1967a). The effect of social companions on mother-infant relations in rhesus monkeys. In D. Morris (Ed.), *Primate Ethology*. London: Weidenfelt & Nicolson.

Hinde, R. A. and Spencer-Booth, Y. (1967b). The behaviour of socially living rhesus monkeys in their first two and a half years. *Animal Behaviour*, **15**, 169–196.

Imanishi, K. (1957). Social behavior in Japanese monkeys. *Psychologia*, **1**, 47–54.

Jensen, G. D. and Bobbitt, R. A. (1965). On observational methodology and preliminary studies of mother–infant interaction in monkeys. In B. M. Foss (Ed.), *Determinants of Infant Behaviour*. Vol. III. London: Methuen.

Jensen, G. D., Bobbitt, R. A., and Gordon, B. N. (1967). The development of mutual independence in mother–infant pigtailed monkeys. In S. A. Altmann (Ed.), *Social Communication Among Primates*. Chicago: University of Chicago Press.

Jensen, G. D., Bobbitt, R. A., and Gordon, B. N. (1968). Sex differences in the development of independence of infant monkeys. *Behaviour*, **30**, 1–14.

Kawai, M. (1965). Newly acquired precultural behavior of the natural troop of Japanese monkeys on Kashima islet. *Primates*, **6**, 1–30.

Kummer, H. (1967). Tripartite relations in Hamadryas baboons. In S. A. Altmann (Ed.), *Social Communication among Primates*. Chicago: University of Chicago Press.

Kummer, H. (1971). *Primate Societies*. Chicago: Aldine–Atherton.

Lancaster, J. B. (1968). Primate communication systems and the emergence of human language. In P. C. Jay (Ed.), *Primates*. New York: Holt, Rinehart & Winston.

Marler, P. (1968). Aggregation and dispersal: Two functions in primate communication. In P. C. Jay (Ed.), *Primates*. New York: Holt, Rinehart & Winston.

Mason, W. A. and Hollis, J. H. (1962). Communication between young rhesus monkeys. *Animal Behaviour*, **10**, 211–221.

Miller, R. E., Banks, J. H., and Ogawa, N. (1962). Communication of affect in "cooperative conditioning of rhesus monkeys". *J. abnorm. & soc. Psychol.*, **64**, 343–348.

Rowell, T. E. (1966). Hierarchy in the organization of a captive baboon group. *Animal Behaviour*, **14**, 430–443.

Varley, M. and Symmes, D. (1966). The hierarchy of dominance in a group of macaques. *Behavior*, **27**, 54–75.

Yamada, M. (1957). A case of acculturation in a subhuman society of Japanese monkeys. *Primates*, **1**, 30–46.

Zuckerman, S. (1932). *The Social Life of Monkeys and Apes*. London: Routledge & Kegan Paul.

CHAPTER 6

Psychotherapy as Interpersonal Communication

THE INTERPERSONAL SIGNIFICANCE OF PSYCHOTHERAPEUTIC CATEGORIES

In our culture considerable resources are expended every day in maintaining special interpersonal relationships that are intended to produce such changes in individuals as will enable them to cope more effectively with the world in which they find themselves. Such psychotherapeutic relationships are entirely made up of interpersonal communications between client and therapist, and the magnitude of the resources we are prepared to divert to them bears witness to the faith most of us have in the potential power of such intercommunication.

At the same time, the way in which we tend to think of the psychotherapeutic process pays relatively little attention to the interpersonal events that are crucial to it but leans heavily on concepts borrowed from individual psychology. In the psychodynamic tradition that traces its origins to Freud's contribution the concept of "resistance" is central to an understanding of the therapeutic process. It involves a defense of the repression of dynamic tendencies within the client so that he need not become aware of them. But in the therapeutic situation this maneuver is just as much an attempted deception of the therapist as it is a self-deception of the client who is not only concerned to hide his repressed feelings and motives from himself but also from others. To this end the client develops an ambiguous style of communication that allows some kind of expression to the repressed material but at the same time prevents it from being recognized for what it is either by himself or by his respondent (Beier, 1966, pp. 35–36). Indeed, at least one unorthodox psychoanalyst came to the conclusion that the communication of all neurotics was marked by a "universal symptom," which he called *duplicity* (Kaiser, 1965). Such individuals, according to Kaiser, "do not stand behind their words"; their communications do not mean what they seem to mean at first, as the transaction proceeds they shift their ground and cannot easily be pinned down to their real meaning. Their communications serve to hide them from others as well as from themselves.

If the interpersonal component forms an essential aspect of the phenomenon of "resistance" it becomes even more salient in any consideration of the concept of "transference." In the classical definition the patient transfers to the therapist attitudes that had their origin in his relationship with his parents and endows the therapist with qualities that in his childhood he attributed to his parents. On this view the transference is a unilateral process that emanates from the patient and for which the therapist is merely the object (Jackson and Haley, 1963). Consideration of the therapist's countertransference takes into account the dyadic nature of the relationship but still expresses it in concepts whose reference is essentially to intraindividual rather than interpersonal processes.

It has been pointed out (Haley, 1963) that the patient's behavior in the classical psychoanalytic session may not constitute an "irrational" regression to infantile response patterns but may be the result of an attempt to cope as well as possible with the paradoxical demands of a situation that is quite unlike any situation he has met in his normal adult life. Among the many paradoxical demands of this peculiar interpersonal situation the following deserve special notice:

(1) The analyst's role is that of an expert, and experts are expected to give advice and direction; yet he leaves the initiative to the patient and refuses to give explicit direction.
(2) There is ambiguity about the voluntary nature of the relationship. On the one hand, the analyst stresses the voluntary nature of the relationship, yet he objects when the patient is late or misses a session, thus giving the relationship a compulsory flavor.
(3) The patient finds that he cannot manipulate the analyst by means of an aggravation or an improvement of his symptoms, yet it is his desire for help with his symptoms that has caused him to enter the therapeutic relationship.

In attempting to cope with these and other peculiar features of the analytic relationship the patient cannot use either his symptoms or normal techniques of adult interpersonal communication. Under these circumstances he may well fall back on social patterns he has not used for many years. But the occurrence of such regressive features does not mean that they necessarily have any existence outside the special interpersonal context of the psychotherapeutic session.

In that session, as in any situation that involves interpersonal communication, the participants *present* themselves to each other in characteristic ways (see Chapter 2). Their relationship exists in the presentations they make of each other to each other. But unlike most ordinary relationships *this* relationship is supposed to lead to some reliable change in the way in which one of the participants presents himself in other relationships.

There are broadly speaking two ways of bringing about such a change. The first has already been mentioned. It involves the therapist engaging in paradoxical presentations that make it difficult or impossible for the patient to embark consistently on any of his own habitual presentations. His repertoire of interpersonal presentations is therefore thrown into flux and the possibility is opened up for the emergence of more adequate ways of relating to others.

But the likelihood that this possibility will be realized depends largely on the mobilization of the second of the major change inducing processes in psychotherapy. This is the process by which the individual cognitively *represents* his interpersonal presentations to himself by means of language. There are three possible relationships between a social presentation an individual makes in an interpersonal encounter and the way he represents his performance if he gives an account of it, either to himself or to others. First, the representation may be an accurate reflection of the presentation to which it refers; second, it may be a distorted reflection; and third, the presentation may run off without it being represented in any form. An individual who presents himself in a dominant manner may be able to give an accurate linguistic description of this fact, or he may represent his behavior as something quite different, even the opposite, or finally, he may be altogether unable to give any kind of cognitive representation of his interpersonal posture.

The lack of congruence between a social presentation and its representation by cognitive reflection sets up an unstable intrapersonal system as soon as the individual becomes aware of it. Under these circumstances there is a tendency to reestablish the appearance of congruence by rejecting the correct representation or by changing the presentation so that it matches the cognitive representation to which the individual wishes to lay claim. Psychotherapy aims at making the patient aware of incongruence between these two levels of response or establishing representations where none existed before. This process is often referred to as "insight," and the hope is that if the new representations of his interpersonal presentations are internalized by the patient strong pressures will be set up to change those aspects of his presentations to which an invidious label has now been attached.

In one sense the lack of congruence between actual presentation and cognitive representation, which characterizes the life of the neurotic to an unusual degree, can be seen as an avoidance of responsibility. By talking about our actions in a way that distorts and falsifies them, or by never directly talking about them at all, we are in fact not taking responsibility for what they really are. We cannot be held accountable for that which we do not recognize as our own.

Patients in therapy commonly use various stratagems to present interpersonal dispositions in a disguised or indirect way, so that they cannot be held responsible for them. Two favorite techniques involve the reporting of dreams and childhood experiences, which enable the patient to offer all kinds of interpersonal presentations without having to take full responsibility for them. The therapist must listen for the hidden agenda in these revelations and constantly ask himself: "Why is the patient presenting this particular material now at this moment, and how does he expect me to react?" (Beier, 1966). The answers to these questions will provide clues to the way in which the patient is seeking to structure his relationship with the therapist, and this in turn will give clues to some of his interpersonal presentations outside the therapy session.

THE TASKS OF THE THERAPIST

The therapist can use two sources of evidence to inform himself about the covert meaning of the patient's communications. First, he may use his own spontaneous reactions to the patient's messages as an indication of the kind of relationship the patient was trying to set up. Do the patient's messages create feelings of being dominated, seduced, hoodwinked, put at a distance, or whatever? The nature of interpersonal communications depends on the type of relationship that they invite the other person to engage in. The therapist should keep a sharp lookout for such implied invitations, using his own unreflecting response as a clue to the kind of engagement he was probably being invited to make. Instead of accepting the invitation, however, he identifies it verbally and confronts the patient with the appropriate cognitive representation of his interpersonal strategy and its implications.

Nonverbal channels of communication provide another major source of evidence about implicit meanings in the patient's communications during psychotherapy. Bodily movements of approach or withdrawal, gestures symbolizing incorporation or rejection, voice qualities expressing domination or compliance, facial expressions of positive or negative affect are such an important part of the presentation the patient directs at the therapist that nonverbal behavior has sometimes been considered the "relationship language" *par excellence* (Ekman and Friesen, 1968). Moreover, these nonverbal signals have an important *metacommunicative* function, providing information about how the accompanying verbal communication is to be interpreted, whether it is to be taken at face value or regarded as a defensive maneuver designed to cover up the patient's real feelings, or considered as a ploy in an attempt to regulate the patient–therapist relationship.

Nonverbal clues are particularly useful to the therapist because they seem to be less susceptible than verbal output to conscious deception or conscious decentering. That is why they have sometimes been described as a *leakage channel* of communication (Ekman and Friesen, 1969). In a well-known pronouncement Freud put it this way:

"He that has eyes to see and ears to hear may convince himself that no mortal can keep a secret. If his lips are silent he chatters with his fingertips; betrayal oozes out of him at every pore" (Freud, 1905). For example, there is the patient who deftly plays with his pencil until he defensively claims perfect efficiency at his work, at which point he loses control of the pencil and drops it to the floor (Mahl, 1968).

The classical psychoanalytic situation, in which the therapist sits invisibly behind the patient, probably enhances the leakage factor in nonverbal communication because the patient is deprived of most of the interpersonal feedback that normally enables him to modify his nonverbal communication, at least to some extent. Freud gave two reasons for adopting the classical psychoanalytic position in which the therapist sits behind the patient: One reason had to do with Freud's own discomfort about being stared at for eight hours a day; but the second reason, which is more interesting in the present context, referred to his desire to hide from the patient those spontaneous changes in facial expression that would provide the patient with unintended feedback about how his communication had been received. Under normal conditions of interpersonal communication each individual monitors his presentation in the light of the response he evokes in the other. In the psychoanalytic situation the patient is deliberately deprived of most of the nonverbal components of his feedback, so that his interpersonal presentations are much less subject to a censorship that has its origin in the uncontrolled momentary reactions of the analyst.

But the encouragement of relatively uncensored presentations by the patient represents only one side of the successful psychotherapeutic relationship. There would be little benefit to the patient if his hidden messages were not picked up by the therapist and "interpreted," that is, subject to cognitive representation. The patient's free flow of presentations must be matched by the therapist's sensitivity to their meaning and by his ability to communicate his conclusions back to the patient in an appropriate manner. It is essential that the therapist pay attention not only to the verbal content of the patient's message but listen closely to what the patient's words conceal and what his tone of voice, his gestures, and facial expressions reveal. The therapist must learn, in the phrase which Theodor Reik borrowed from Nietzsche, to "listen with the third ear" (Reik, 1948). His job is not only to listen to how the patient represents things in words but how he presents himself in his interpersonal encounters. This does not mean that the therapist will always be able to identify the exact source of his information, the precise gesture, fleeting facial expression, or subtle tonal inflection that form the basis of his overall impression. But he must cultivate an attitude of exceptional openness to these communication channels and allow them due weight in the formulation of his impression. He must "hear" those aspects of the patient's presentation to which the patient himself is deaf. Having listened effectively he must formulate a verbal representation of what he has heard and find an acceptable way of communicating this formulation to the patient.

Therapists differ in the skill with which they carry out these tasks. There are those who notice only the most obvious postures that the patient presents in his interpersonal relationships, and there are others who may be sensitive to the finer nuances but who seem unable to communicate their insight to the patient in terms that are meaningful and acceptable to the latter. The therapeutic skill that is involved here has been labeled "accurate empathy" by those working in the client-centered tradition of psychotherapy. It is a skill that must be clearly distinguished from mere proficiency in the application of diagnostic labels. The effective therapist is not the one to whom impersonal judgments of the "I understand the dynamics that make you act that way" type come easily, but the one who is able to enter into the patient's presentation by way of "trial identification," so as to grasp its inner meaning and the kind of experience that accompanies it (Truax and Carkhuff, 1967).

What is meant by "accurate empathy" in this context is not simply a passive receptiveness to the patient's plight, but the ability to communicate this understanding to the patient in a form that will hit home. We are not talking about an attitude or personality attribute of the therapist but about an interpersonal skill (Truax and Mitchell, 1971, pp. 318–319). Effective therapeutic listening is of little consequence unless it affects the kind of communication that takes place between therapist and patient. Good listening is a necessary but hardly a sufficient condition of therapeutic effectiveness.

Much of the classical literature on psychotherapy is dominated by two fundamental premises about its purpose. The first premise involves the assumption that psychotherapy is essentially a technique for dealing with intrapsychic conflicts; the second premise assigns the key role in the therapeutic process to the development of insight or greater self-awareness. Together, these premises lead to a vision of psychotherapy from a purely individual perspective. The focus is on what happens *within* the participants in the therapeutic process rather than on what happens *between* them. Even when the dyadic nature of the therapeutic relationship is recognized by the introduction of concepts like *countertransference* the perspective remains limited to intraindividual rather than interindividual processes.

The preoccupation with insight and internal conflicts leads to a description of psychotherapy in terms of its results rather than in terms of the actual processes that constitute the therapeutic relationship. No doubt psychotherapy often has an impact on internal conflicts and is capable of generating insight, but explaining its workings in terms of these effects is rather like explaining the mechanism of the automobile by saying that it is a device for getting one to and from one's place of work. If we want to understand the processes that make it possible for psychotherapy to have its desired effects on individuals we must start with the fact that it involves at least two people. Its intraindividual effects are generated by certain patterns of social interchange; the motor of therapeutic change lies in interpersonal processes. If it were not so the same effects might as well be produced by individual meditation or by the perusal of enlightening literature.

If therapeutic effectiveness depends on certain interpersonal transactions between therapist and patient it should be possible to establish empirical relationships between these interpersonal variables and appropriate measures of therapeutic outcome. Such measures might include ratings of therapeutic effectiveness by therapists and by patients, personality changes in patients that can be psychometrically tied down, and the use of a scale of change in the patient that is derived from one's definition of the purpose of psychotherapy. The most frequently used example of this last type of measure is the "depth of self-exploration" scale developed in the tradition of client-centered therapy. From the interpersonal perspective developed in the present context "depth of self-exploration" can be seen as closely related to the establishment of congruence between social presentations and their representation by cognitive reflection.

A first approximation to the measurement of interpersonal variables in psychotherapy can be achieved by the development of reliable rating scales for therapist interpersonal skills. This has been quite successfully done for "accurate empathy," discussed above, as well as for "genuineness," that is, the nonphony, nondefensive quality of the therapist's approach to the patient, and "nonpossessive warmth," a warmly receptive, nondominating attitude on the part of the therapist. Numerous research studies have succeeded in demonstrating a positive relationship between these therapist interpersonal skills and favorable therapeutic outcome. This body of work has been thoroughly reviewed by Truax and Mitchell (1971).

INTERPERSONAL TECHNIQUES OF THE THERAPIST

However, the establishment of relations between therapist interpersonal skills and therapeutic outcome can give us only a limited view of what actually happens in the psychotherapeutic encounter. It is a view that is limited by the scope and perspective of the theory from which the basic dimensions of therapist behavior are derived, and it may lead us to overlook equally important aspects of therapist behavior that do not happen to be emphasized by the theory. To get beyond this limitation we need a more descriptive and a less interpretive definition of the relevant variables. A further limitation arises out of the fact that "therapist interpersonal skills" are dispositional variables that do not tell us anything about the flow of specific communicational events that constitutes the psychotherapeutic process. It is useful to know that therapists differ in genuineness, nonpossessive warmth, and so on, but in order to understand the psychotherapeutic process it is also important to discover just *how* these and other qualities are communicated to the patient, and how the patient in his turn influences their expression.

An interesting beginning in developing a process language for communication in psychotherapy has been made by Rice (1965) who has shown that systematic naturalistic observation of therapists' behavior leads to a classification of vocal style that can be related to case outcome. Three properties of vocal style were used to distinguish between various types of therapeutic interview: (1) fresh, stimulating, highly connotative, imaginative quality of language as contrasted with the use of commonplace words and phrases; (2) voice quality, which may be (a) *expressive* (wide pitch range, considerable and irregular emphasis, high energy used in a controlled way), (b) *usual* (limited pitch range, moderate amount of energy and inflection), (c) *distorted* (marked pitch variation, regular emphasis producing a kind of singsong quality); (3) functional level (whether the therapist, in responding to the patient's message, focuses on the patient's immediate inner experience or on something outside the patient or joins the patient in observing and analyzing the self as an object).

Three kinds of therapeutic interviews could be distinguished in terms of the most usual combination of these qualities. Type I interviews were characterized by commonplace language, even and relatively uninflected voice quality, and reflection of the patient's self-observation. Type II interviews differed from Type I chiefly in terms of the preponderance of distorted voice quality. Type III interviews contrast with Type I on all three vocal properties. They are marked by an expressive voice quality, focus on the patient's immediate inner experience and fresh, imaginative use of language.

The presence of Type II interviews either early or late in therapy was characteristic of therapies that were seen as unsuccessful by both therapist and patient. Type III interviews were related to successful outcome (as viewed by both therapist and patient) only when they appeared late, but not when they appeared early in therapy. In other words, they seem to be a correlate but not a predictor of therapeutic success. There is evidence (Rice, 1973) that the kind of therapist participation characteristic of Type III interviews influences the style of patient participation after a number of therapy sessions. It seems to affect patient voice quality, and to promote the patient's exploration of his inner experience in an immediate and differentiated fashion. It seems likely that the effect of the therapist's style on therapy outcome is mediated by the influence that it has on the patient's style of participation in the therapeutic process.

This is one example of a process that takes us to the very core of the psychotherapeutic endeavor. It is very clear that the practical effectiveness of psychotherapy is at best minimally related to the theoretical content of psychotherapeutic systems. Therapists with the most diverse theoretical orientations are all able to claim some therapeutic successes. It seems likely, therefore, that such successes are due to features that are common to psychotherapies practiced under the aegis of quite diverse theoretical orientations. These common features are usually to be found in the area of interpersonal confrontation. With the exception of systems based on various forms of autosuggestion all approaches to psychotherapy involve the creation of a special system of interpersonal transactions. It is in this area that we must look for the processes and principles that determine the success or failure of psychotherapy.

Entering psychotherapy means participating in a special kind of interpersonal communication. Any changes that psychotherapy produces in an individual depend on this participation. Let us not be misled by an inappropriate model of the kind of causality that is involved here (see Chapter 10). Psychotherapy is not something that is *done to* the patient, it is not something that is administered like a drug, but something that requires his active participation. The manner of this participation will determine the effects that psychotherapy has on him as an individual. It is the function of the psychotherapist to create the conditions for effective participation by the patient. The psychotherapist's style of communication should be such as to stimulate those aspects of the patient's communication that are associated with therapeutic change. Much research still needs to be done to enable us to identify all the aspects that are relevant in this context. But we are beginning to know something about the way in which the psychotherapist's style of communication influences the patient's participation in the psychotherapeutic interchange.

Before dealing with the quality of the patient's communications we might note that their sheer volume is likely to vary with the ambiguity and the amount of feedback provided by the therapist's remarks. In interview situations ambiguous interviewer remarks, in contrast to specific ones, are associated with longer interviewee responses. On the other hand, reduction in interviewer feedback leads to a reduction in the verbal productivity of the interviewee (Siegman and Pope, 1972). In both cases interviewee uncertainty is increased, but in the first case the uncertainty affects only a particular message, while in the second case it affects the whole relationship with the interviewer. The interviewer who is interested in maximizing interviewee productivity should therefore increase the ambiguity of individual messages while providing the interviewee with adequate feedback.

But the sheer volume of an interviewee's messages will usually be of less interest to an interviewer or therapist than their content. What can a therapist do to encourage the patient's communications related to specific topics? In the first place, he should take up these topics if and when they are raised by the patient. If a patient expresses hostility or dependency, for example, and the therapist responds by avoiding the matter, the patient is much less likely to continue such expressions than if the therapist directly takes up the topic (Schuldt, 1966; Varble, 1968).

If the therapist does address himself to a topic introduced by the patient he may do so in a number of ways, and the result will not always be the same. For instance, he may respond in a warmly accepting manner, or he may respond by disagreement or disapproval. Opinions are divided about what is the best course to follow. As mentioned before, the client-centered school of psychotherapy has emphasized the beneficial effects of therapist warmth and acceptance, but there is now clear evidence (Heller, 1968, 1972) that interviewer disagreement or disapproval leads many subjects to persist in talking about precisely those topics that elicited these negative responses. This illustrates the presence of an element of challenge in many highly effective interview and therapy situations. After all, communication in these situations is a two-way channel, and interviewees or patients may reveal more about themselves in taking up what they feel to be a personal challenge than in basking in the interviewer's unconditional approval. It is certain that individuals will differ greatly in their manner of handling this aspect of the interview or therapy situation. One should not make the mistake of supposing that there is one best method that will necessarily provide the optimum conditions for promoting self-disclosure among all persons.

This does not mean that all generalizations about the relative effectiveness of different types of therapeutic intervention are futile. Such a generalization follows from one of the fundamental purposes of the psychotherapeutic endeavor, which we have earlier defined as the effecting of change in the patient's interpersonal presentations through the medium of their cognitive representation. Interpersonal presentations manifest themselves subjectively as feelings and affects. The attachment of appropriate cognitive representations to interpersonal presentations can therefore be accomplished by encouraging the patient's reflective verbalization about his affects and feelings. This is something the therapist is able to do by taking up any material of this type produced by the patient. It has been shown that when the therapist follows up the theme of the patient's affect verbalization this encourages further affect verbalization by the patient (Isaacs and Haggard, 1966). Moreover, the patient is more likely later in the session, to return spontaneously to the content in connection with which the therapist dealt with affect. The responses the patient makes under these conditions are also marked by particular concern with his current motivational state and his ability to relate to others. These effects of therapist attention to patient affect verbalization would seem to be highly desirable in terms of most theoretical orientations to the process of psychotherapy.

PSYCHOTHERAPY AS A TWO-WAY INFLUENCE PROCESS

The practical application of any conclusions about the relative effectiveness of therapeutic interventions and conditions is subject to considerable limitations that have their origin in the fact that the therapist is usually not free to vary his behavior autonomously but is constrained by the behavior of the patient. As we have already emphasized, psychotherapy is not something that is *done to* the patient but something that requires the patient's active participation. This makes it inevitable that it is not only the therapist who produces effects on the patient but also the patient who produces effects on the therapist. Insofar as it constitutes a system of interpersonal communication the psychotherapeutic relationship is as inadequately represented by a one-way, unidirectional model of influence as are other such systems. In the Introduction it was pointed out that the effective analysis of interpersonal communication always required the use of causal models based on two-way or reciprocal influence. In recent years considerable evidence has accumulated that psychotherapy is certainly no exception to this rule.

In a study involving hospitalized schizophrenics Rogers and his co-workers (1967) concluded that characteristics of the patient influenced the nature of the relationship between him and the therapist and in some degree determined the therapist conditions available to him.

In analyzing an example of psychotherapy reported by Rogers, Truax (1966) was able to show that therapeutic conditions were not uniformly distributed, but were systematically related to certain patient categories. For example, the therapist was more empathic and positive when the client showed evidence of insight, discrimination learning, and expressive style similar to that of the therapist.

It has also been demonstrated that the functioning of therapists can be influenced by the experimental manipulation of "client" behavior. In one such study (Heller, Myers, and Kline, 1963) unsuspecting therapists responded in a more friendly fashion to actors simulating essentially friendly "patients," and in a more hostile manner to essentially hostile simulated "patients." This kind of finding has often been interpreted in terms of the principle of *reciprocal affect*, which states that in any interpersonal situation the affect elicited in one person is similar in kind and in proportion to the affect communicated by the other. Other studies using actors to simulate friendly and hostile "patients" support the conclusion that therapists respond in a negative manner when hostility is directed at them (Gamsky and Farwell, 1966).

Once psychotherapy is seen as a two-way influence relationship a whole new level of analysis is opened up. For certain purposes the individual characteristics of patients and therapists are still of interest, but when a particular patient–therapist pair are brought together a dyadic system is set up whose properties cannot be simply deduced from the characteristics that each of the participants brings to the situation. The system properties of therapist–patient dyads must be studied in their own right if psychotherapy is to be understood as essentially a special process of interpersonal communication.

Even such primitive and contentless measures as sound–silence patterns of dialogue in interviews show the influence of interpersonal factors. When the length and frequency of conversational pauses are compared for interviewers who are successively paired with different subjects their pattern of pauses tended to vary in consistently different ways with different subjects. Conversely, subjects showed a different pattern of vocalization and pauses depending on whom they interacted with. The temporal pattern of an individual's conversational behavior is therefore modified by the temporal patterning of other individuals with whom he interacts (Feldstein, 1972).

Similar synchronous relationships between interviewer and interviewee have been demonstrated for duration of utterances (Matarazzo *et al.*, 1963), for loudness, for precision of articulation, and for speech rates (Webb, 1972). Other studies (Jaffe, 1964) have shown that over a series of therapeutic interviews there is a convergence between therapist and patient in such measures as sentence length, utterance length, specificity (usage of "a" versus "the"), and interpersonal orientation (ratio of usage of "I" versus "you"). Using the types of voice quality described earlier Rice was able to show that a patient's increase of "focused voice quality" over a series of twenty interviews correlated with relatively successful therapeutic outcome. It appears likely that this is a function of therapist's voice quality, there being a clear correlation between therapist's expressive voice quality and patient's focused voice quality by the middle of the series of therapeutic interviews. It appears that the voice quality of therapist and patient show a mutual influence over time.

In a major study of psychotherapy as a dyadic system Lennard and Bernstein (1960) were able to show a clear convergence over a series of psychotherapeutic session in "primary system reference." This category is a measure of therapist–patient role relations, i.e. the mutual obligations of therapist and patient vis-à-vis each other. Such references frequently involve discussions of the purpose of psychotherapy. A similar therapist–patient convergence occurs with regard to affective propositions, directed toward or expressing feelings or emotions. Some therapist–patient dyads show an increased sensitivity to this area of concern over time while others do not. A reciprocal relation was also demonstrated between the information fed into the system by therapists and patients. Patient silences or brief verbalizations are associated with therapist statements of high informational specificity.

Most studies of therapist–patient synchrony have used verbal measures but his should not make us lose sight of the fact that this synchrony extends to nonverbal behavior as well. In the analysis of filmed psychotherapy sessions it is possible to distinguish congruent and incongruent postures and movements. One example of postural congruence is the so-called "mirror" form where one person's posture is the mirror of the other with a precise reversal of laterality, so that one person's left side is equivalent to the other person's right. Upper body congruence involves an arrangement in which the head, shoulders, and trunk position is equivalent for both subjects and is held that way for a distinguishable period of time. Lower body congruence involves a similar arrangement for hips and lower limbs. In congruent body movement the motion starts from a congruent body posture, is congruous and synchronous for its duration, and ends in a congruous posture. Performing a frame by frame analysis of filmed psychotherapeutic interactions Charny (1966) was able to show that the duration of postural congruence increased in the course of psychotherapy while noncongruent postures decreased. He was also able to show that during noncongruent periods there was greater use of the first person and greater use of negative statements pertaining to thought, action, and feeling. Statements made during noncongruent periods are highly self-oriented and often self-contradictory. On the other hand, patient statements during congruent periods are more likely to engage the therapist directly and are more likely to involve the patient–therapist relationship. This was particularly true of upper body congruence, which appears to be a naturally occurring unit indicative of a state of therapeutic rapport or relatedness. Further research along these lines promises to shed additional light on the dyadic patterning of the therapeutic relationship.

The mutual influence of patient and therapist makes it quite hazardous and misleading to predict the behavior in psychotherapy of either of them on the basis of purely individual data. Such therapist resources as accurate empathy and patient propensities to demonstrate different degrees of self-exploration do not constitute invariable personal dispositions but are properties that will emerge in different degrees in different therapeutic dyads. In one study that demonstrates this quite directly three patients were seen separately by five therapists (van der Veen, 1965). No therapist offered the same conditions of congruence and accurate empathy to any two patients, and no patient showed the same degree of problem expression or experiencing (exploration of immediate experience) with any two therapists. The precise level of therapeutic conditions offered and patient responses varied from one dyad to another. Different patients elicited different therapeutic conditions from different therapists, and different therapists elicited different therapeutically relevant behavior from different patients. Whatever propensities therapists and patients brought to the therapeutic situation were decisively modified by their interaction once the process of interpersonal communication got under way. The specific characteristics of each therapeutic dyad could not have been effectively predicted from the behavior of each of the participants in other therapeutic dyads.

Other studies in which the same therapists were successively paired with the same patients have emerged with essentially similar results. Moos and Clemes (1967) paired four therapists and four patients in counterbalanced order. For both therapist and patient measures significant patient–therapist interactions were found in the proportion of feeling words and the proportion of action words used as well as in the number of reinforcements (mm-hmm's) emitted. Interestingly enough, therapist reinforcements did not correlate with any of the measured patient variables, whereas patient reinforcements correlated significantly and positively with therapist's use of feeling words and significantly and negatively with therapist's use of action words. In a similar study Moos and MacIntosh (1970) were able to show significant patient–therapist interactions for the total number of words spoken by both therapists and patients.

Such findings are clearly at variance with the classical Rogerian view according to which therapist variables are essentially "traits" that are offered in a nonselective fashion to the client. They are also at variance with the verbal conditioning paradigm of psychotherapy that is based on a model of one-way influence that passes from therapist to patient. In a two-way influence model the effects of patient reinforcements on therapists must also be considered, and in fact these studies show patients to be much more effective sources of reinforcements than therapists. In general, therapists varied their behavior much more with different patients than patients varied their behavior with different therapists.

The study of interpersonal communication in psychotherapy once more shows the inappropriateness of unidirectional causal models in which one participant is regarded as the source of influence and the other as its target. In reality we have a dyadic system with its own properties that cannot be reduced to the individual contributions of its members. For the analysis of such systems concepts like convergence and divergence are far more appropriate than simplistic cause and effect models whose seductive attraction stems from their historical success in some of the physical sciences.

CONCLUSION

Psychotherapy represents the mobilization of interpersonal communication processes for the purpose of producing specific changes in individuals. That psychotherapy is basically an interindividual process seems quite obvious, yet it needs emphasizing in view of the fact that most theorizing in this area tends to focus on intraindividual states and events. This may take the form of an analysis of the psychodynamics of the patient or of the personality characteristics of effective psychotherapists. In either case the actual exchanges that occur between therapist and patient or between counselor and client are lost from view. Yet the fact that therapists of the most diverse theoretical persuasion are able to register some measure of success suggests that the effectiveness of psychotherapy depends on certain interpersonal events that are common to different forms of psychotherapy. It is these events that provide the motor of therapeutic change.

The first step toward an understanding of the interpersonal transactions that constitute psychotherapy must involve a recognition of the fact that psychotherapy is not something that can be administered to the patient, but rather something that requires his active participation. It is not only the therapist who exerts an influence on the patient, but also the patient whose behavior affects the therapist in a manner that the latter ought to recognize if he is not to flounder blindly into a potentially destructive situation.

Therapists are not machines that impartially dish out a programmed system of reinforcements to all comers, but are themselves profoundly affected by the responses that patients make to their interventions. Whatever the predispositions that therapists and patients bring to the therapeutic situation, their behavior is significantly affected by the feedback they receive from each other in the course of treatment.

Insofar as the therapist becomes sensitive to his own unreflecting responses to the patient's behavior he will be able to recognize the direction in which the latter's tactics of interpersonal communication are pointing. Patients in therapy invariably attempt to impose a particular structure on their relationship with the therapist. In other words, they attempt to present their end of the relationship in a certain manner, and this is simultaneously an invitation to the therapist to assume the appropriate reciprocal role that would confirm the patient's presentation of the relationship. However, the therapist declines to provide the patient with the kind of feedback that would constitute an appropriate response to this invitation in everyday life. He may do this in a variety of ways, by sitting out of sight of the patient so as to deprive the latter of nonverbal feedback, by being noncommittal and merely reflecting the patient's statements, or by administering a prearranged program of reinforcement. The common feature of these tactics is the refusal of the kind of feedback that would permit the patient to structure the relationship on his terms. This breaks up the usual pattern of the patient's interpersonal presentations and creates conditions for their change.

Such change is desirable because the problems that individuals bring to the psychotherapeutic situation generally involve difficulties in the establishment and maintenance of social relationships. These difficulties commonly arise out of ambiguities in the individual's interpersonal communications. The messages that the patient or client addresses to others tend to proceed on two levels, an overt level that contains the ostensible purpose of the message, and a covert level that contains the "hidden agenda" of the social transaction. Communications on the second level remain covert in the double sense that the individual seeks to hide their meaning both from himself and from others. Psychotherapists must therefore become skillful in detecting not only what the patient's communications reveal, but also what they conceal.

This detection involves the verbal representation of unacknowledged aspects of the patient's communications. When these representations are communicated to the patient, the latter has the choice of rejecting them or of changing his social presentation so as to establish congruence between the presentation and its verbal representation. Before therapy, the covert element in his social presentations were either not represented at all or represented in a distorted form. It is the common purpose of all "insight therapies" to establish congruence between social presentations and their verbal representation. Once this congruence has been achieved the conditions for effective therapeutic change have been created. The conflict between overt and covert aspects of his social presentations has now been reflected on the verbal level where it can be reached by the interventions of the therapist and where the establishment of congruence is more easily achieved than on the nonverbal level. For effective therapeutic change it is of course necessary that the congruencies that have emerged on the level of verbal representations be reflected back to the level of social presentation.

REFERENCES

Beier, G. (1966). *The Silent Language of Psychotherapy*. Chicago: Aldine.

Charny, E. J. (1966). Psychosomatic manifestations of rapport in psychotherapy. *Psychosomatic Medicine*, **28**, 305–315.

Ekman, P. and Friesen, W. V. (1968). Nonverbal behavior in psychotherapy research. In J. M. Shlien (Ed.), *Research in Psychotherapy*. Vol. III. Washington, D.C.: American Psychological Association.

Ekman, P. and Friesen, W. V. (1969). Nonverbal leakage and clues to deception. *Psychiatry*, **32**, 88–106.

Feldstein, S. (1972). Temporal patterns of dialogue: Basic research and reconsiderations. In A. W. Siegman and B. Pope (Eds.), *Studies in Dyadic Communication*. New York: Pergamon Press.

Freud, S. (1905). Fragment of an analysis of a case of hysteria. *Collected Papers*, Vol. 3, p. 94. New York: Basic Books, 1959.

Gamsky, N. R. and Farwell, G. F. (1966). Counselor verbal behavior as a function of client hostility. *J. counsel. Psychol.*, **13**, 184–190.

Haley, J. (1963). *Strategies of Psychotherapy*. New York: Grune & Stratton.

Heller, K. (1968). Ambiguity in the interview interaction. In J. M. Shlien (Ed.), *Research in Psychotherapy*. Vol. III. Washington, D.C.: American Psychological Association.

Heller, K. (1972). Interview structure and interviewer style in initial interviews. In A. W. Siegman and B. Pope (Eds.), *Studies in Dyadic Communication*. New York: Pergamon Press.

Heller, K., Myers, R. A., and Kline, L. V. (1963). Interviewer behavior as a function of standardized client roles. *J. consult. Psychol.*, **27**, 117–122.

Isaacs, K. and Haggard, E. (1966). Some methods used in the study of affect in psychotherapy. In L. A. Gottschalk and A. M. Auerbach (Eds.), *Methods of Research in Psychotherapy*. New York: Appleton-Century-Crofts.

Jackson, D. D. and Haley, J. (1963). Transference revisited. *J. nerv. ment. Dis.*, **137**, 363–371.

Jaffe, J. (1964). Verbal behavior analysis in psychiatric interviews with the aid of digital computers. In D. McK. Rioch and E. A. Weinstein (Eds.), *Disorders of Communication*, chapter 27. Baltimore: Williams & Wilkins.

Kaiser, H. (1965). *Effective Psychotherapy*. New York: Free Press.

Lennard, H. L. and Bernstein, A. (1960). *The Anatomy of Psychotherapy*. New York: Columbia University Press.

Mahl, G. F. (1968). Gestures and body movements in interviews. In J. M. Shlien (Ed.), *Research in Psychotherapy*. Vol. III. Washington, D.C.: American Psychological Association.

Matarazzo, J. D., Weitman, M., Saslow, G., and Wiens, A. N. (1963). Interviewer influence on duration of interview speech. *J. verb. Learning and verb. Behavior*, **1**, 451–458.

Moos, R. H. and Clemes, S. R. (1967). Multivariate study of the patient–therapist system. *J. consult. Psychol.*, **31**, 119–130.

Moos, R. H. and MacIntosh, S. (1970). *J. consult. & clin. Psychol.*, **35**, 298–307.

Reik, T. (1948). *Listening with the Third Ear*. New York: Farrar, Straus & Giroux.

Rice, L. N. (1965). Therapist's style of participation and case outcome. *J. consult. Psychol.*, **29**, 155–160.

Rice, L. N. (1973). Client behavior as a function of therapist style and client resources. *J. counsel. Pschol*, **20**, 306–311.

Rogers, C. R., Gendlin, G. T., Kiesler, D. V., and Truax, C. B. (1967). *The Therapeutic Relationship and Its Impact: A Study of Psychotherapy with Schizophrenics*. Madison: University of Wisconsin Press.

Schuldt, W. J. (1966). Psychotherapists' approach-avoidance responses and clients' expressions of dependency. *J. counsel. Psychol.*, **13**, 178–183.

Siegman, A. W. and Pope, B. (1972). The effects of ambiguity and anxiety on interviewee verbal behavior. In A. W. Siegman and B. Pope (Eds.), *Studies in Dyadic Communication*. New York: Pergamon Press.

Truax, C. B. (1966). Influence of patient statements on judgments of therapist statements during psychotherapy. *J. clin. Psychol.*, **22**, 335–337.

Truax, C. B. and Carkhuff, R. R. (1967). *Toward Effective Counseling and Psychotherapy: Training and Practice*. Chicago: Aldine.

Truax, C. B. and Mitchell, K. M. (1971). Research on certain therapist interpersonal skills in relation to process and outcome. In A. E. Bergin and L. Garfield (Eds.), *Handbook of Psychotherapy and Behavior Change: An Empirical Analysis*. New York: Wiley.

van der Veen, J. (1965). Effects of the therapist and the patient on each other's therapeutic behavior. *J. consult. Psychol.*, **29**, 19–26.

Varble, D. L. (1968). Relationship between the therapist's approach-avoidance reactions to hostility and client behavior in therapy. *J. consult. & clin. Psychol.*, **32**, 237–242.

Webb, J. T. (1972). Interview synchrony: An investigation of two speech rate measures. In A. W. Siegman and B. Pope (Eds.), *Studies in Dyadic Communication*. New York: Pergamon Press.

CHAPTER 7

The Study of Disturbed Communication in Families

No social context can compare with the family in terms of the poignancy with which it draws attention to the problematic nature of human communication. Members of families spend half a lifetime or more attempting to communicate with one another and often the result is nothing but misunderstanding and mutual alienation. The failure of communication is the commonest complaint of disenchanted marriage partners and parents and children locked in intergenerational conflict. Small wonder that more thought and more research on problems of interpersonal communication have been generated in the area of the family than in any other.

What is the reason for the frailty of successful communication in family contexts? It is not that there is a lack of desire to communicate. In fact, the depth of frustration produced by the failures of communication attests to the strength of the underlying intention. So do the ever-repeated attempts at resuming the dialogue in spite of repeated rebuffs. But obviously good intentions are not enough in this situation. In spite of the best intentions the process of communication goes awry again and again and leads to outcomes that were not desired by anyone. It is as though, once initiated, the communication process develops an autonomy of its own and proceeds to unfold in a manner of speaking behind the backs of the participants.

In this connection it may be useful to make a distinction that originated with the philosopher Jean-Paul Sartre and has been introduced to the field of family interaction studies by Laing and Esterson (1964). The distinction is one between *praxis* and *process*, where the former refers to social actions that can be traced to definite decisions and intentions, while the latter involves events that just seem to happen without anyone intending them. Events in the realm of social praxis are directly intelligible to the participants but process events are not. It is the task of systematic research in this area to render the *process* of communication intelligible. Only when this is done will intelligent intervention in these events be possible and their possibly malignant course become reversible.

This view implies that family members (and for that matter members of other groups too) are not normally aware of everything that they communicate by their actions and statements, nor are they aware of all the effects that the messages of others have on themselves. It also implies that the control that individuals have over the messages that they actually transmit is far from perfect. One may intend to create harmony and light by one's statements but the net effect may be nothing but discord and confusion, and this may be as much due to the nature of the message as to the perversity of the receiver. My tone of voice, my change of topic at certain moments, or my failure to respond to the implications of certain statements may have consequences that completely negate the content of what I intend to communicate, and what is more, I may have no inkling of what I am doing. My partner in communication may be aware only of certain disagreeable consequences without being able to put his finger on their precise cause. And so the altercation may proceed with mounting misunderstanding to an unsatisfactory conclusion.

It is easy to become trapped in such situations unless it is possible to make the unintended processes of communication intelligible to one another. This will be the easier the less one's involvement in the situation and the smaller the weight of past misunderstandings that the relationship has to carry. Family situations are therefore particularly intractable in terms of hopes for spontaneous insights by the participants. The assistance of an objective bystander in the form of a counselor or therapist may be required. But the insights of such a specialist are of limited validity. Some of them are based on practical intuition and do not necessarily advance our ability to identify the precise elements that have given the interaction process its peculiar form. Other aspects of communication may be too subtle for the sensibilities of even the most skillful practitioner who has no opportunity to react to a particular interaction sequence more than once. Then again, the practical need to concentrate on individual families makes it impossible to adequately test generalizations about different types of family interaction in a clinical context. For all these reasons systematic research provides the most effective tool in the long run for rendering the processes of family communication intelligible.

MEASURES OF FAMILY COMMUNICATION

It is one thing to recognize the need for systematic research in family communication in principle, it is quite another to translate this realization into practice. Research gives no guarantee of new insights unless it addresses itself to the right questions and has at its disposal techniques that are adequate to the problem. Not all studies in the field of family interaction throw light on problems of interpersonal communication because they do not necessarily address themselves to questions that are relevant to the topic of communication.

In fact, the traditional approach to studies of family interaction quite definitely excludes any consideration of interpersonal perspectives. Because this approach is based on the traditions of individual psychiatry and psychology its variables are personal qualities and not interpersonal processes. Thus the cognitive style or the personality traits of parents may be correlated with those of their children without raising questions about the interaction processes that produce such correlations. From this point of view communication in the family remains an intervening system that is not studied directly. This is a kind of "black box" approach to the family where the inputs and outputs of the system consist of the personality characteristics of its members. It is only these characteristics that are directly assessed, while family interaction is simply assumed to mediate between them without being itself the object of study. It is clear that this approach does not enable us to raise or answer questions about the nature of communication processes in the family.

Not that the process of family communication lends itself very readily to direct investigation. Indeed, the complex of innuendos, subtle attempts at influence and counterinfluence, ambiguity, multilayered statements, voluble silences, and mutually conflicting messages is enough to defeat the best efforts of even the most determined and skillful investigator. We must therefore approach this potential Pandora's box of problems in manageable stages, trying not to raise questions that our available techniques will not enable us to answer. There are three levels at which these issues may be posed. Each successive level of investigation becomes more ambitious in terms of the questions that are raised about the actual substance of family communication.

At the first level our measures are still based on the *outcomes* of communication processes without any attempt at studying those processes directly. However, if these outcome measures are interpersonal in nature, rather than purely individual personality measures, we are able to take a first step toward the elucidation of the interaction system that constitutes the family. Such interpersonal variables may involve an assessment of how family members perceive their relationship to one another, or a measure of their patterns of dominance or collaboration when they are faced with a common task or decision. Such patterns are revealed in the outcome of decision situations, but there is no attempt to analyze the actual content of messages that pass back and forth during the interaction process itself.

We can push our analysis a stage further by examining the *process* of interaction instead of its outcomes. The first step toward this goal involves the overall rating of the quality of the interaction. At this stage we make no attempt at dissecting the communication process into its component messages but merely aim at a global assessment of its general qualities. This involves the use of skilled observers. The components of such an analysis consist of rating scales, a defined set of dimensions that are thought to characterize the interaction process. Warmth, permissiveness, dominance, or intrusiveness would be examples of such dimensions. The disadvantages of this approach do not only lie in the fact that they may tell us more about the semantic space of the raters than about the nature of the processes taking place among the family members whose interaction is being observed. There is the additional problem that it is extremely difficult to construct rating scales that refer to truly interpersonal events. Most of the scales used in this context are based on the personal style of individual interactants and so tell us little about the pattern of action and reaction that constitutes the actual process of interpersonal communication.

It has therefore become increasingly common to make the transition to the third level of analysis that involves an attempt at dissecting the communication process into its message components and characterizing these in terms of their interpersonal significance. Instead of relying on a global assessment of a whole interaction sequence each separate unit of the sequence is categorized so that the process as a whole can be characterized by the patterning of the units. This yields the most complete description of what actually passes between individuals in the course of interpersonal communication, but it is also a time-consuming procedure that is not free of its own problems.

Outcome Measures

It is instructive to illustrate each of these levels of analysis by appropriate examples that serve to bring out the advantages and limitations of each type of approach. As a first example of an attempt at studying family interaction in terms of interpersonal outcomes we may take Haley's (1962) experiment on coalition formation. Father, mother, and child are placed at a round table separated by partitions so that they cannot see one another, nor are they permitted to talk. Their only means of communication consists of signal buttons that light up in another family member's cubicle when pressed. By pressing these buttons each participant in the experiment can signal his or her desire to form a coalition with one or other of the other participants. A coalition consists of a simultaneous pressing of two other buttons by two family members, which has the effect of running up a score for each of them. The longer the two buttons remain depressed the higher the score, and each individual is instructed to aim at getting the highest score. To win this game a person must shift coalitions and win points with each of the others while avoiding the odd-man-out position. The pattern of button pressing for each person is recorded during the game and can be used to analyze the pattern of coalition formation in the family group.

In comparing families that contained a schizophrenic child with normal families Haley found that the former had more difficulty in forming and maintaining coalitions and had longer continuous periods of time when no two family members were in coalition. In a variant of the game the families were asked to decide together before starting which of them was to win. The schizophrenic families were significantly less likely to achieve the agreed outcome than the normal families.

In a study by Caputo (1963) it was also shown that parents of schizophrenics had more difficulty in reaching agreement about their discrepant answers on parental attitudes than normal parents. Ferreira (1963) obtained similar results in studies of the resolution of opinion differences in schizophrenic families.

The situation faced by family members who participate in such experiments is of course highly artificial, and it is an open question whether this distorts their normal pattern of interaction. Single experiments of this type are more important for their methodological hints than for their substantive contribution to the understanding of family interaction styles. An obvious next step in this type of research is the conducting of several experiments on the same set of families to discover whether there is any consistency of interaction patterns from one setting to another.

An example of a somewhat less artificial task situation designed to yield outcome measures for family interaction is provided by a study conducted by Ferreira and Winter (1965). In this case the family members were presented with a number of situations to which many alternative answers were possible. For example, they were asked to indicate what films they might want to see, countries they might want to visit, magazines to which they might wish to subscribe, and the color scheme of their next car. These questions had to be answered individually and then again as a family group. This meant that they had to discuss their choices because the final decision was supposed to apply to all of them. Three outcome measures were employed: the amount of spontaneous agreement that existed among family members before discussion, the time taken to complete the joint questionnaire, and the number of instances where a particular individual's choice became the family choice. Comparison of families with a schizophrenic, maladjusted, or delinquent child revealed a number of differences among these categories and between them and normal families. The latter showed more spontaneous agreement before discussion, needed less time to make their family decisions and arrived at a better fulfillment of family members' individual choices.

What both these studies have in common is that the measures used reflect the outcome of the interaction process rather than the process itself. We do not know what passed between the family members when they discussed their joint choices in the second study or when they planned who was to win in the first study. We only know such things as their success in satisfying individual choices or their success in achieving their announced goal. This means that the obtained group differences are difficult to explain because information about the actual dynamics of interaction is lacking.

Process Measures

To overcome these limitations it is necessary to pay some attention to the interaction process itself. As stated before, the first stage in this enterprise is to make global assessments of the quality of interaction as a whole. For this purpose the interaction may be observed either in an unstructured situation or else the family members may be given some common task like completing stories or solving problems. Quite a large number of dimensions have been used in devising rating scales in this context. These include stimulation, emotional interchange, tension reduction (Yarrow, 1963), affect, anxiety, reactivity, responsiveness (Caldwell and Hersher, 1964), intrusiveness, competence, intensity (Escalona, 1969), domination, rejection, and direction (Schulman, Shoemaker, and Moelis, 1962). Typically, such rating scales are used in the context of parent–child interaction, mainly in reference to the mother's behavior, which is then correlated with certain "outcome" variables characteristic of the child. The paradigm is generally one that envisages one-way effects from parent to child rather than a truly interactional framework, which leaves room for the effects that the child has on the parent. Global rating scales do not readily lend themselves to an interactional framework because the specific action–reaction patterns tend to get lost in the overall assessment.

Quite apart from this limitation global rating scales suffer from the drawback that they leave us in ignorance about the specific instances of behavior that formed the basis for the judgments made by the raters. They do not convey information about the nature of the actual interchanges that form the basis of communication among family members.

An alternative way of arriving at an overall characterization of interaction patterns is to limit our categorization to relatively molecular behavioral acts and to examine sequences of such acts for the emergence of regular patterns. This leads us to the third stage of analysis of interpersonal communication in the family.

There are two levels at which the analysis of individual communicative acts may be pursued. in the first place we may concentrate on those aspects of communicative acts that are essentially independent of their content. This includes such aspects of interaction sequences as the pattern of who speaks to whom, who follows whom, who initiates a discussion, who does the most talking, and who the least. The analysis of the content of interchanges forms a further stage in the process of analysis.

Examples of noncontent measures of family interaction are provided by a number of studies. Drechsler and Shapiro (1963) have compared the relative frequency of parent to parent and parent to child communications in families with different types of pathology. Haley (1964, 1967) has examined the *order* in which family members speak during a discussion. In a family group consisting of mother, father, and child each of the speakers might be followed by either of the other two. These sequences can show interesting regularities and patterns. Thus if we designate each participant by the appropriate initial we might get a communication sequence that looks like this:

MCFMCFMCFMCFMCFMCFM---   and so on.

In this case there is perfect regularity in the sequence of speakers with mother always following father (except at the beginning), child always following mother, and father always following child.

In practice such perfect regularity will never occur but there may be statistically significant approximations to it. It is possible to test the sequential data for significant deviations from a completely random order of speaker sequence, but in doing so we must be careful to correct for unequal contributions by the participants (Waxler and Mishler, 1970a). In the above example, father, mother, and child each speak the same number of times but this will seldom be true in practice. We are much more likely to get a sequence that runs like this:

MFMCFMCFMFMFMCFMF

In this case mother and father each speak seven times but the child speaks only three times. However, it is still true that when the child does speak he always follows the mother and never the father, so that the sequence still departs from a purely random order. A disturbed child is quite likely to speak less frequently than the parents, and if we do not take this into consideration we will end up with spurious deviations from a random speaking order. Some of the statistical techniques developed in the framework of information theory are particularly suitable for the analysis of such patterns because they allow us to separate the contributions of unequal frequency of speech acts from the contribution of actual regularities of patterned sequences (Raush, 1965). The application of these techniques is still in its infancy, although they appear to be quite promising.

Another type of noncontent measure of family interaction involves the use of time scores, that is to say, the number of seconds each participant in a family discussion speaks, the length of overlapping speech sequences (Ferreira, Winter, and Poindexter, 1966), or the length of silences in the course of a discussion (Ferreira and Winter, 1968). Interesting differences in regard to such measures can be demonstrated to exist between normal families and families with a disturbed child. However, without the use of content measures it is hardly possible to explain the reasons for these differences.

A further possibility for the application of noncontent measures of family interaction lies in the use of observations of who speaks to whom. In a family consisting of the parents, an older child, and a younger child, a joint discussion is unlikely to involve a completely random distribution of the messages addressed to the various participants. Typically, the younger child has the smallest number of messages addressed to him and the older child receives fewer messages than the parents (Murrell and Stachowiak, 1967). This approach provides an alternative technique for the investigation of family coalitions, for it would be possible to spot a family member who was being conspicuously ignored by the others, and the formation of exclusive cliques among any two family members who preferred to communicate with each other would also become apparent. The normal coalition appears to involve the two parents, but it is possible that in some disturbed families cross-generational coalitions may become more prominent.

Specific distortions of the flow of addressed communications in three-member family groups may be of considerable psychological interest. For example, it is not without significance if a son shows a marked tendency to address himself to his mother rather than to his father. Two independent groups of investigators have reported a clear tendency for schizophrenic sons to follow this pattern when compared with normal control families (Lennard and Bernstein, 1970; Mishler and Waxler, 1968). The fathers in these schizophrenic families generally remain somewhat on the fringes of the family interaction, also receiving rather fewer messages from the mothers and addressing fewer messages to the sons, though these differences are not as striking as those relating to the son's infrequent address of the father. This pattern is strikingly present only in the case of schizophrenic sons, not in the case of schizophrenic daughters.

Such findings appear to provide at least partial support for theories that link the development of schizophrenia in boys to the failure of the father to provide a dominant same sex role model that provides a basis for clear identity formation in the son (Fleck, Lidz, and Cornelison, 1963). Of course such a configuration may not be specific to schizophrenia, but may equally well be associated with other types of deviation from more or less normal personality development. Adequate data on this question are still lacking.

The differential use of the possible address channels in a family is only one measure of a general feature of interpersonal communication, namely, procedures of *attention control*. In discussing communication systems among primates in Chapter 5 we saw that the distribution of attention was of fundamental significance in determining the course and outcome of interaction. Indices of attention control are therefore quite important parameters of any process of interpersonal communication. Participation rate, the number of times an individual intervenes in a discussion of given length, and the average length of his statements are two other possible measures of attention control. The rationale for using statement length in this context is that it provides a measure of the person's success in holding the floor and so imposing himself on the attention of the rest of the group. By and large, this latter measure shows up the same differences between normal families and those with schizophrenic sons as does the "who speaks to whom" measure, with the normal fathers holding the floor for longer periods than the fathers of schizophrenic sons (Mishler and Waxler, 1968).

The plotting of patterns of statements in terms of the family member to whom they are addressed yields a somewhat static picture of the process of attention control. Such patterns are after all the outcome of a dynamic balance of forces that point in different directions. One can think of each participant in the discussion as experiencing a certain pressure to communicate with the others. In a triadic situation any one member may be excluded from effective participation by a coalition formed by the other two, a condition under which his pressure to communicate will meet with resistance. He can attempt to overcome this resistance by intruding on the discussion and so breaking up the previous coalition. This is how speaker sequences change. But an intrusion attempt is not necessarily successful; the coalition partners may ignore the third party's attempt at cutting in and resume their dyadic interchange. The final sequence of speakers in a discussion will therefore depend on the balance between the strength of each member's need to participate and the relative imperviousness of each dyadic coalition to intrusion by another person.

These forces can be measured more directly than by merely noting the final speaker sequence. An interruption would be a strong form of an attempt at intrusion. But some attempted intrusions are more subtle. A statement can be categorized as an intrusion when its originator was not involved in the immediately preceding verbal exchange and was neither the initiator nor the target of this exchange. An intrusion can be regarded as successful if it yields at least one communication directed at the "intruder" by one of the other interactants. In an interesting application of these measures Lennard, Beaulieu, and Embrey (1965) demonstrated significantly lower intrusion rates in families with a schizophrenic child than in normal families. While it is not clear whether this is a reaction to the child's condition or an antecedent factor, such observations do demonstrate the sensitivity of this type of measure to differences in family communication patterns.

As a final example of communication measures that do not depend on a coding of content we may take indices of disrupted communication, such as incomplete sentences and phrases, disconnected words, repetition of words and phrases, as well as laughter and contentless sounds. Such measures will often be found to be quite highly correlated with one another, leading to a characterization of two speech styles: one highly controlled and somewhat pedantic, where there are relatively few instances of disrupted communication, and another more spontaneous and informal style marked by a relatively high incidence of disrupted speech. In a careful study by Mishler and Waxler (1968) it was shown that parents changed to a less spontaneous form of communication in the presence of their schizophrenic child, while they showed as much speech disruption as normal parents in the presence of one of their other children who was not schizophrenic. Whether this pattern preceded the child's schizophrenic breakdown or not, it does mean that the peculiarly stilted nature of the parents' communication with him makes it more difficult for him to break through their defensive screen, which keeps at bay ambiguous feelings and ideas that are difficult to express. Such a situation is unlikely to be helpful when there are already difficulties in getting through to others.

Other applications of measures of speech disruption readily suggest themselves. The degree to which married couples adopt a stilted communication pattern with each other may be related to the quality of their relationship, and changes to or from the rather disrupted pattern of spontaneous speech in different situations or in the presence of different family members may yield important clues about the influence of various factors on the life of the family.

MEASUREMENT OF COMMUNICATION CONTENT

The value of noncontent measures of communication in the family is limited to the investigation of such features of interaction as coalition formation and attention control. If we wish to study other aspects of family interaction it becomes necessary to use measures based on the content of messages. The nature of these measures will depend on what aspects of interpersonal relationships we are interested in exploring. Communication between individuals serves various functions and interpersonal communication in the family is no exception. It may serve such diverse functions as the exchange of information, the attempt to influence others and the expression of affective reactions. Like other systems of face-to-face relationships the family involves various types of exchange among its members, the system as a whole being constituted by the regularity and pattern of these exchanges. Let us consider each type of exchange in turn.

In the first place the family can be considered as a problem-solving group whose members exchange information with a view to arriving at a solution to common problems. In doing this they may develop characteristic styles of cognitively structuring their environment. Such styles are simultaneously reflected in distinctive patterns of communication and in characteristic patterns of cognitive functioning among family members. In this context the question of *causal precedence* may not be particularly useful or important. It is true that individual cognitive styles may impose a certain form on family communication, but on the other hand, it is difficult to believe that persistent patterns of information exchange in the family remain without effect on patterns of individual thinking. No simplistic cause–effect model is likely to prove adequate in a situation that is probably marked by constant interaction between the cognitive styles that individuals bring to the interpersonal situation and the effects that that situation has on them.

David Reiss (1967, 1970) has introduced an important distinction between the *expressive form* of family members' communications to one another and their *experiential sensitivity*. The first aspect is concerned with those features of the communication that can be categorized by an independent observer without reference to the situation facing the communicator at the time the communication was made. Two major components of expressive form are the level of abstractness of the communication and its clarity in directing attention to critical features of the task situation. It is obvious that both these components can be assessed by considering the form and content of the communication quite abstractly without reference to the interpersonal situation in which it occurs. A particular message may have a content that is more or less abstract and more or less clear in its reference to this or that feature of a problem. An uninvolved rater will be in a position to judge these features quite effectively without reference to the interpersonal experience of the individuals who are the source or target of such messages.

This is not the case with the second major feature of informational exchanges, namely, their experiential sensitivity. The question here is one of the degree to which a communication is based on an accurate perception of the amount and kind of information available to and required by other family members. For example, an individual who gives the appropriate reply to a request for information in the course of a group problem-solving task shows more experiential sensitivity than one who ignores such a request or gives vague or misleading information. The efficiency with which members of family groups exchange information provides a good overall measure of their experiential sensitivity. In these cases the measure of information exchange is relative to the situation faced by the interactants and is not based simply on the form of individual messages.

The two general features of information exchange, expressive form and experiential sensitivity, do not have the same relationship to the cognitive style of the family. It is likely that the level of experiential sensitivity provides the context within which expressive form operates. Depending on this context the same forms of communication can have different effects. Thus an abstract level of communication may contribute little or nothing to the effectiveness with which the family solves its problems if such communications generally take place in a context of poor experiential sensitivity in which messages are not attuned to the cognitive requirements of other family members. On the other hand, the potential created by a high level of experiential sensitivity may not be fully exploited because of a poverty of expressive form. Such a situation may be relatively common in families from a culturally impoverished environment. In any case, where inadequacies in the exchange of information among family members lead to problems of adjustment the basis of such inadequacies must be carefully diagnosed, because the remedy will not be the same if there are deficiencies in the area of expressive form or if these deficiencies exist rather in the area of experiential sensitivity.

Communication within the family also serves other functions than information exchange. One such function involves the regulation of the power and influence of family members. Like all face-to-face groups the family constitutes not only a system in which information is disseminated but also a system in which power and influence are distributed one way or another. This distribution depends on the differentiation of status that is based on such variables as age and sex. While status differentiation in the family is influenced by general social norms these norms are only effective insofar as they are reflected in the actual behavior of family members toward one another. A particular distribution of power and status always involves certain patterns of interpersonal communication and excludes others (Farina, 1960). Such patterns are necessary to maintain a particular status structure or to modify it. The attempt to maintain or to modify existing status relationships is an important aspect of communication in the family.

There are two important aspects in the communication of power and influence within the family. First, such communications are not equally distributed over all members of the family, so that it is possible to distinguish a characteristic influence structure. Either the father or the mother, for example, may be the predominant source of influence attempts over a child, and in addition a hierarchy of power assertion may exist among the children. However, the establishment of such an overall influence structure has only a limited significance for the exploration of interpersonal relationships in the family because most influence attempts typically lead to attempts at counterinfluence that may be subtle but nonetheless effective. Influence patterns in the family are seldom one-way and apparently nondominant partners in a relationship have a way of getting back at the dominant partner so that it is often difficult to say who is dominating whom.

For studying the actual process of the communication of influence in the family it is therefore more important to analyze the *mode of expression* of such communications than to simply assign them to a source. The crucial dimension of this mode of expression involves the *directness* with which attempts at influence and counterinfluence are communicated. A parent may insist on having his way by directly asserting his right to be obeyed because of his status, superior knowledge, and so on. On the other hand, he may avoid such direct power assertions and dominate the child by a series of questions that force the child into a corner from which there is no escape but yielding to the parent. The degree of parental dominance may be the same in the two cases but the effect on the child is likely to be very different. There is evidence (Alkire *et al* ., 1971) that adolescents whose parents are more prone to use the less direct forms of influence are more likely to develop problems in their family relationships, while the problems of adolescents whose parents use more direct forms of authority assertion are more likely to extend outside the home in the form of antisocial or negative behavior.

The degree to which authority relationships are disguised by the pattern of communication in the family may vary all the way from indirect power assertion to complete mystification. The messages exchanged between family members may serve the function of disguising rather than expressing underlying claims to power and influence. Instead of asserting their point of view directly the members of the family may have recourse to pretense and distortion refusing to be nailed down to a position that they actually hold. Such behavior is part of a pattern of *pseudomutuality* in which an appearance of harmony is preserved at all costs because any direct confrontation is experienced as an intolerable threat to family relationships. It has been suggested (Wynne *et al*., 1958) that a pervasive pattern of this kind is characteristic of the family relationships of schizophrenics. Indeed, there is some evidence (Lerner, 1965) that the parents of schizophrenics are prone to deny and disguise previously expressed opinions when confronted by differing opinions on the part of the other parent. However, further research is needed in this area to determine whether the prevalence of these patterns is peculiar to the families of schizophrenics or whether it can equally well be associated with other forms of disturbance.

Affective Expression

Much interpersonal communication in families serves the expression of affect. In interacting with one another family members not only exchange information and seek to influence one another but also react emotionally. Three major issues arise in connection with such affective reactions: (1) What is their quality, in particular, what is the ratio of positive communications that express acceptance, solidarity, and relaxation, to negative communications that express rejection, tension, and antagonism? (2) How much spontaneous emotional expression do family members permit themselves in their communication with one another? (3) How are emotional expressions distributed over individuals playing various roles in the family?

The most commonly used instrument for answering these questions has been the Bales IPA scale, which involves the coding of interaction units into twelve categories, six of which refer to the "social–emotional area" and six to the "task area." Three of the social–emotional categories involve positive reactions—"solidarity," "tension release," and "agreement," and three of them involve negative reactions—"disagreement," "tension," and "antagonism." The ratio of the total of positive acts to the total of negative acts can be used to characterize the overall quality of family interaction. Similarly, the ratio of the total number of statements in the social–emotional area to the number of statements in the task area can be used as a measure of the overall level of emotional expressiveness in a particular segment of family interaction. The relative predominance of task-area interactions over social–emotional interaction would seem to indicate a somewhat muted and controlled level of emotional expressiveness. Some evidence has been reported (Mishler and Waxler, 1968) that such lowered levels of expressiveness are more characteristics of families with a schizophrenic child than of normal families. This would seem to reflect a collective defensiveness against the expression of feelings in schizogenic families that would make it difficult for the members of such families to react spontaneously to the demands placed on them by other family members. The reaction may therefore take indirect and bizarre forms.

However, the use of the IPA system in the study of family interaction is quite problematic. Reassuring levels of reliability in the coding of the categories have been difficult to achieve (Waxler and Mishler, 1966) and indices based on these categories have not been found particularly useful in discriminating among the interaction patterns of families exhibiting widely differing types of deviance (Winter and Ferreira, 1967). This is particularly true of the area of emotional expressiveness. The multidimensional coding categories of the IPA system will need to be replaced by more specific scales before further progress can be made in the systematic investigation of emotional expressiveness in family interaction. Some steps in that direction may be mentioned. The common semantic meaning of individual words expressing affect may be taken as a basis for coding, irrespective of context (Mishler and Waxler, 1968). Or statements can be rated in terms of a dimension of "distantiation," which includes the use of such devices as talking about absent persons, referring to present persons in the third person and talking about the experimental procedure (McPherson, 1970), all of them ways of avoiding the direct expression of affect toward family members with whom one is presently interacting. The spontaneity of topic change in family discussions is another possible index of emotional freedom (Riskin and Faunce, 1970). While the use of such measures looks promising they all require further practical test.

The distribution of affective communications among family members occupying different status positions has generally been studied in the context of the theory of family role specialization of Parsons and Bales (1955). According to this theory the paternal role tends to be specialized in the direction of "instrumental" functions concerned with the family's adaptation to externally imposed tasks while the maternal role is more directed toward the "expressive" function of internal maintenance of family relationships and the social–emotional needs of family members. However, direct studies of family interaction have provided little support for this theory, especially in relation to the suggestion that the roles of husbands and wives are essentially complementary in respect to the instrumental–expressive distinction. The most expressive wives are also apt to be the most influential in the task area (Kenkel, 1957), and in many families fathers are distinctly predominant in both the expressive and the instrumental role (Straus, 1967). Most interesting is the observation that when the interaction of families is compared in an experimental laboratory situation and in the home situation the task–emotional differentiation between fathers and mothers appears only in the laboratory, whereas at home the instrumental orientation of the fathers drops while that of the mothers increases (O'Rourke, 1963). It is clear that the distribution of emotional expressiveness among family members varies according to the situation and that global generalizations in terms of patterns supposedly characteristic of various family roles will not hold up (Waxler and Mishler, 1970a, 1970b).

This raises some serious questions about the general representativeness of samples of family communication obtained in a laboratory context. It is all too easily assumed that when family members communicate with one another under artificial conditions they respond essentially to the experimental conditions crucial to the research design. In actual fact their response to the presence of an interviewer, a tape recorder and the unique nature of the experience to which they are being exposed may distort their interaction pattern so much that no conclusions about their day-to-day interaction at home are possible. Quite frequently a central preoccupation of family members in a research situation is constituted by their efforts to preserve the private features of their day-to-day conduct from public view (Vidich, 1956). Moreover, if an interviewer is present during the family discussion he is not often ignored but is treated as an audience whose support and sympathy is available for solicitation. Such an audience is not generally present in the home situation.

There are many other technical problems that cast doubt on the validity of family interaction research in the laboratory. It is a difficult and usually arbitrary decision to choose a particular time sample as providing a representative example of communication processes in a particular family. The use of purely quantitative measures also raises problems because trivial events may occur frequently and vital ones rarely. Measurement variables may be chosen with an eye to ease of counting and reporting in reputable journals rather than with an overriding concern for what is really significant in family communication. For these kinds of reasons some investigators have suggested that research on family interaction should ideally be conducted in the context of extended family therapy (Framo, 1965) where family dynamics are necessarily exposed to long-term study that eliminates the artificiality of the single experimental session. Of course even under these conditions the problems of measurement and quantification can hardly be avoided if systematic data are required and if precise, general hypotheses are to be tested.

RESPONSIVENESS AND DISQUALIFICATION

There is a sense in which most of the categories in terms of which we have been discussing family interaction miss the crucial point of the communication process. This process consists, after all, of a sequence of connected events that follow one another in a pattern that is far from random. The successive statements that individuals make to one another hang together and perhaps their most significant property is the nature of their connection to one another. This connection travels in two directions, including both the statement's relationship to what has preceded it and its relationship to what follows it in the sequence of communicative acts. No cumulative measure of the characteristics of acts peculiar to a particular type of family or a particular family member can express the sequential properties of interpersonal communication.

The crucial feature of these sequential properties lies in the fact that each message in an interchange has a certain "demand" aspect (Ruesch and Bateson, 1951); it requires a response of a certain kind. In Gestalt terms, every message in an exchange between persons is a figure that lacks "closure." The response that follows may contribute to this closure, may address itself to the implicit demand, or it may not. In this way we are able to distinguish between appropriate and inappropriate responses. The next statement in the sequence may relate itself to the intent and meaning of the previous message or it may be based on a misunderstanding or a deliberate evasion. In some cases the lack of connection between statement and response may even strike us as bizarre.

Appropriate responses to messages need not confirm them. A direct disagreement may be an equally appropriate response, as long as it addresses itself to the intended meaning of the original message. The crucial distinction between appropriate and inappropriate responses depends on the identification of a response category that constitutes a *disqualification* rather than an acceptance or a straight rejection of the previous message. A disqualification involves an invalidation of either the response or the message that evoked it (Watzlawick, Beavin, and Jackson, 1967). Such invalidation may be achieved in many different ways, including self-contradiction, blatant inconsistency, changing the subject, misunderstanding, going off at a tangent, interpreting metaphors literally, and interpreting the message in terms of a personal reflection on either of the interactants. Resource to disqualification is very characteristic of people who find themselves obliged to communicate in some way but wish to avoid the commitment that is normally inherent in communication.

The crucial significance of the quality of responsiveness in communication arises from the fact that in communicating with one another people define or "present" (Chapter 2) their relationship to one another. These relationships always imply a certain definition of the social identity of the individuals engaged in them. Status relationships imply the interaction of individuals whose identity is defined by a certain status, solidary relationships imply identification by membership of a particular group, and so on. The response that one individual makes to the communication of another is therefore more than a reaction to a particular message, it is also a response to the individual who is the source of the message and as such it helps to define his social identity in the context of a particular relationship. Confirmation of another's statement is more than just a matter of intellectual agreement, it also confirms the other as a person, validates certain of his claims at self-presentation. Even disagreement with another's statement may imply such confirmation because it implies at least some recognition of what is being rejected and therefore does not necessarily negate the self-presentation of the other.

It is disqualification of the other's message that carries the implication of an invalidation of his self-definition because it does not honor the claim for recognition that every message entails. In recognizing the meaning and intent of a message and addressing myself to its implied demand I also recognize the originator of the message as a person. In disqualifying a message and refusing to recognize its nature I invalidate the claim to self-definition that it implies. If I show by my inappropriate response that a message has not registered I am at that moment refusing confirmation of the personality that is the source of the message.

The significance of occasional acts of disqualification should not be exaggerated. They occur from time to time in most interaction sequences including those that take place in families. Their effect will depend on their pervasiveness and on the kind of reaction to them that is encouraged and permitted.

Lack of responsiveness in the form of disqualification can take many forms. At the simplest level the previous statement is simply ignored; a question may remain unanswered and in addition there is not even any recognition that a question was put. Or one person finishes another's sentence with content that is clearly irrelevant to the intent of the first speaker. Usually, it is necessary to take the metacommunicative aspects of statements into account in detecting the presence of disqualification. It will be remembered that metacommunication involves communication about communication, explicit or implicit aspects of messages that label them as messages of a certain kind. For example, a particular statement may be labeled as a question, as an answer, as part of a continuing topic of conversation, or as a statement about the environment rather than about the speaker. Disqualification generally involves a redefinition of the metacommunicative aspects of messages. Thus what was meant to be a question may be interpreted as an answer or vice versa; and what was meant to be a statement about the environment may be interpreted as a statement about the speaker.

Sluzki *et al*. (1967) provide some instructive examples of the commonest forms of disqualification. In one case an elaborate statement by the son about his relationship to his sister is interrupted by the mother saying:: "I don't want to speak all the time, doctor." Here there is an abrupt change of subject without any labeling of the topic switch. Evasion is a favorite form of disqualification. In addition to a change of subject there may be a pretense that the switch in fact constitutes a response to what the previous speaker intended. Thus an adolescent son who says to his mother: "You treat me like a child," and is answered by: "But you are my child," experiences a disqualification of his intended meaning, which referred to his relative age and not to his biological status. Or a child whose question is answered by : "Well, a mother knows about these things" experiences disqualification because his question is invalidated by reference to the status difference between mother and child.

Disqualifications naturally occur within a sequence of messages and must themselves be followed by some kind of response. The manner of dealing with disqualifications may be crucial for their ultimate effect. In ordinary discourse disqualifying statements are commonly followed by some explicit comment on the incongruity or a request for clarification. In this manner the misunderstanding may be cleared up. Or the whole matter may be dropped, one of the interactants may withdraw from the scene, or both of them may start afresh on a new basis. The disqualification may therefore remain an isolated episodic event without further repercussions.

On the other hand, one disqualification may lead to another counterdisqualification, and so on, until the whole communication sequence becomes more and more confused and bizarre. If this pattern becomes established as the characteristic form of communication in a family there may well be serious consequences. For disqualification excludes both agreement and disagreement by definition. Faced by a sequence of disqualifications and counterdisqualifications the participants in the interaction are unable to reach either a position of concensus about the subject matter nor are they able to define the issue they disagree about. They simply talk past one another and are thus unable to define their relationship to one another. It has been suggested (Wynne and Singer, 1963) that this pattern of confused communication is characteristic of the families of schizophrenics. The surface of the discussion may seem clear in the sense that each individual statement is relatively coherent, but the connection between one person's statements and the next is bizarre.

THE DOUBLE-BIND CONCEPT

Faced with the pervasiveness of such communicational patterns the individual may withdraw from human communication as much as possible, or he may conclude that there are hidden clues and messages that would make sense out of an otherwise uninterpretable set of human relationships. In a situation in which it is the characteristic fate of most messages to be disqualified he may also come to disqualify his own messages, engaging in bizarre speech in which the different components disqualify one another. In this way it is possible to regard many of the symptoms of schizophrenia as aspects of pathological communication.

The best known example of a communicational theory of schizophrenia is the concept of the *double-bind*, first put forward by Bateson *et al.* (1956). A crucial feature of this concept is the presence of *self-disqualification*, that is to say, the existence of disqualification, not between successive messages of different individuals but between different messages of the same individual. The classical example of the individual caught in a double-bind situation is the schizophrenic patient who puts his arm around his mother when she comes to visit him. Thereupon she stiffens, he withdraws his arm, and she says: "Don't you love me any more?" Another example would be the mother who shows her dislike of her son's friends and then scolds him for being unsociable. Bateson *et al.* (1956) see the double-bind as involving a conflict between two negative injunctions at different levels, each carrying at least the implication of punishment. For the double-bind to produce its pathological effects it is also necessary that the victim be prevented from escaping from the situation and that his relationship to the source of the double-bind be intense.

In its original form the double-bind theory leads to many conceptual problems (Schuham, 1967). For example, it is not clear why the conflicting messages must necessarily be defined as negative injunctions involving a threat of punishment. This is only a special case of a general class of paradoxical messages, and there is in fact no evidence that it is precisely this special type of self-disqualification that is associated with the pathology of schizophrenia. Second, it is not clear how the difference in the "level" of the two injunctions is to be interpreted. Bateson *et al.* (1956) speak of a difference in abstractness, but it seems much more accurate to refer to a distinction between a communication and its attached metacommunication, as Watzlawick, Beavin, and Jackson (1967) have done more recently. These authors define the double-bind as involving a message "which is so structured that (a) it asserts something, (b) it asserts something about its own assertion and (c) these two assertions are mutually exclusive. Thus, if the message is an injunction, it must be disobeyed to be obeyed; if it is a definition of self or the other, the person thereby defined is this kind of person only if he is not, and is not if he is. The meaning of the message is therefore undecidable" (p. 212).

Different versions of the double-bind theory, however, agree in emphasizing that pathological consequences can only be expected if the double-bind occurs in the context of a relationship that is intense, if it occurs repeatedly, and if escape from the bind is blocked. It is only if the victim is prevented from leaving the framework established by the self-disqualifying message, for instance by commenting on its inconsistency, that he is caught in the characteristic dilemma of having to react in some way and yet being unable to react appropriately.

The most serious source of misunderstanding in the concept of the double-bind undoubtedly lies in its implicit distinction between one person who is seen as the source of the bind and another person who is seen as its victim. In its original formulation the theory seemed to assume that both mutually disqualifying messages originated with the same person, usually the parent, and that the other individual simply acted as the recipient of this paradoxical communication. In other words, it seemed to be essentially a theory of *self-disqualification*. Subsequently, it has become more and more apparent that the distinction between the originator and the so-called victim of the double-bind is difficult to uphold in most practical instances. The common situation is one in which both participants in an interaction mutually disqualify each other's messages, so that both of them are equally "bound" and the labeling of one of the participants as the "victim" becomes somewhat artificial. In the previously quoted example the schizophrenic patient first places his arm around his mother, then withdraws it and blushes. So his mother is as much the victim of a paradoxical communication as he is. Their disqualification of each other's messages is mutual, both of them actively contribute to the unsatisfactory interaction and neither is simply a passive victim.

Subsequent redefinitions of the double-bind situation have generally recognized the need for this correction (Weakland, 1960), and it is perhaps more accurate to use the term "transactional disqualification" (Sluzki *et al*., 1967) for these situations than the term "double-bind." The important point is that two or more people are involved in a sequence of incongruent messages that mutually disqualify each other. This means that in their intercommunication they cannot confirm each other unambiguously as taking up a certain position in their relationship. Because the validity of their communications is in doubt they cannot honor each other's claims to stand in this or that relationship to each other. Straightforward agreement or disagreement makes such confirmation possible but mutual disqualification leaves each in doubt as to his position vis-à-vis the other. This amounts to a mutual failure at confirming the social identity that the participants have in their interaction (Laing, 1961). If one of the participants has been consistently exposed to such interactions from an early age it may indeed have serious consequences for the development of a stable self-concept.

Experimental tests of various aspects of the double-bind theory have proved extremely difficult and their results are generally unsatisfactory. One reason for this is that the theory involves no specific predictions about the nature of the various communication channels that may be used to carry the various components of self-disqualifying messages. As different channels will commonly be used to carry the communication and its disqualifying metacommunication there seems little point in examining messages that use only one channel, the verbal one, for evidence of double-binds (Ringuette and Kennedy, 1966). Nor is it particularly illuminating to use the retrospective reports of schizophrenic patients which may be subject to all kinds of distortions (Berger, 1965). Where the effects of incongruent messages in different communication channels are investigated the results may depend entirely on which channels one happens to pick. Thus one study reports no relationship between psychopathology and incongruity between messages using the verbal and the postural channel (Beakel and Mehrabian, 1969), while another study does find evidence of a relationship between disturbances in children and mothers' use of incongruous messages in the verbal, vocal (tone of voice), and visual (facial expressions, gestures, etc.) channels (Bugental *et al.*, 1971). Systematic empirical research in this area may prove rather illuminating.

CONFIRMATION AND DISCONFIRMATION

If disqualifying communications remained isolated occurrences in human relationships they would probably have little significance. What makes them important is their repetition, and in families this repetition typically demonstrates a regularly recurring pattern. Over a period of time the communications among family members do not follow a random sequence but tend to repeat certain themes. These themes are typically concerned with the relationship of the family members to one another. Families are certainly no exception to the rule that when people communicate their messages not only *represent* a certain content but also *present* a certain type of relationship among the communicators. These relationships always imply a certain set of reciprocal social identities among the participants, they may be the identities of persecutor and victim, of dominator and dominated, of helper and helped, and so on. In the regular patterning of their interactions individuals confirm these reciprocal social identities for each other (Buber, 1957).

But this process is always subject to the possibility of pathological forms of self-confirmation. People may "play games" with one another (Berne, 1966) and confirm one another in regressive identities that are at variance with their claims to mature adulthood. Or different family members may engage in "collusion" (Laing, 1961), engaging in a tacit agreement to confirm one another in fantasied identities that have little in common with their real selves. However, the most pernicious form of the process of mutual self-disconfirmation probably occurs when family members habitually engage in transactional disqualification of one another's communications. For in that case they are put in what has aptly been called an untenable position—they can only assume a particular identity by not assuming it, they are met with disconfirmation of claims to a particular identity whatever they do. If it is true that this pattern is in fact characteristic of the families of at least some types of schizophrenics then we are led to the fascinating speculation that the apparently nonsensical communications of such schizophrenics are in fact the only possible way of responding to their situation. Since any communication defines the sender's view of his relationship with the receiver some schizophrenics avoid a definition, which their past experience has made impossible for them, by not communicating. "Schizophrenese, then is a language which leaves it up to the listener to take his choice from among many possible meanings which are not only different from but may even be incompatible with one another. Thus it becomes possible to deny any or all aspects of a message" (Watzlawick, Beavin, and Jackson, 1967, p. 73). The gap between the empirical techniques described in the earlier parts of this chapter and the theoretical sweep of these final speculations will help to give the reader a sense of the challenge faced by research on family communication.

CONCLUSION

The consideration of empirical techniques used in the study of disturbed interpersonal communication in families provides an appropriate occasion for a discussion of methodological problems that are common to all attempts at investigating interpersonal communication empirically but that emerge with special force in the context of family relationships. Systematic empirical study of a range of phenomena demands the isolation of variables that are objective and quantifiable, so that their functional interrelationships can be explored. But the variables that most readily lend themselves to objective measurement are usually not the ones that are most significant for an understanding of communication processes under natural conditions.

Thus the outcomes of these processes are usually much more easily represented in objective quantitative terms than the processes themselves, but they do not really advance our understanding of what takes place during interpersonal communication as such. Similarly, the use of content-free measures of communication, while objective, does not provide much insight into the essential characteristics of human interchanges. Moreover, there is evidence that the course of interpersonal communication in well-established groups like the family is rather different under natural conditions than under the artificially contrived conditions that are often necessary if objective measurements are to be obtained. Therefore, we still have to rely rather heavily on clinical material for the illustration of explanatory concepts that attempt to come to grips with the most significant features of disturbed interpersonal communication.

These features involve the quality of responsiveness that emerges when we examine the content of a sequence of interchanges between two or more individuals. Each statement in such a sequence is normally linked to preceding and succeeding statements in that it takes previous statements into account and is itself taken into account by subsequent statements. This means not only that the next statement constitutes a response to the overt content of the previous statement, by agreement, disagreement, modification, amplification, and so on, but also constitutes a validation or invalidation of the implicit interpersonal demands contained in the previous statement. In other words, individuals respond to one another not only on the level of explicit verbal representations but also on the level of implicit presentations of their relationship. Each segment in a sequence of interchanges communicates an invitation to define the relationship of the participants in a particular manner. This invitation can be accepted or rejected. Its rejection implies a rejection of the social identity that the other party had laid claim to, because social identities are conferred by shared definitions of social relationships.

Responses to communicative acts proceed on two levels, just as the acts themselves. On the one hand, they address themselves to the truth value of messages on the level of representation, confirming or disconfirming the claim to objective veracity that such acts contain. On the other hand, such responses are also addressed to the self-presentation that communicative acts imply, validating or invalidating these presentations, thereby granting or withholding recognition of implied claims about the definition of the relationship that exists between the communicators. Disturbed communication among members of a family generally involves a pervasive invalidation or "disqualification" of communicative acts.

However, such disqualification may not originate in responses to communications but in the communicative acts themselves. In such cases we may speak of "self-disqualification," which involves the invalidation of one part of a message by another part. Here we have an ambiguous message that simultaneously presents two mutually exclusive definitions of the relationship between the communicating individuals. It is impossible to make an adequate response to such ambiguous messages because by validating one aspect one must necessarily invalidate the other aspect. The most likely response to such ambiguity is to answer it by a similarly ambiguous message because in that case one throws the responsibility for making a decision between two incompatible interpretations back to the other person. In this way family members may become locked in long sequences of mutual self-disqualification in which the definition of their relationship to one another always remains blurred. If an individual is consistently exposed to such a disturbed pattern of communication in the family he may repeat this pattern in all his interpersonal relationships and come to be labeled as seriously disturbed or insane.

Unfortunately, this aspect of disturbed communication in families does not very readily lend itself to objective measurement. It must therefore be approached clinically or else indirectly by the study of parameters of family communication that can be regarded as manifestations of this fundamental disturbance. Such parameters will be of two kinds, those that relate to the receptivity or sensitivity of family members to one another's needs, and those that relate to the directness with which fundamental relationships in the family are expressed. An ambiguous style of communication marked by mutual disqualification is likely to manifest itself in a low level of sensitivity and a preference for indirect methods of expression.

Both these aspects have received some empirical confirmation. On the one hand, disturbed family communication has been shown to be associated with low levels of "experiential sensitivity," i.e. accurate perception of the amount and kind of information available to and required by other family members. On the other hand, the expression of affect and of power relationships in the family tends to take on a veiled, indirect form when family communication is disturbed. Hopefully, the gap that still exists between such observations and the formulation of the nature of the underlying disturbance will be closed by future research.

REFERENCES

Alkire, A. A., Goldstein, M. J., Rodnick, E. H., and Judd, L. L. (1971). Social influence and counterinfluence within families of four types of disturbed adolescents. *J. abnorm. Psychol.*, **77**, 32–41.

Bateson, G., Jackson, D. D., Haley, J., and Weakland, J. (1956). Toward a theory of schizophrenia. *Behavioral Science*, **1**, 251–264.

Beakel, N. G. and Mehrabian, A. (1969). Inconsistent communications and psychopathology. *J. abnorm. Psychol.*, **74**, 126–130.

Berger, A. (1965). A test of the double-bind hypothesis of schizophrenia. *Family Process*, **4**, 198–205.

Berne, E. (1964). *Games People Play*. New York: Grove Press.

Buber, M. (1957). Distance and relation. *Psychiatry*, **20**, 97–104.

Bugental, D. E., Love, L. R., Kaswan, J. W., and April, C. (1971). Verbal–nonverbal conflict in parental messages to normal and disturbed children. *J. abnorm. Psychol.*, **77**, 6–10.

Caldwell, B. M. and Hersher, L. (1964). Mother–infant interaction during the first year. *Merrill-Palmer Quart.*, **10**, 119–128.

Caputo, D. V. (1963). Parents of the schizophrenic. *Family Process*, **2**, 339–356.

Drechsler, R. J. and Shapiro, M. I. (1963). Two methods of analysis of family diagnostic data. *Family Process*, **2**, 367–379.

Escalona, S. K. (1969). *The Roots of Individuality: Normal Patterns of Development in Infancy*. London: Tavistock.

Farina, A. (1960). Patterns of role dominance and conflict in parents of schizophrenic patients. *J. abnorm. & soc. Psychol.*, **61**, 31–38.

Ferreira, A. J. (1963). Decision making in normal and pathologic families. *Arch. gen. Psychiat.*, **8**, 68–73.

Ferreira, A. J. and Winter, W. D. (1965). Family interaction and decision-making. *Arch. gen. Psychiat.*, **13**, 214–223.

Ferreira, A. J. and Winter, W. D. (1968). Information exchange and silence in normal and abnormal families. *Family Process*, **7**, 251–276.

Ferreira, A. J., Winter, W. D., and Poindexter, E. J. (1966). Some interactional variables in normal and abnormal families. *Family Process*, **5**, 60–75.

Fleck, S., Lidz, T., and Cornelison, A. (1963). Comparison of parent–child relationships of male and female schizophrenic patients. *Arch. gen. Psychiat.*, **8**, 1–7.

Framo, J. L. (1965) Systematic research on family dynamics. In I. Boszormenyi-Nagy and J. L. Framo (Eds.), *Intensive Family Therapy*. New York: Harper & Row.

Haley, J. (1962). Family experiments: A new type of experimentation. *Family Process*, **1**, 265–293.

Haley, J. (1964). Research on family patterns: An instrument measurement. *Family Process*, **3**, 41–65.

Haley, J. (1967). Speech sequences of normal and abnormal families with two children present. *Family Process*, **6**, 81–97.

Kenkel, W. F. (1957). Influence differentiation in family decision making. *Sociology and Social Research*, **42**, 18–25.

Laing, R. D. (1961). *The Self and Others*. London: Tavistock.

Laing, R. D. and Esterson, A. (1964). *Sanity, Madness and the Family*. London: Tavistock.

Lennard, H. L. and Bernstein, A. (1970). *Patterns in Human Interaction*. San Francisco: Jossey-Bass.

Lennard, H. L., Beaulieu, M., and Embrey, N. G. (1965). Interactions in families with a schizophrenic child. *Arch. gen. Psychiat.*, **12**, 166–183.

Lerner, P. M. (1965). Resolution of intrafamilial conflict in families of schizophrenic patients. I: Thought disturbance. *J. nerv. & ment. Dis.*, **141**, 342–351.

McPherson, S. (1970). Communication of intents among parents and their disturbed adolescent child. *J. abnorm. & soc. Psychol.*, **76**, 98–105.

Mishler, E. G. and Waxler, N. E. (1968) *Interaction in Families*. New York: Wiley.

Murrell, S. A. and Stachowiak, J. G. (1967). Consistency, rigidity and power in the interaction of clinic and non-clinic families. *J. abnorm Psychol.*, **72**, 265–272.

O'Rourke, J. (1963). Field and laboratory: The decision making behaviors of family groups in two experimental conditions. *Sociometry*, **26**, 422–435.

Parsons, T. and Bales, R. F. (1955). *Family Socialization and Interaction Process*. Glencoe, Ill.: Free Press.

Raush, H. L. (1965). Interaction sequences. *J. Personal. & soc. Psychol.*, **2**, 487–499.

Reiss, D. (1967). Individual thinking and family interaction: I. Introduction to an experimental study of families of normals, character disorders, and schizophrenics. *Arch. gen. Psychiat.*, **16**, 80–93.

Reiss, D. (1970). Individual thinking and family interaction: V. Proposals for the contrasting character of experiential sensitivity and expressive form in families. *J. nerv. & ment. Dis.*, **151**, 187–202.

Ringuette, E. L. and Kennedy, T. (1966). An experimental study of the double bind hypothesis. *J. abnorm. Psychol.*, **71**, 136–141.

Riskin, J. and Faunce, E. E. (1970). Family interaction scales: I. Theoretical framework and method. *Arch. gen. Psychiat.*, **22**, 504–537.

Ruesch. J. and Bateson, G. (1951). *Communication: The Social Matrix of Psychiatry*. New York: Norton.

Schuham, A. I. (1967). The double-bind hypothesis a decade later. *Psychol. Bull.*, **68**, 409–416.

Schulman, F. R., Shoemaker, D. J., and Moelis, I. (1962). Laboratory measurements of parental behavior. *J. consult. Psychol.*, **26**, 109–114.

Sluzki, C. E., Beavin, J., Tarnopolsky, A., and Veron, E. (1967). Transactional disqualification: Research on the double bind. *Arch. gen. Psychiat.*, **16**, 494–504.

Straus, M. A. (1967). The influence of sex of child and social class on instrumental and expressive family roles in a laboratory setting. *Sociology and Social Research*, **52**, 7–21.

Vidich, A. J. (1956). Methodological problems in the observation of husband–wife interaction. *Marriage and Family Living*, **18**, 234–239.

Watzlawick, P., Beavin, J. H., and Jackson, D. D. (1967). *Pragmatics of Human Communication: A Study of Interactional Patterns, Pathologies and Paradoxes*. New York: Norton.

Waxler, N. E. and Mishler, E. G. (1966). Scoring and reliability problems in interaction process analysis: A methodological note. *Sociometry*, **29**, 28–40.

Waxler, N. E. and Mishler, E. G. (1970a). Sequential patterning in family interaction: A methodological note. *Family Process*, **9**, 211–220.

Waxler, N. E. and Mishler, E. G. (1970b). Experimental studies of families. In L. Berkowitz (Ed.), *Advances in Experimental Social Psychology*. Vol. 5. New York: Academic Press.

Weakland, J. (1960). The "double bind" hypothesis of schizophrenia and three-party interaction. In D. D. Jackson (Ed.), *The Etiology of Schizophrenia*. New York: Basic Books. Pp. 373–388.

Winter, W. D. and Ferreira, A. J. (1967). Interaction process analysis of family decision-making. *Family Process*, **6**, 155–172.

Wynne, L. C. and Singer, M. T. (1963). Thought disorder and family relations of schizophrenics, I. A research strategy. *Arch. gen. Psychiat.*, **9**, 191–198.

Wynne, L. C. Ryckoff, I., Day, J., and Hirsch, S. (1958). Pseudomutuality in the family relations of schizophrenics. *Psychiatry*, **21**, 205–220.

Yarrow, L. J. (1963). Research in dimensions of early maternal care. *Merrill-Palmer Quart.*, **9**, 101–114.

CHAPTER 8

The Development of Interpersonal Communication in Children

EARLY BEGINNINGS

The complete helplessness of the newborn human infant makes the mother's task a hard one. What makes it particularly hard is the fact that the object of her labor and attention gives her no sign of human recognition. In the absence of such feedback it is not always easy to maintain the conviction that one is attending to the needs of a germinal human personality. Small wonder then that many mothers have initial feelings of strangeness or distance toward their infants and look anxiously for signs of sociability in them (Robson, 1967).

Their search is first likely to be rewarded during the third or fourth week when the "social smile" makes its appearance. At this stage, a specifically human stimulus, a high-pitched voice, elicits smiling more consistently than any other stimulus (Wolff, 1963). Up to this time there had been smilelike mouth movements unrelated to social stimuli, but now the eyes participate in the smile—they appear bright and focused.

Soon after this a further radical development occurs. The infant clearly focuses on the mother's face while he smiles and makes eye contact with her. For many mothers this developmental step produces a real change in their relationship to the infant. Now they have a sense of human contact, a sense of personal recognition, a feeling of joy at the thought that the baby has a social personality after all. The baby is now fun to be with, and the mother is likely to spend much more time playing with it. Very soon the infant's smiling response becomes prepotent over other responses, and the feeding infant may interrupt his sucking and smile in response to the human voice.

Somewhat later the voice seems to lose some of its effectiveness in eliciting the infant's smile and is more likely to produce vocalization on the part of the infant. Smiling is now particularly evoked by the human face, especially the area around the eyes. When he is a little older the infant will scan the face and break into a smile as soon as eye contact has been established. At first, the smiling response appears indiscriminately in the presence of any human face, but by the fourth month some infants smile preferentially at the mother and not at strangers (Ambrose, 1961). This is part of a general development in which the infant shows differential social responses to his mother and to other individuals (Ainsworth, 1969). He smiles and cries in a distinctive way upon her departure. In other words, his interpersonal communication now begins to become discriminating.

Unlike other primates it is not until the latter part of the first year of life that the human infant is able to initiate physical contact with an adult. But long before that he is able to establish a face-to-face relationship by making eye contact with another human being. Eye contact lays the basis for interpersonal communication in man. It begins that fundamental two-way process of communication—looking at and being looked at—that will continue to play an important role in all of the individual's human relationships.

THE IMPORTANCE OF ROLE TAKING

The acquisition of speech constitutes a major leap in the child's possibilities for interpersonal communication. No longer limited to the nonverbal level he can now begin to be influenced and to influence others by means of the highly differentiated medium of language.

However, we must draw a clear distinction between the child's acquisition of linguistic competence, his knowledge of the rules of syntax and the meaning of words, and his effective use of this knowledge for purposes of interpersonal communication. Learning the rules for making meaningful statements and learning how to use such statements for purposes of effective communication are two entirely different processes. This crucial distinction arises from the fact that for effectively addressing statements to another individual I need to know more than the rules and words of the language; I also need to take into consideration the situation of the listener and my relationship to him. In addition, there must be a real motivation to communicate. The use of speech in interpersonal communication therefore raises an entirely different set of considerations than the acquisition of mere linguistic competence. It raises questions about the rapport between speaker and listener and about their desire to communicate. Communication competence is not by any means to be equated with linguistic competence.

Children achieve a reasonable measure of linguistic competence by the age of three-and-a-half (McNeill, 1966), but it is easy to show that their communication competence continues to undergo major development after that age and does not approach adult levels even at age ten. This was demonstrated in an experiment (Krauss and Glucksberg, 1969) in which two children sat at a table facing each other, separated by an opaque screen. Each child had a set of six wooden blocks with different novel designs stamped on them. One child's blocks were laid out at random, the other child's were stacked in a certain order. The task of the second child was to get the first child to stack his blocks in the same order as his own by describing the succession of novel figures that identify the blocks. After each attempt the two stacks were compared by the children to see how well the one child got across the description of the figures to the other child. Then the attempt was repeated with a different order for the blocks and a new inspection of the completed stacks at the end. It was found that over a succession of eight such attempts the ability of kindergarten children to communicate the nature of the identifying figures did not improve at all. These children had not profited from the

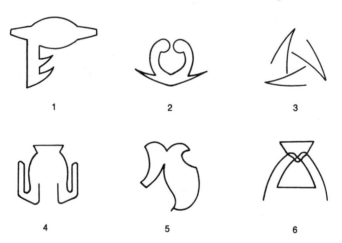

Fig. 3   The six noval figures in this experiment (From Krauss, R. M. and Glucksberg, S. The development of communication: Competence as a function of age. *Child Development*, 1969, **40**, 255–266).

comparison of stacks at the end of each attempt. Although they could see which figures had been misidentified, this did not enable them to give a better description next time. Older children, however, did show a progressive decline of misidentifications of figures, indicating that they were learning to identify each figure in such a way that their partner would know which figure they meant. The improvement over eight trials was most marked in grade five children and less marked in grade one children. As they get older children are better able to reformulate their communications to make them more appropriate to the listener's requirements.

This process of taking into account the listener's requirements involves putting oneself in the place of the listener and deciding what would be useful information from his point of view. The child who describes one of the novel figures as being "like mommy's hat" is looking at the problem from an idiosyncratic point of view, failing to consider that this information is useless from the point of view of his partner. Effective communication, on the other hand, needs to be adapted to the position of the listener, and this can only happen if the child adopts this position instead of his initial idiosyncratic point of view. There is good evidence to suggest that the development of communication capacity in the child is strongly linked to the growth of his ability to change perspectives, to take into account the perspective of the listener as well as his own. Young children are poor at communicating information because they remain firmly tied to their own point of view, failing to take into consideration that of their partner.

This fact is nicely illustrated by a series of experiments reported by Flavell and his collaborators (1968). In one of these the child is shown how to play a game by example and gesture and then has to explain the game verbally to another individual who may be blindfolded. The adequacy of the child's verbal explanation is scored in terms of its potential effectiveness in actually conveying all the information needed to play the game. (For example, it would not be effective communication to a blindfolded listener if the child pointed to a certain part of the game board, saying, "and then you move it there.") It is found that there is a fairly regular increase in the adequate game information conveyed by children from grade two to grade eleven. Moreover, the gap between the adequacy of the information conveyed to blind and to sighted listeners narrows. That is to say, whereas the information given to the blind listener was grossly less adequate than the information given to the sighted listener by children at grade two or three level, there was hardly any such difference for the older children. This means that the older children were taking into account the special position of the blindfolded listener to whom many extra explanations would have to be given. The younger children hardly seemed to take into account the difference in their own position and that of the blind listener. The ability to put oneself in the place of the listener appeared to increase with age.

In another experiment in this series the child was given the tasks of selling a tie to a stranger (there was a prize for success) and persuading his father to buy him a television set. The situations were hypothetical but the children entered into them very readily. Here are some examples of attempts at persuasion at different grade levels:

> Grade three: "Here's a tie .... Do you want to buy it? ... Give it to him, he don't say no more."

> Grade seven: "Ah ... oh, ah ... hello, sir. I'd like to introduce a new kind of tie that we have brought out. I'm sure that you would like it. It's a—it would be a wonderful Christmas present, or a birthday present, and of course you could wear it anywhere you want yourself. It doesn't cost very much. It's a very handsome tie, and you could match it with all your shirts, I'm sure."

> Grade eleven: "Well, you're the perfect type. Oh, you notice in this tie this blue is the exact color of your eyes. Oh, I bet you could never find a match like that again. Oh, that gray shirt you've got on, the gray is the exact same color. Oh, it would just go so nice with that shirt. All the people have been trying to get this tie but I've been saving it because I liked it so much I thought I might buy it myself, but seeing it looks so good on you, I guess I'll sell it to you."

> Grade three: "Oh Daddy, oh Daddy, please let me buy a television. I always wanted a television. Oh please, Daddy, please."

> Grade seven: "Say, Dad, a lot of kids at school I know are getting televisions for Christmas. Can I have one? Gee, I know a lot of kids that want one, gee. I could really use it, you—for some of the educational programs, you know, that are on TV, and they're real good, and for homework at night some of our teachers want to watch 'em, and—you know, Johnnie always wants to watch cowboys, and ... and everything, and I—I'll never get a chance to watch it down there, so why can't I have it in my room? C'mon Dad, please."

> Grade eleven: Well, Dad, I have a problem. Since we here in Rochester have only two stations, uh—for a choice of television

watching, and—uh—we have a very large family, and—so we probably have many different interests. You like to watch the baseball game, I like to watch Alfred Hitchcock, and if they come at—at the same time . . . somebody's going to be left out. Since I have the largest room in the house, all the conveniences of the room and everything—to put another television, wouldn't it be a very good idea if I had one up there? I don't know what he'd say. Well, the expense wouldn't be bad, because you could buy it on installments, or you could even get a second-hand one. Probably pick one up very cheap at a second-hand store, maybe you'd have to sink a little money into it, but—it probably wouldn't be bad at all. And the kids could come up there and watch their programs, while we—while you're watching yours, and—and there's only two stations anyway, so—two TV sets would be just fine.

As the young persuaders get older they not only use many more arguments but also change to arguments that are clearly based on an appreciation of their target's point of view. Such arguments include the mention of advantages or benefits to others, the use of personalized appeals (e.g. "it will look good on you"), anticipation of economic objections, and appeals to bandwagon or prestige effects. The use of a combination of several such argument types shows a significant increase, especially from the grade three to the grade seven level.

It seems quite evident that the improvement in the child's capacity for interpersonal communication on the verbal level depends on his increasing facility in seeing things from the point of view of the person he is addressing. This facility is a form of *role taking*, not to be confused with *role enactment* (Sarbin, 1954). The latter involves an overt adoption of the role's attributes in one's behavior, for example, the girl who enacts the maternal role toward her doll. But role taking refers to a covert, cognitive process that analyzes the role attributes of the other so that one will be better able to relate to him. It involves the ability to shift from one's own point of view and to adopt the perspective of the other.

This process of perspective shifting is precisely what Jean Piaget alludes to in his account of the transition from egocentric to operational thought. As used by Piaget the term *egocentricity* refers to the young child's inability to distinguish between his own momentary point of view and the point of view of others. Cognitive judgments are therefore based on the perspective or point of view that the child adopts at the moment, without being corrected by other possible perspectives or points of view.

This is shown quite literally in an experiment reported by Piaget and Inhelder (1956) in which the child is placed in front of a scale model of three mountains and is asked to select from a series of photographs the one that would represent the appearance of the mountains if he were looking at them from some other indicated position. For example, he might be asked to show what the mountains looked like from the side opposite to the one he now occupies. Young children could not solve this problem; some of them would only select the photograph representing their own perspective, no matter from which position the scene was supposed to be seen. They could not free themselves from their own momentary point of view and were thus unable to put themselves in the place of someone looking at the scene from a different point of view. Piaget would call their behavior *egocentric*; they were unable to take the role of the other.

The overcoming of egocentrism involves the development of the ability to shift one's point of view rapidly, to *decenter* one's attention from one's momentary perspective to consider simultaneously other possible perspectives. One can then consider various aspects of the situation at the same time and allow them to correct one another. This becomes particularly interesting when the people whose point of view is being considered are themselves part of the situation they are considering. What happens when the scene is not being considered by people who look on it as spectators but by people who are participants?

In that case we are confronted with a role-taking participation task. Suppose the scene is not one of three mountains but one of three people interacting. There might be a figure of a man, a woman, and a child in front of a house or some trees, and the child might be asked to make up a little story describing their interaction. They might be planning a picnic, for example, or the mother and the child might be welcoming the father home at the end of the day. The child would be left free to make up any little scene he likes. But these interpersonal scenes would not look quite the same to all their participants. The father coming home might be feeling his tiredness, the child might be looking forward to a romp in the garden, and so on. But it would need a certain degree of sophistication to realize that this would be so, and that each participant in an interpersonal situation would bring his own perspective to it.

Feffer and Gourevitch (1960) got children between six and thirteen to make up a story about each of a number of simple three-person pictures. Then the children were required to retell their initial story from the point of view of each actor in turn. The stories of the younger children were dominated by the concrete perceptual properties of the pictures and by the impact of the point of view adopted in the initial story. Among the older children the description of the actors in the story became more abstract, taking in thoughts, intentions, emotions, and general attributes. At the same time the children introduce appropriate changes of perspective when they retell their story from the point of view of each of the actors. These shifts in perspective soon become mutually consistent. Mother notices that father looks sad and concludes that he had a bad day at the office. Father sees that mother looks tired because she spent most of the day cleaning up. The statements that one of the participants makes about the others are consistent with the others' description of their condition. The child's achievement of consistent shifts of perspective reflects the growth of his role-taking skills. Scores can be assigned to different levels of role-taking skill so that the higher scores reflect greater consistency in the elaboration of each particular role and in the descriptions of the same role behavior described from the perspectives of different participants. In the Feffer and Gourevich study there was a positive relationship between the level of role-taking skill a child had reached on the RTT and his level of performance in a more conventional Piaget-type cognitive task. It was therefore suggested that the same kind of cognitive skill was likely to be involved.

Be that as it may it is clear that the development of interpersonal communication skills in children is fundamentally dependent in the development of role-taking skills. It is the ability to take different points of view simultaneously and consider a scene from a coherent set of perspectives that makes effective interpersonal communication possible.

THE "PRIVATE SPEECH" CONTROVERSY

The absence of effective interpersonal communication manifests itself in young children in the phenomenon of "private speech," or "egocentric speech," as Piaget (1926) prefers to call it. This is the type of speech in which nothing is in fact communicated—two children might be talking but they do not talk to each other. One type of private speech is the collective monologue:

PETER: I'm throwing it, I'm throwing it.
PAUL: This box is heavy.
PETER: How far it goes, how far it goes.

PAUL: It's full of stones.
PETER: I'll run after it.
PAUL: It won't move, it won't move.
PETER: See you there.
PAUL: I'm going to empty it.

The two children talk past each other. They both busily verbalize in each other's presence but they do not get through to each other.

According to Piaget there is a lack of communication because of a lack of desire to communicate. The young child's egocentrism makes him use speech in a nonsocial way. He does not realize that to get through to the other person the other's point of view has to be appreciated. A lot of the time the young child uses speech purely expressively, he wants to get something off his chest, not to get across to someone else.

On this point there is a long-standing disagreement between two points of view, one represented by Piaget, the other by the Russian psychologist Vygotsky (1962). The latter did not agree with Piaget's theory of egocentricity; he did not believe that the failure of communication in private speech necessarily indicated a lack of desire to communicate. What it did indicate was the child's failure to distinguish between himself and the other as listener. In private speech, according to Vygotsky, the child is really addressing himself; he is using speech as a self-directive instrument. Such speech has more than a purely expressive function, it serves the function of self-communication. Such speech has self-guiding properties that Vygotsky calls "parasocial." According to Vygotsky there is a social intent behind private speech, but this intent does not distinguish clearly between self and other as listener.

This difference in Piaget's and Vygotsky's points of view about private speech is much more than a verbalism because it leads to different predictions about the circumstances that will favor private speech. If Piaget is right then private speech is essentially an immature form of speech and should decline clearly as age and intelligence increase. If there is anything to Vygotksy's view private speech has a positive cognitive role to play at a certain stage, because verbal self-directions help task performance. The relationship of private speech to age and intelligence should therefore be curvilinear, increasing at first, and only later decreasing when silent inner speech takes over. Studies reported by Kohlberg, Yaeger, and Hjertholm (1968) seem to support Vygotsky's rather than Piaget's predictions.

Of course private speech is a rather mixed bag. If it is analyzed into its components a definite age hierarchy emerges as follows: (1) word play and repetition, (2) remarks to nonhuman objects, (3) describing own activity, (4) questions answered by the self, (5) self-guiding comments, (6) inaudible muttering, and (7) silent inner speech, This makes it possible to see to what extent private speech represents a transitional stage towards mature inner thought. Existing studies of age trends seem to be much more clearly in line with this type of interpretation than with one that relegates all private speech to the immature form of a manifestation of "egocentrism."

CONCLUSION

If confusion is to be avoided we must make a clear distinction between linguistic competence and communication competence. The former is concerned with the knowledge of correct forms of speech, the latter with the ability to use this knowledge effectively in communicating with other people.

Communication competence involves one factor that is not involved in linguistic competence, namely, the ability to take the point of view of the person who is addressed. The young child lacks this ability and has to acquire it gradually through a process that Piaget calls *decentering*, the capacity to take into account different perspectives on the same subject matter. It is not enough to know the forms of correct communication, it is also necessary to know how to apply them in specific situations. A certain sensitivity to the experience of the other person is required if communication is to be successful and if individuals are not to talk past one another.

It would be wrong, however, to conclude from this that the young child lacks the desire to communicate, that he is primarily concerned with self-expression rather than communication. What it does suggest is an initial difficulty on the part of the child in distinguishing between the self and the other in the role of listener or addressee. The young child, like the older child, addresses communications both to himself and to others, but at first he does not realize that he is in a privileged position as far as the receipt of communications is concerned, and that things that are taken for granted by himself must first be clarified for others. This is a peculiarity of verbal communication, because it is only this channel that can be used both for communication with oneself and for communication with others. Nonverbal channels, like gaze direction, lack this ambiguity and therefore show a highly socialized form of communication from a very early age.

REFERENCES

Ainsworth, M. (1969). Object relations, dependency and attachment: A theoretical review of the infant–mother relationship. *Child Development*, **40**, 969–1025.

Ambrose, J. A. (1961). The development of the smiling response in early infancy. In B. M. Foss (Ed.), *Determinants of Infant Behaviour*. Vol. 1. London: Methuen.

Feffer, M. and Gourevitch, V. (1960). Cognitive aspects of role taking in children. *J. Personal.*, **28**, 383–396.

Flavell, J. H. (1968). *The Development of Role-Taking and Communication Skills in Children*. New York: Wiley.

Kohlberg, L., Yaeger, J., and Hjertholm, E. (1968). Private speech: Four studies and a review of theories. *Child Development*, **39**, 691–736.

Krauss, R. M. and Glucksberg, S. (1969). The development of communication: Competence as a function of age. *Child Development*, **40**, 255–266.

McNeill, D. (1966). Developmental psycholinguistics. In F. Smith and G. A. Miller (Eds.), *The Genesis of Language*. Cambridge, Mass.: M.I.T. Press.

Piaget, J. (1926). *The Language and Thought of the Child*. London: Routledge & Kegan Paul.

Piaget, J. and Inhelder, B. (1956). *The Child's Conception of Space*. London: Routledge & Kegan Paul.

Robson, K. S. (1967). The role of eye-to-eye contact in maternal–infant attachment. *J. Child Psychol. & Psychiat.*, **8**, 13–25.

Sarbin, T. R. (1954). Role theory. In G. Lindzey (Ed.), *Handbook of Social Psychology*. Vol. 1. Cambridge, Mass.: Addison-Wesley.

Vygotsky, L. (1962). *Thought and Language*. Cambridge, Mass.: M.I.T. Press.

Wolff, P. H. (1963). Observations on the early development of smiling. In B. M. Foss (Ed.), *Determinants of Infant Behaviour*. Vol. 2. London: Methuen.

CHAPTER 9

Cultural Differences in Interpersonal Communication

SOCIAL CLASS

In everyday life we commonly use speech as a clue to an individual's social class. When talking to a stranger we soon decide whether he speaks like a truck driver or a member of one of the professions. Systematic studies bear us out: middle-class speakers tend to talk more, use more varied vocabulary, and employ more varied grammatical constructions than blue-collar speakers.

These observations immediately lead to two questions: (a) Are class differences in communication limited to the verbal sphere or do they extend to the nonverbal level? (b) Precisely what is the significance of differences in language use for interpersonal communication?

In regard to the first question we do have some evidence that class differences in communication exist also on the nonverbal level. This evidence comes from studies of mother–child interaction in different social classes. One study, for example, finds that mothers of low socioeconomic status engage in more physical contact with their five-year-old children than mothers of high socioeconomic status. On the other hand, there was more reciprocal eye contact among the high-status mother–child pairs (Schmidt and Hore, 1970).

Other studies indicate that at the age of five or six youngsters from low-status homes are more influenced by paralinguistic cues than are their age mates from high-status homes. This finding emerges from experiments in which children have to carry out instructions spoken in a "positive," a "neutral," or a "negative" tone of voice. While the tone of voice made no difference to the way middle-class children responded to

161

the instructions, it did make a difference to the lower-class children who responded best to the instructions spoken in a "positive" tone (Kashinsky and Wiener, 1969).

Such findings afford us a few fascinating glimpses into the almost uncharted area of subcultural differences in the use of different channels for interpersonal communication. It looks as if people of different socioeconomic status place different weights on various communication channels and probably do not use these channels in exactly the same way. This is an area in which further research is very much needed.

The question about the significance for interpersonal communication of different patterns of language use has received rather more attention from research workers. It has been suggested that differences in language use are indicative of different *styles* of communication characteristic of various social classes. For example, when children are asked to describe abstract figures or faces with different expressions to other children who cannot see these stimuli, differences between middle-class and working-class children appear (Heider, 1971). Middle-class children use far more words to describe the figures and faces; they are also more inclined to give descriptions of the physical properties of parts of the figure, while working-class children are more likely to give metaphorical descriptions of the whole figure, e.g. "it looks like someone who is scared." This difference is reminiscent of variations between the formal mode of speech used with a stranger and the informal mode of speech used with a friend (Ervin-Tripp, 1969). The latter mode tends to consist of shorter and more metaphorical statements. Perhaps the working-class children were quicker to adopt another child as a friend, while the middle-class children continued to treat him as a stranger and spoke to him in a more formal way.

If this turned out to be the correct interpretation of the observed class differences it would be an example of what sociolinguists have called *register* (Houston, 1969). A register consists of certain language styles that have in common their appropriateness to a particular social situation. Rural black children, for example, have been found to have two registers, one for use in school or with persons in authority, and the other for use with friends or members of the family. The school register uses a simplified syntax while the nonschool register shows a complete set of syntactic patterns.

The concept of "register" has much in common with the concept of "code" as used by some students of this area. Bernstein (1964), for example, distinguishes between what he calls "elaborated" and "restricted" codes. The latter are characterized by simple, short, and often unfinished sentences lacking subordinate clauses; there is a limited vocabulary and much stereotyped expression. This code relies heavily on implicit shared meaning and on nonverbal channels for the transmission of new information and of the specific intentions of the speaker. By contrast, an elaborated code involves a wider range of vocabulary and of syntactic structures and involves the *verbal* representation of specific features of the situation and the special perspectives of speaker and listener. It is claimed that while working-class children acquire only restricted codes, middle-class children acquire both codes and are able to shift from one to the other, for instance, using an elaborated code in school and a restricted code when communicating with friends.

This claim had proved to be somewhat controversial for a variety of reasons. For instance, in one study boys of different social class origins were asked to write two letters, a formal and an informal one (Robinson, 1962). If middle- and working-class boys differ in that the former are able to switch to an elaborated code while the latter are not, then the difference between them should be particularly marked in the formal letter. In fact, there were fewer language differences in the formal than in the informal letter. Field observations have given no support to the notion that lower-class individuals are limited to a restricted language code. The example of black rural children who have two registers has already been noted. Other sociolinguistic studies of naturally occurring interaction have found shifts to relatively elaborated codes among lower-class speakers (Chandler and Erickson, 1968), and studies of lower-class black language have shown that while it is different from standard English it is no less complex, rich, or sophisticated (Baratz and Shuy, 1969).

One must also consider the possibility that the distinction between two extreme types of code or register may constitute an oversimplification. What we may have in reality is a continuum of language styles whose use varies with the function that the utterance serves. At one end we would have a type of discourse in which the topic is of central importance, rather than the relationship between the speakers. In that case we would expect an elaborated code to be used. At the other extreme we would find a type of discourse in which the topic is irrelevant and only the relationship between the speakers is of importance. These situations would be characterized by the use of a restricted code. But between these extremes we may get intermediate forms in which both the topic and the relationship of the speakers is relevant (Williams and Naremore, 1969). Such forms may occur when one recounts an experience or gives instructions. In this case elements of both elaborated and restricted codes may coexist. The particular code used by an individual will depend on the kind of function he wishes his utterances to serve, and this function will be determined by the social context.

Such considerations raise problems for research on class differences that is based on laboratory situations rather than on naturalistic observation. It is highly unlikely that individuals of low socioeconomic status will perceive the laboratory situation in the same terms as individuals of high socioeconomic status. The latter are likely to be more at ease with the experimenter and to have a clearer understanding of the purpose of the study. On the other hand, low-status individuals may be preoccupied by their problematic relationship to the experimenter and may perceive the entire situation as alien and strange. Given these differences in the way the laboratory setting is interpreted we would expect differences in the language code or register used. But it would be dangerous to generalize such differences to situations outside the laboratory (Sroufe, 1970).

Another pitfall to be avoided when considering social class differences in verbal communication is the notion that lower-class language is somehow more simple or primitive than middle-class language. The fact is that the basic structuring principles on which language is founded appear to be universal and most linguists now assume that languages do not differ greatly in their underlying structures or in their formal characteristics. In all languages sentences are hierarchically structured and their interrelationships are at equally complex (Houston, 1970). The learning of the rules for constructing sentences requires a certain ability to abstract, irrespective of what the content of those rules may be in this or that language. Lower-class language or black language may be different from middle-class language but the rules for constructing sentences are of equal difficulty and complexity in all cases.

That is why the concept of "cultural deprivation" acquires rather dubious overtones when used in this context. It implies that middle-class English is the standard against which other forms of English are to be measured and compared to which they involve varying degrees of "deprivation." While it is true that the lack of standard middle-class English may constitute an insuperable block to upward social and economic mobility, it does not follow that there is any intrinsic deprivation involved. In this area we should be prepared to use the same perspective of cultural relativism that we generally use when comparing two cultures. In comparing, say American and Japanese culture, we would be content with noting differences and it is most unlikely that we would consider one culture "deprived" relative to the other. The same approach ought to guide our study of subcultural differences (Tulkin, 1972). If it does not, our standard is simply an expression of class bias that may be a suitable basis for social engineering but not for an objective account of subcultural differences.

A UNIVERSAL NONVERBAL LANGUAGE?

It is obvious that persons who do not share the same or a similar language cannot speak to one another. But what about nonverbal communication? As we know, men do not speak to one another only in words. Gestures, tone of voice, facial expression, posture, and spatial orientation all play an important role in human communication. Could it be that there are universal elements in nonverbal communication that allow people to convey some meaning in the absence of a shared verbal language?

If such elements exist they must be well hidden by an enormous cultural overlay for the cultural diversity of nonverbal expression is almost as well documented as the diversity of spoken language. In fact, there is more room for misunderstanding in the nonverbal than in the verbal area. If two people do not share a spoken language there is simply no verbal communication; but in nonverbal communication the same element, the same gesture, facial expression, and so on may have an entirely different meaning in two cultures. This can easily lead to misunderstanding, which may be worse than no communication at all. Suppose that two cultures have different norms regarding the appropriate interpersonal distance in various situations. Then when members of the two cultural groups meet, each will attempt to establish the interpersonal distance that he deems appropriate to the occasion. As a result the person whose culture prescribes a relatively large interpersonal space will experience the other person's attempts to reduce that space as an offensive intrusion. The other person in turn is made to feel uncomfortable by the apparently "standoffish" attitude of his partner. And so the ground is prepared for all sorts of misunderstandings.

But is it a fact that cultures differ in their prescriptions for appropriate interpersonal distance? Until quite recently we had to make do with impressionistic evidence on this point, but this has now been supplemented by more systematic, quantitative observations. In one such study (Watson and Graves, 1966) North American and Arab students were observed sitting at a table talking to one another. As had been expected on the basis of impressionistic accounts, the Arabs sat significantly closer to one another than the North Americans. Moreover, the Arabs turned to face one another to a much greater extent than the North Americans whose orientation to one another was more oblique. In addition, the Arabs engaged in more eye contact, spoke more loudly, and occasionally touched one another, whereas touching never occurred among the North Americans. This study therefore reveals systematic intercultural differences, not only in one, but in several channels of nonverbal communication. Each one of these channels could give rise to misunderstanding when members of the two cultures meet.

The only universal element in such situations appears to be the general human need for *some* norm to regulate such features of social interaction as interpersonal distance, touching, eye contact, and loudness of speech. The actual content of these norms varies from culture to culture, but it is unlikely that there are cultures that leave these aspects of social interaction entirely to chance. Norms operate by defining the limits of acceptable and appropriate behavior in various situations. These limits may be fairly wide at times, but *some* limit is always imposed. A society that is more permissive than ours about touching among males may very well regard the extremes of no touching or constant touching as inappropriate for certain situations. Similarly, there are always some limits on the amount of eye contact or loudness of speech under various circumstances. It is only the demand for some normative limits, not the nature of these limits, that appears to be a universal characteristic of human nonverbal communication.

But what about all those aspects of communication that cannot be quantified like interpersonal distance or amount of eye contact? What about gestures like head nodding or the quality of facial expression? Is the meaning of these actions universal across cultures, or is their significance based on social conventions?

Universalists have had no difficulty in pointing to behavioral patterns that have the same meaning in many culturally and geographically separate societies. On the other hand, relativists have usually managed to come up with a few instances that contradict the claim that the same meanings are universally communicated by the same gestures. Head nodding, for instance, is found as a sign of assent or approval in cultures as far apart as the European, Bantu African, Papuan, Balinese, Samoan, and Japanese (Eibl-Eibesfeldt, 1970a). However, among the Aino of northern Japan head nodding is reported to be unknown, the pygmy Negroes in remote parts of Malaya say "yes" by thrusting the head sharply forward, and the Abyssinians are said to indicate assent by throwing the head back and raising the eyebrows (Labarre, 1947).

Shaking the head indicates "no" in many different cultures, but the Sicilians say it by laying back the head, the Abyssinians jerk the head to the right shoulder, the Dyaks of central Borneo contract their eyebrows. Universalists meet such examples by suggesting that there may be several primary forms of showing rejection or disapproval, one of which is then conventionally adopted by a particular culture for the generalized "no" communication (Eibl-Eibesfeldt, 1970b).

There are gestures and expressions that do appear to have some cross-cultural validity. Bowing, where it is used, generally indicates submission, and smiling is a universal sign of appeasement in the interpersonal context. There are other gestures that appear to have the opposite meaning in different cultures. Hissing in many western countries means disapproval of a performance, but the Basuto of South Africa applaud by hissing. Spitting is a widespread sign of disgust and contempt, yet among the Masai of East Africa it is a sign of affection and benediction.

Relativists (Birdwhistell, 1963) tend to ignore the remarkable cross-cultural convergence that exists for many gestures and expressions, universalists are continually looking for new patterns that show generality across cultures. Eibl-Eibesfeldt (1970b), for example, has filmed observations that seem to show that the flirting behavior of girls agrees "in the smallest detail" among native inhabitants of Samoa, Papua, France, Japan, and parts of Africa and South America. This behavior pattern runs off as follows: The girl first smiles at the person to whom the flirting behavior is directed and lifts her eyebrows with a quick jerky movement upward, then she turns away with the head turned to the side, a lowered gaze and dropped eyelids. Frequently the girl then covers her face but continues to look at her partner out of the corners of her eyes. Impressive though these observations are, the thoroughgoing relativist would probably have little difficulty in coming up with contradictory data from other cultures.

THE ROLE OF CULTURE IN THE FACIAL EXPRESSION OF EMOTIONS

As long as we confine ourselves to bodily gestures we are unlikely to get a clear answer to the question of whether nonverbal communication is entirely based on learned, conventional patterns, or whether it contains an innate component. If we favor the latter point of view we will stress the high degree of cross-cultural generality that many of these gestural patterns possess, if we favor the relativist position we will stress the exceptions. It would be useful to study aspects of interpersonal communication that do not have the "all-or-none" quality of gestural patterns but that can be analyzed in terms of definite components. Facial expression gives us the material for just such a study. It is known to be linked to emotional expression, and it can be varied by appropriate movements. The fact that it is linked to emotional expression gives it meaning, so that we can ask questions about the generality of emotional meaning that a given facial expression possesses. The fact that it can be varied allows us to investigate the range of any community of meaning we may find.

Charles Darwin believed that a definite facial expression was innately associated with each of the fundamental emotions, and that has always been the universalist position. To the relativist, on the other hand, the link between facial expression and emotion is entirely governed by cultural convention (e.g. the Japanese learn to smile even when they are sad). If the relativist is right members of different cultures should show little more than chance agreement in labeling the emotional meaning of a particular facial expression. If Darwin was right there should be substantial agreement across cultures on the appropriate emotional label for a certain face.

In order to decide the issue Izard (1971) presented posed photographs supposedly representing eight fundamental emotions to nine groups of university students (American, English, German, Swedish, French, Swiss, Greek, Japanese, and African). The subjects were given a list of emotional labels, (interest–excitement, enjoyment–joy, surprise–startle, distress–anguish, disgust–contempt, anger–rage, shame–humiliation, and fear–terror), and asked to match these labels with the appropriate photographs. Intercultural agreement on the "correct" matching for each emotion was much greater than chance, a result that is not compatible with the extreme relativist position, which considers the facial expression of emotion to be entirely a matter of cultural convention.

However, certain aspects of the study did suggest that culture plays some role in the recognition of emotions. Seven of the nine groups tested belong to the area of western culture, and it was precisely the two groups that did not belong to this area, the Africans and Japanese, that were significantly less successful in "correctly" matching photographs and emotional labels. The only significant difference among the seven western groups was that between Greeks and Americans. It is therefore plausible to assume that at least six of the western groups have common conventions about emotional expression that are different than the cultural conventions of Africans or Japanese. Unfortunately, the Africans were the only group who were tested in what was to them a foreign language, and it is impossible to say how much this affected their performance. The failure of the Japanese to attach the expected verbal label was essentially limited to four of the eight emotions, on the other four emotions their agreement with western subjects was really quite high. In the light of these ambiguities the universalist position cannot be rejected.

On the other hand, it is always possible for a thoroughgoing relativist to claim that whatever agreement in emotional labeling is found across cultures is due to common exposure to movies and television where actors strike conventional poses that are pretty similar the world over. It is also likely that people learn to interpret the conventional expressions of another culture by contact with members of that culture. In order to test these possibilities it is necessary to include in one's study people who have had minimal contact with Westerners or western mass media.

The results of two such studies are now available (Ekman and Friesen, 1971; Ekman, 1972). Subjects were drawn from two isolated neolithic groups in New Guinea that had had minimal exposure to Westerners and no exposure to western mass media. These people were shown two or three photographs of posed emotional expression and were asked to match them with simple stories that clearly involved a particular emotion. In most cases their performance showed very high agreement (80–100%) with similar judgments made by members of literate cultures. The New Guineans were also asked to pose various emotions, and photographs of these poses were then shown to college students in the United States. The latter were able to apply the correct emotional label with better than chance accuracy in the case of the emotions of happiness, anger, disgust, and sadness.

The fact that visually isolated people are able to recognize and to pose the facial expression of certain emotions constitutes strong support for the view that there is an innate basis for the expression of at least some emotions. At the same time the influence of culture cannot be denied. Neither the extreme position of universalism nor that of complete cultural relativism can be seriously entertained in the face of the available evidence. Clearly there is an interaction between innate mechanisms and cultural conventions. The question is only how we are to conceive this interaction.

Suppose we start with the assumption that there is an innate basis for the facial expression of certain fundamental emotions like happiness, anger, fear, disgust, sadness, and surprise. Then culture can influence these expressions in three ways (Ekman, 1972): In the first place, it determines which emotion will be elicited in different situations. A funeral may be defined as an occasion for sadness in one culture or an occasion for joyful celebration in another. In comparing gestures and facial expressions across cultures we must always be careful to make sure that the eliciting event has the same meaning in the cultures that are to be compared. Differences of expression between cultures may simply mean that the event eliciting the expression has a different meaning in these cultures and hence gives rise to different emotions. There are certainly some events, like a sudden loud noise or a bad smell, that elicit much the same emotional expression in all cultures. But this is not the case for most interpersonal situations whose emotional meaning is usually culturally determined.

The second way in which culture affects emotional expression is based on the fact that people react to their own emotions, and these reactions are usually culturally determined. For example, people may react to the arousal of anger in themselves with fear or shame, or they may react to the arousal of fear with anger or disgust. These reactions are often immediate and may lead to an expression that is a blend of the original emotion and the reaction to it. Such expressions will be hard to classify. It is even possible that the reaction suppresses the original emotion, so that in an anger-arousing situation we do not see the anger but only the reactive fear, and in a fear-arousing situation we do not see the fear but only the reactive disgust.

This brings us to the third way in which culture distorts primary emotional expression. The fact is that emotional expression is subject to voluntary control, it may be artificially posed, deliberately intensified or deintensified, or masked by a different expression. These techniques of managing emotions have been called "display rules" (Ekman and Friesen, 1969), and they are strongly controlled by cultural norms. For instance, in many competitive situations in our culture it is expected that the winner will deintensify his expression of happiness while the loser should deintensify or mask with happiness his primary feeling of sadness. In the middle-class subculture it is also expected that urban males should mask or at least deintensify expressions of fear and sadness in almost all public places. In many societies the masking of fear and anger by an outward show of happiness is mandatory for everyone, or at least for people of a particular social status.

Slow motion film projection is a useful tool in the discovery of display rules. It makes it possible to detect facial expressions that are too brief to be detected by ordinary observation or that have been aborted by the intervention of a different expression prescribed by the display rules.

In the light of all the evidence it seems clear that the interpersonal expression of emotion involves both universal, pancultural components, and features that are strongly influenced by culture. An extreme position on this issue simply cannot account for all the data. In order to disentangle the complex interaction between the various factors involved future research will have to turn increasingly to slow motion films and to the microanalysis of facial expression. In this way it will be possible to get away from crude, global judgments of expression to a detailed analysis of changes in the facial musculature. One interesting possibility is that different parts of the face differ in their susceptibility to deliberate control. For example, the lower face may be more easily influenced by display rules than the muscles around the eyelids that continue to show the original emotion.

Facial expressions are not a language in the sense that an arbitrary combination of elements is given a particular meaning in each culture, nor are they simply preprogrammed instinctive patterns that run off in the presence of an innately established pattern of releasing stimuli. They are rather complex resultants of a few innate programs and specific cultural influences.

CONCLUSION

The existence of cultural and subcultural differences in the employment of different channels of interpersonal communication leads to two important questions: (1) does it make sense to speak of "cultural deprivation" in the sphere of verbal communication, and (2) is there a universal language of nonverbal communication?

The answer to the first question must take into account the fact that members of different cultural groups develop a variety of "registers" or "codes" of verbal communication whose employment depends on the way in which social situations are defined. Such registers or codes are styles of verbal expression that are considered appropriate to particular social settings, and groups such as social classes differ in their styles as well as in their definition of the situations to which these styles are assigned. Some styles involve a simplified form of verbal communication but no group is limited to such styles—given the appropriate social occasion, members of all groups are capable of displaying the full range of linguistic complexity. The use of simplified styles is likely to depend on different interpretations of social situations rather than on any lack of linguistic or communicational competence.

Questions about the existence of a universal language of nonverbal communication are often obscured by a failure to distinguish between different ways in which culture can affect nonverbal communication. It is not enough to speak of cultural programming in general. Culture may affect the way in which a given social context is defined, it may affect the directness or intensity with which a particular reaction is communicated, or it may affect the individual's response to his own immediate reaction, resulting in a complex communication in which a universal core is hidden by layers of culturally determined forms. When care is taken to allow for these diverse cultural influences it does seem in some cases that a core of universally recognized signs is left. This applies particularly to the facial expression of affective states.

REFERENCES

Baratz, J. C. and Shuy, R. W. (Eds.) (1969). *Teaching Black Children to Read*. Washington, D.C.: Center for Applied Linguistics.

Bernstein, B. (1964). Elaborated and restricted codes: Their social origins and some consequences. In J. Gumperz and D. Hymes (Eds.), The ethnography of communication. *American Anthropologist Special Publication*, **66**, 55–69.

Birdwhistell, R. (1963). The kinesic level in the investigation of emotions. In P. H. Knapp (Ed.), *Expression of the Emotions in Man*. New York: International Universities Press.

Chandler, B. J. and Erickson, F. D. (1968). *Sounds of Society: A Demonstration Program in Group Enquiry*. Washington, D.C.: United States Government Printing Office.

Eibl-Eibesfeldt, I. (1970a). *Liebe und Hass*. Munich: R. Piper.

Eibl-Eibesfeldt, I. (1970b). *Ethology: The Biology of Behavior*. New York: Holt, Rinehart & Winston.

Ekman, P. (1972). Universals and cultural differences in facial expressions of emotion. In J. K. Cole (Ed.), *Nebraska Symposium on Motivation*. Vol. 19. Lincoln: University of Nebraska Press.

Ekman, P. and Friesen, W. V. (1969). The repertoire of nonverbal behavior. *Semiotica*, **1**, 49–98.

Ekman, P. and Friesen, W. V. (1971). Constants across cultures in the face and emotion. *J. Personal. & soc. Psychol.*, **17**, 124–129.

Ervin-Tripp, S. M. (1969). Sociolinguistics. In L. Berkowitz (Ed.), *Advances in Experimental Social Psychology*. Vol. 4. New York: Academic Press.

Heider, E. R. (1971). Style and accuracy of verbal communications within and between social classes. *J. Personal. & soc. Psychol.*, **18**, 33–47.

Houston, S. H. (1969). A sociolinguistic consideration of the black English of children in northern Florida. *Language*, **45**, 599–607.

Houston, S. H. (1970). A reexamination of some assumptions about the language of the disadvantaged child. *Child Development*, **41**, 947–963.

Izard, C. E. (1971). *The Face of Emotion*. New York: Appleton-Century-Crofts.

Kashinsky, M. and Wiener, M. (1969) Tone in communication and the performance of children from two socio-economic groups. *Child Development*, **40**, 1193–1201.

Labarre, W. (1947). The cultural basis of emotions and gestures. *J. Personal.*, **16**, 49–68.

Robinson, W. P. (1965). The elaborated code in working class language. *Language and Speech*, **8**, 243–252.

Schmidt, W. H. O. and Hore, T. (1970). Some nonverbal aspects of communication between mother and preschool child. *Child Development*, **41**, 889–896.

Sroufe, L. A. (1970). A methodological and philosophical critique of intervention-oriented research. *Developmental Psychol.*, **2**, 140–145.

Tulkin, S. R. (1972). An analysis of the concept of cultural deprivation. *Developmental Psychol.*, **6**, 326–339.

Watson, O. M. and Graves, T. D. (1966). Quantitative research in proxemic behavior. *American Anthropologist*, **68**, 971–985.

Williams, F. and Naremore, R. C. (1969). On the functional analysis of social class differences in modes of speech. *Speech Monographs*, **36**, 77–102.

CHAPTER 10

The Study of Interpersonal Processes: Some General Reflections

ONE-WAY AND TWO-WAY INFLUENCE

Twentieth-century developments of the mass media and their large-scale use in advertising and propaganda have inevitably led to a specifically modern preoccupation with the techniques and implications of controlling and manipulating the thought and behavior of human beings. Recent utopias have typically addressed themselves to the problems and challenges created by the new possibilities of psychological control, whether pessimistically, like Huxley's *Brave New World*, or optimistically, like Skinner's *Walden Two*. But whether the new techniques of manipulation are seen as a specter or as a promise there is never any doubt about their power. The generation that witnessed the crucial developments in the modern techniques of psychological control has been understandably fascinated by them, so much so, that it has been generally reluctant to see their limitations.

For the prophets of psychological control the crucial social relationship is that between controllers and controlled. Whether they applaud or deplore the fact the prophets have placed at the center of their scheme of things an asymmetric relationship in which social influence is effective by a one-way channel. Instead of the traditional dichotomy between the rich and the poor they see the dichotomy between controllers and controlled. In this scheme of things the former are effectively removed from the influence of the latter. Society is conceived on the model of the psychological experiment in which the experimenter calls the tune, manipulating the subject while being himself immune to influence attempts on the part of the latter.

One must wonder about the adequacy of this model. While counterinfluences from subject to experimenter may be effectively eliminated in the psychological experiment, especially if the subject happens to be a pigeon or a rat, it is doubtful whether this distinction of roles can ever be maintained in all its purity outside the laboratory. In real-life situations audiences have ways of making their feelings known, and would-be controllers and manipulators are apt to find themselves swallowing their own medicine in liberal doses.

Even if the one-way influence model turns out to be applicable to certain types of relationship it is not of much help in improving our understanding of a large part of human interaction. For all their exposure to the mass media and to authoritarian institutions people still marry, have children, make friends, and talk to their colleagues; and in the relationships between spouses, between parents and children, and between friends and colleagues, influence is never just a one-way street, it is always reciprocal. The clear distinction between controller and controlled brakes down as soon as we leave the psychological laboratory or the bureaucratic institution and enter the sphere of family life or of ordinary sociable interaction among peers. How does a couple decide on the size of their family? What determines a child's choice of occupation or a change of topic in an ordinary conversation? Rarely do such matters involve unilateral decisions, more usually they depend on a complex interchange between the individuals concerned. While different levels of dominance can certainly be distinguished in interpersonal relationships, this is always a matter of degree and never permits the neat division into controllers and controlled that formal authority relationships imply.

As a matter of fact the democratization of relationships between spouses, between parents and children, and between colleagues has gone hand in hand with the increasing bureaucratization of public life and the growth of techniques of mass control. It is certainly possible, though hardly susceptible of proof, that this correlation indicates a genuine causal link, and that the spread of egalitarian principles in the private sphere is at least in part a compensatory reaction to the growing sense of being manipulated by the organs of public power.

Psychologists have frequently approached the study of human behavior with their own version of what may be called "management ideology." They have been primarily interested in developing techniques of control that would make it possible to divert human behavior from its natural path, the justification being that the natural path all too often led to psychological disorder, individual maladjustment, and intergroup hostility. Their preoccupation with prediction stems much less from its use to test the claims of rival theories (genuine examples of such use of prediction are relatively rare in Psychology) as from their conviction that prediction was a necessary prerequisite to effective control. They have therefore accumulated a mass of laboratory findings that can only be successfully applied in those real-life situations where the distribution of power is about as uneven as it is in the psychological laboratory. Much psychological research is only applicable in settings that make it possible to control the individual's response options quite drastically, so that he can neither remove himself from the influence of the crucial stimuli nor subvert the controller's purpose by exerting any effective counterinfluence of his own. Educational and medical institutions often provide fair approximations to settings of this type.

But this orientation has led to the relative neglect of those vast areas of human interaction that do not lend themselves to an analysis in terms of unilateral control. The large literature on *behavior modification*, for example, contains little that is relevant to an understanding of how people influence one another in everyday life. We know something about how teachers can modify the behavior of deviant children but nothing about how those children commonly modify the behavior of the teacher. And we know much more about the exercise of influence by persons in authority than we know about the mutual effect that peers have on one another. In fact, as Psychology has become more strongly committed to its version of managerial ideology studies of peer relations (with the single exception of College students) have become distinctly less popular.

Yet the exploration of what happens among peers can be distinctly illuminating, even when it is undertaken from the point of view of behavior modification. One study of nursery school children, for example, found that the giving and receiving of positive reinforcement were reciprocal activities (Charlesworth and Hartup, 1967). Those children who gave the most reinforcement to their peers also received the most in terms of Skinner's "generalized reinforcers," like attention, approval, affection, submissiveness, and tokens (giving tangible objects). Moreover, the giving and receiving of each category of reinforcement were significantly correlated: the children who gave the most attention and approval tended to receive the most and those who received the most affection tended to give the most. This study demonstrates that in situations that have not been artificially pre-programmed reinforcement is a reciprocal matter and its dispensing is not the prerogative of particular individuals. In ordinary social situations the person seldom simply reacts to others, rather he *interacts* with them according to a discernible pattern. If we treat social behavior merely in its reactive aspects and ignore the interactive aspects we emerge with a very distorted picture of what normally takes place between individuals.

REINTERPRETATION OF SOCIALIZATION STUDIES

Perhaps the clearest example of the one-sidedness of the reactive model is provided by research on socialization. Almost all of this rather extensive body of research is concerned with unidirectional influences passing from various caretakers, usually the parents, to the child. The influence that the child exerts on his caretakers is usually ignored. This is quite in line with an ideology of control, but it leads to a plethora of mutually contradictory and nonsignificant results that can only be made to fit into any sort of pattern by strictly limiting oneself to a single source of information, namely, the mother (Yarrow, Campbell, and Burton, 1968). Studies of the effects of maternal control techniques on the child are as plentiful as studies of child control of adults are rare.

One recent study that deliberately attempted to demonstrate the reality of child effects on adult behavior employed two nursery school teachers who each attempted to treat some groups of children in a highly nurturant manner and other groups of children in a manner that minimized nurturant interaction (Yarrow, Waxler, and Scott, 1971). When their behavior with the children was carefully observed it was found that neither of them was able to carry out their program consistently with all the children under their care. Predictably, they adjusted their behavior to the kinds of demands that were made on them by different children. Children who made frequent bids for help or attention received far more than their share of nurturant responses (in the form of interest, help, attention, and affection) from the adult than children who made few such bids. On the other hand, when the adult was trying to impose a regime of low nurturance bids for help and attention from the children more frequently met with rejection and criticism. Moreover, under this condition there was an appreciable correlation between negative adult responses to bids by the child and negative contacts *initiated* by the adult. The treatment that the child receives is therefore clearly a product of his own behavior and the program the adult is trying to follow. The child who makes many bids for attention gets very different treatment under the two conditions, and the adult metes out different treatment, depending on what child she is dealing with. The treatment received by any particular child can only be predicted by taking into account both the program the adult is trying to follow and the relevant aspects of the child's own behavior.

The results of socialization studies are usually expressed in the form of a correlation between some aspect of parental behavior and some aspect of child behavior. This correlation is then interpreted as providing evidence for the effect that parental treatment has on the child, although, as every student knows after his Introductory Psychology course, a correlation between two events tells us nothing about the causal relationship that may or may not exist between them. A correlation between child and parent behavior is as likely to have been produced by a parental adaptation to the demands of the child as the other way around (Bell, 1968). Or, still more likely, it will be the result of an interaction between the two. To attribute to the parent the function of providing the stimulus and to the child the function of providing the response is to prejudge the issue in terms of an ideology of control that leaves no room for the psychology of interpersonal interaction.

One way of checking on the accuracy of the model that treats parent–child relations in terms of unidirectional effects from parent to child is to carefully observe sequences of parent–child interaction in order to assess whether any given sequence is typically initiated by the parent or by the child. Take the infant's crying and fussing for example. Is it generally a response to something the parent has done, or is it more frequently a stimulus to the parent to do something? At least one study of fifty-four mother–infant pairs (Moss and Robson reported by Bell, 1971) has shown that the infant's crying or fussing is significantly more likely to precede maternal contact than to follow it. Such a result merely confirms by systematic observation what is generally known, namely, that the infant's cry is a potent stimulus for eliciting maternal behavior.

Other studies of the sequential patterning of mother–infant interaction have emerged with similar findings. In one case three-event sequences were studied in which one member of the pair initiates and terminates an interaction sequence while a response from the other member of the pair occurs in the middle (Gewirtz and Gewirtz, 1965). It happened that sequences initiated and terminated by the infant were significantly more frequent than those initiated and terminated by the mother. This certainly casts the infant in the role of one who shapes maternal responses, perhaps to a greater degree than he allows himself to be shaped by maternal attempts at control.

One way of thinking about the parent–child relationship in interactional terms is to regard each participant as showing upper and lower limit control behavior. Each member of the dyad attempts to optimize the stimulation he receives from the other member. If the other's behavior produces a significant drop from this optimum level the partner will engage in lower limit control behavior, which consists of attempts to restore the stimulation received from the other to the desired level; if, on the other hand, the other's behavior produces a level of stimulation that is significantly above the optimal level, upper limit control behavior will be elicited, and this consists of attempts to cause the partner to reduce or cease the behavior that is the cause of the undesirable level of stimulation (Bell, 1968, 1971).

It is easy to apply this scheme to the analysis of mother–child interactions. A sequence may start by the infant waking up in his cot and beginning to fuss. This is not a strong enough stimulus to produce a maternal response, so the fussing gradually changes into crying, which may be thought of as lower limit control behavior on the part of the infant who is seeking a maternal response. When the crying has gone on awhile the mother initiates upper limit control behavior by coming over to the infant, picking him up, and seeking to soothe him. She is successful and he eventually becomes quiet. She may now engage in lower limit control behavior in her turn by talking to him, tickling him, and jogging him in an attempt to induce him to smile or vocalize. He may in fact vocalize, but after a while she begins to lose interest and cuts down on her talking and playing; at this point he smiles at her and this lower limit control behavior on his part causes her to resume her previous rate of talking and tactile stimulation. In this way mother and infant are constantly fashioning each other's responses, the infant relying partly on unlearned behavior and partly on learned contingencies that have been acquired through operant conditioning in previous interactions.

This type of analysis can be extended to parent–child interaction far beyond infancy. Take the adolescent's struggle for independence, for example. At this stage the child becomes interested in taking over control over ever larger segments of his own behavior, and in the usual case this control is only reluctantly relinquished by the parent. The adolescent therefore seeks to confine the parent's controlling behavior within ever narrower limits, while the parent continues to impose upper limits on the child's behavior. A compromise is often the result, leaving each party with the feeling that their attempts at control have met with some success. For example, the adolescent would really like the freedom to stay out all night, while the parent would actually like him to be home by 9 p.m.

Neither may state his optimum outcome openly, but they engage in an interchange that results in an agreement for the adolescent to be home by midnight. Both have influenced each other and both have contributed to the final decision, so each feels that his attempt at control has been successful.

This seems the most reasonable way to interpret the results of a study (Danziger, 1975) in which the independent reports of mothers and their adolescent sons were compared in respect to who they thought was responsible for certain decisions affecting the son. These decisions covered such questions as the time at which the son was expected to be home, what shoes he was to buy, what friends he could bring home and when, what time he was expected to go to bed, and so on. It emerged that both mother and son had a marked tendency to claim responsibility for more decisions than they were given credit for by the other. In a given case a mother and son might both claim sole responsibility for determining the son's bedtime and so on. The tendency for both son and mother to claim a larger share of responsibility for themselves than they assigned to each other seems to suggest that in many cases controls on the behavior of adolescents cannot be attributed to a single source but represent the outcome of an interaction process to which both child and parent have contributed. It seems that in such situations one is more likely to perceive the effectiveness of one's own influence attempts than that of one's partner. That is why it is useless to base the measurement of variables like "parental control" on the report of only one of the partners in the interaction. Such a procedure is based on the assumption of a unidirectional flow of influence in a situation that in fact depends on the contributions of both partners in an interaction.

TWO FURTHER EXAMPLES OF INTERACTION PROCESSES

Let us complete our illustration of the interactive nature of human relationships by quoting two further studies involving adolescents or adults, one experimental, the other a field study. Milgram's (1963) by now classical study of obedience has sometimes been interpreted as though it represented the acme of one-way influence effects. A majority of the subjects in his famous experiment were induced to administer apparently extremely painful electric shocks to other individuals simply because it was demanded of them by the experimental procedure. They sheepishly and irresponsibly continued to inflict intense suffering on others because they seemed unable to resist the authoritative demands of the experimenter. Helpless victims of one-way influence? Not quite, as a more recent modification of the experimental procedure has shown (Tilker, 1970). In this case the subjects were exposed to varying amounts of feedback from the "victim." One group received no feedback at all; a second group received auditory feedback in the form of the victim's pleas, cries, and complaints; and a third group was exposed to the sight of the victim's contortions under the influence of severe electric shocks as well as the auditory feedback. Verbal protests by the subjects about the conduct of the experiment increased in direct proportion to the amount of feedback they received from the victim. Moreover, while only one out of fifteen subjects in the no-feedback condition physically stopped the experiment, four out of fifteen subjects in the auditory feedback condition and eight out of fifteen subjects in the auditory plus visual feedback condition resorted to physical interference to stop the experiment.

It is therefore quite clear that the transformation of individuals into helpless carriers out of orders is greatly facilitated by interference with the normal feedback obtained in face-to-face interaction with the victim, a lesson to which the crews of bomber aircraft have borne witness thousands of times. The contrast between authoritarian institutions, in which influence flows in only one direction, and ordinary face-to-face encounters, in which influence is always tempered by counterinfluence, emerges with particular force in this context.

Our final illustration of interaction effects in face-to-face behavior will be taken from the field of therapeutic intervention. Most studies of the effectiveness of psychotherapy rely simply on before and after therapy measures, a procedure that makes it impossible to assess the role of therapist–patient interaction. The technique of measuring adjustment only before and after and not *during* therapy implies a one-way influence model in which the client is the recipient and the therapist the source. If therapy is unsuccessful this procedure throws no light on *why* it fails. It is possible, for example, that a client may show considerable improvement in the earlier stages of therapy, only to backslide later on. To allow for this possibility it is necessary to assess *both* therapist and client behavior at various stages in the course of therapy. If client improvement shows a fluctuating course it may be possible to relate the outcome to changes in therapist–client interaction.

This is just what was done in a study of a rehabilitation program directed at adolescent members of street gangs in Chicago (Caplan, 1968). Six levels of input by counselors and eight levels of adjustment of the boys were distinguished and weekly ratings of both the boys and their counselors were conducted by independent observers over a period of a year. The scale of counselor input varied from merely providing social and recreational services on a group level to the point where the time and resources of the counselor are largely preempted by his effort to assist a single boy. The scale of boys' adjustment varied from a level at which the boy is not receptive to personal counseling to the level of "success" where the boy stands on his own feet, stays in school, or holds down a job independently of counselor influence. All the stages, except the last one, are in fact instrumental stages that trace the development of the relationship between the boy and his counselor through noncooperation to ever greater "receptivity" on the part of the boy. Only the last stage involves independence from the counselor.

After a year of therapeutic intervention only 7% of the boys were at the final "success" stage of adjustment, but 33% were at the penultimate stage, and 38% were at the stage before that. What was stopping their jump to the final stage? Inspection of the records kept over a year showed that 61% of the boys had in fact reached the penultimate stage of success at one time or another, but many of them subsequently slid back to lower levels of adjustment instead of going on to the final improvement. This process of advancing to the penultimate stage of adjustment and then backsliding was repeated several times in the course of a year by quite a number of the boys. What produced this negative outcome? A large part of the answer is provided by the behavior of the counselors. When a boy reached the higher stages of adjustment they typically redoubled their efforts to move him to the final stage by devoting more of their time and resources to him. When the boys slid back they tried even harder, often producing a return to the penultimate stage, which was followed by yet more counselor input that duly resulted in a repetition of backsliding. Clearly, the increased effort by the counselors produced an effect very different from the intended one. What was intended only as a means to the final goal of independent adjustment became an end in itself for most of the boys who discovered that the way to secure the maximum amount of involvement and interest from the counselor was to engage in repeated cycles of improvement and backsliding without ever making the transition to independence. The more-of-the-same recipe followed by the counes- lors was in fact keeping the boys in a state of dependence and undermining the success of the program.

Counseling and psychotherapy cannot be considered as one-way influence processes. The progress and backsliding of the client is likely to have all kinds of consequences for the behavior of the therapist, and some of these reactions may inhibit rather than facilitate a successful outcome of the therapeutic process. If the success rate of psychotherapy is to be improved it will have to be studied in terms of the interaction between therapist and client over a period of time. It will then be possible to sensitize the therapist to those aspects of the client's behavior that produce counterproductive reactions from the therapist. But the existence of interaction patterns that inhibit therapeutic progress will never be discovered unless psychotherapy is recognized for what it is—an interaction process in which both participants produce effects on each other.

FEEDBACK AND REDUNDANCY

It is time to draw some general conclusions from the contrast between relationships governed by an ideology of control in which influence follows a unidirectional path and relationships of interaction in which influence flows in both directions at once. The former type of relationship is generally explicable in terms of traditional scientific principles of linear cause–effect chains. A command may flow down established lines of military or civilian authority step by step so that each level of authority acts as a cause that produces effects on the next lower level. This process is quite analogous to physical processes in which causes and effects are linked in a linear, chainlike manner. Explanations in terms of *antecedents* and *consequents* or *stimuli* and *responses* are quite appropriate to this type of structure.

But interpersonal communication commonly involves a *circular* rather than a *linear* pattern of interaction. Person *A* has some influence on person *B* and the latter then acts back on *A* to produce new behavior that again acts on *B*, and so on. This is the phenomenon known as *feedback*. Systems involving feedback differ in several important respects from systems based on linear cause–effect chains. In the latter there is a clear beginning and a clear end to the causal chain. This means that the output of any part of the system can be predicted from a knowledge of its input and causes and effects can be clearly identified by isolating the appropriate single variables. If an individual has no way of acting back on a source of influence we can study the effect of the source by treating it as the independent variable and the individual's response as the dependent variable. But if the source and the target of influence are continually changing places neither of them can be unambiguously described in terms of a single variable identified either as the cause or the effect. Two individuals in interaction are simultaneously the causes and the effects of each other's behavior.

While time can be treated as having only two states—"before" and "after" in the single variable approach it must be assigned more values in the study of interaction or feedback processes. When two individuals are interacting it would make little sense to sum all the acts of each of them and treat this as a "variable." For the action of individual A at time t_x has already been modified by the action of individual B at time t_{x-1}, and each successive action represents the outcome of different combinations of influences. The sum of B's actions is not simply the resultant of the sum of A's actions but each separate action is determined by its particular place in the sequence of interactions. The absence of linear causality in feedback systems does not mean that the order in which events occur has to be random. On the contrary, the feedback systems constituting interpersonal communication commonly show highly consistent regularities. For example, the contributors to a two-way conversation regularly alternate in the roles of speaker and listener; certain linguistic forms like questions are followed by a certain type of content, namely answers, with a frequency that is considerably above chance. Such orderliness in the sequence of interaction is called *redundancy*.

When we study circular interaction systems the search for redundancy replaces the search for simple cause–effect relationships that characterize the investigation of linear systems. Redundancy is an expression for the degree to which the events in a system deviate from a purely chance order. An everyday word that expresses the same idea is *pattern*. When we study interactional sequences we do not look for single causes and effects so much as for recurring patterns. Such patterns have this in common with causal effects that in both cases we are looking at the *constraints* that produce a nonrandom order of events.

In looking for pattern or redundancy in interactional systems we are in the same position as a person who is trying to learn the rules of chess by watching a number of games. By keeping track of the moves he would soon discover the rule that each player moves alternately, and later he would discover the rules governing the moves of individual pieces. If he watches enough games he will discover the rule that white always moves first, that the loss of the king means the loss of the game, that certain combinations of moves tend to occur together in recognized openings, and so on. It all amounts to a list of constraints that prevent the game from being a random movement of pieces. Such constraints or patterns may be identified qualitatively, although the deviation from randomness may require statistical demonstration.

In one sense the discovery of redundancies in interaction systems amounts to no more than description. It is possible to go one step further and to speculate about the reasons for the existence of the observed regularities. But at the moment so much remains to be done in merely discovering the patterns existing in different forms of interaction that speculation about the reasons for the existence of such patterns is frequently premature. In another sense the identification of the patterns followed by the interactive process constitutes more than a mere description because it establishes the actual constraints under which the system is operating. It amounts to an identification of the forces that necessarily impose a certain form on the system, although we may remain ignorant of the actual nature of these forces. In this respect an analysis in terms of redundancy is no less and no more "scientific" than a cause–effect analysis of linear event chains. What is unscientific, however, is the treatment of feedback systems in terms that are applicable only to linear systems.

One-way influence systems differ from two-way systems in that the relationship on which the system is based is a unilateral one—A affects B and not vice versa. This is not true for systems involving two-way influence. Hence one-way interactions can be studied by summing all the instances of some property of A or of B, the number of presentations of a message or the degree of "nurturance," for example. But feedback systems show the property of *nonsummativity*, elements occurring at one point in the communication sequence cannot be summed with elements occupying a different place in the sequence. It is the *sequence* of events rather than their sum that becomes the object of study. In other words, there has to be a shift from a focus on individuals to a focus on the process of communication between them.

NEGLECT OF COMMUNICATION PROCESSES

When two individuals communicate there is some sort of interaction between them. But the study of social interaction is not the same as the study of interpersonal communication. In most studies of social interaction the process of communication is simply taken for granted or perhaps is treated as an "intervening variable" whose existence is inferred from its results. It is always possible to study social interaction purely in terms of its results without looking at the interpersonal processes that produce these results.

For example, we can study the conditions under which people offer help to others by manipulating the social environment of the potential helper or the situation of the "victim" without ever raising the question of *how* the potential helper becomes aware of the social situation that required his help. Our variables may include such factors as the presence of other people or variations in the characteristics of the person who needs help, but unless we raise questions as to how information about the victim who needs help or about other potential sources of help gets to the subject of our experiment we are not studying interpersonal communication.

Again, we may study the effect of differences in group composition on the performance of group members without looking at the communication of group members among each other. Or we can study sociometric choices or interpersonal attraction as a function of the individual characteristics of the persons involved without relating this to communication patterns among people who choose one another.

When we perform studies of this type we study social interaction in terms of its antecedents and its consequents but we do not concern ourselves with the process of interaction as such. There is a certain input in the form of groups of varying composition, individual characteristics or descriptions of social situations and a certain output in the form of offers of help, work performed or friendship choices, and we look for functional relationships between input and output without using data about what happens in the middle. We may manipulate variables like "status" or "ego involvement" without enquiring how people communicate status differences or involvement to one another.

As long as we study social interaction in this manner the data of social psychology are not essentially different from the data of individual psychology—they are aggregate data based on the properties of individuals (Krippendorff, 1970). What such data tell us is that individuals have certain effects on one another, they do not tell us how such effects are produced.

In studies of social interaction it is very common for measurements to be made *before* social interaction takes place and *after* it has run its course, but no measures of the interaction process itself are attempted. Such a procedure has a certain pragmatic usefulness and may tell us what manipulations to perform if we wish to produce a given result, but it also has certain drawbacks. It means that our theorizing about interpersonal interaction has to be limited to individual cognitive organization, as in balance theory, or to the outcome rather than the process of interaction, as in social exchange theory. It also means that the application of our findings to situations outside the laboratory is often highly problematical because the conditions of interpersonal communication have changed, and we know nothing about the likely effect of such changes.

For example, numerous experimental studies have been carried out on so-called mixed-motive interaction in the Prisoner's Dilemma game. In this situation a person has the choice of either trusting his partner, playing cooperatively and cutting his losses or not trusting his partner, playing competitively and running the risk of either gaining or losing much. Each player has two alternatives. If both of them choose alternative A they both win a small amount or both incur a small loss, if both choose alternative B they both incur a large loss, but if one chooses A and the other B, then the one who chooses B wins and the other loses. Under the usual laboratory conditions the players are isolated from each other and cannot communicate. The result is a preponderance of competitive choices. However, when subjects are allowed to communicate both visually and by talking the proportion of cooperative responses increases to a startling degree (Wichman, 1970). Now, it is clear that the results of laboratory studies on isolated subjects cannot be generalized to the more common real-life situation where those involved are able to communicate with one another. Because social interaction outside the laboratory generally involves interpersonal communication laboratory studies of social interaction that do not take this factor into account are unlikely to form a useful basis for predictions in real life situations.

In some ways the present situation of the social psychology of human interaction is reminiscent of the situation that characterized the study of individual intelligence for some time. As long as studies of intellectual development limited themselves to intelligence test data they had to confine themselves to the *yield* that intellectual processes produced (Piaget, 1960). Theorizing on this basis generally produced no more than a list of intellectual "faculties." To obtain some insight into the cognitive processes that were involved in different kinds of intellectual "yield" it was necessary to conduct investigations into problem solving that addressed themselves to the question of *how* individuals arrived at right or wrong solutions. The student of social interaction actually has an advantage in taking the critical step towards the investigation of processes because unlike the operations of individual intelligence the processes of interpersonal communication are for the most part amenable to direct public inspection.

SELF-PRESENTATION AND SOCIAL IDENTITY

If the study of the actual processes of interpersonal communication is to be taken seriously, it is necessary to make a clear distinction between those aspects of communication that convey information about the world outside the communicators, and those aspects that establish the nature of the relationship between the communicators. We refer to the former as a process of *representation* and the latter as a process of *presentation*. It is this latter process that is frequently neglected in studies of interpersonal communication. By "presenting" themselves in a certain manner human individuals define their roles in any particular relationship and hence assume certain social identities. The relationship of speaking and listening identifies one person as the speaker and the other as the listener. A dominance relationship identifies one person as the dominant one and the other as the submissive one. The existence of a relationship involves roles that identify the carriers of these roles.

Through their "presentational" aspects interpersonal communications establish social relationships and impose social identities. Conversely, these presentational aspects can only be understood in the context of ongoing social relationships. A refusal to reciprocate self-revealing statements, for example, has a very different meaning in a psychotherapeutic relationship and in a relationship among peers. Again, the use of a very careful and pedantic style of speech is likely to have a different significance in a family group and in a work group. The same feature of communication may have different command aspects in different social contexts. That is why it is necessary to consider the *social matrix* if we are to arrive at a real understanding of interpersonal communication (Berlo, 1960). General considerations about interpersonal communication do not carry us very far; we must also consider such communicating in the context of different role systems such as the family, psychotherapeutic relationships, and sociable interaction among peers. Such diverse social contexts also force us to look at different features of interpersonal communication because in different contexts different features become important.

One reason why it is important to concentrate on the "presentational" aspects of communication is because most disturbances of interpersonal communication involve these aspects. When two people have difficulty in communicating with each other, in getting through to each other, this is less often due to a failure to understand each other's representations as a failure to agree on the presentational aspects of the situation. If a husband says to his wife: "This steak is burnt again," the quarrel that ensues is not over the correctness of the information conveyed but over the implication that she is a careless cook and a poor housekeeper. She may refuse to accept the role that he seeks to impose on her. The presentational aspects of communications do not have to be validated by the person for whom they are intended. If they are not validated there is no agreement on the definition of the relationship and hence a disturbance of interpersonal communication that may manifest itself in a quarrel, a withdrawal from further communication, and so on.

The presentational aspects of communication touch people in a way that the representational aspects seldom do. For the demands implied in interpersonal communication pertain to the social identity of the communicators, a matter that is seldom a matter of indifference to them. People care about the way in which their roles are defined by others because it is difficult to maintain a self-concept that is grossly at variance with such definitions. They are sensitive to the interpersonal implications of communications because these implications indicate how they are regarded by others. In validating a particular demand they accept a particular definition of their own role and ultimately of their own self. If this definition is at variance with their self-concept, and if they want to preserve this self-concept, they must either withdraw from the relationship or refuse to validate the presentational aspects of the other's communication. In either case there is a disturbance of communication and often an emotional upset.

We must recognize that when individuals interact they are always engaged in a double exercise. Not only do they semantically represent the world about them for one another's benefit, they also present to one another those social identities that define the social order within which they move. Social messages therefore have a dual significance, mediating the relationship of the communicators both with the world and with one another.

CONCLUSION

Before one begins the systematic investigation of any area of human behavior it is advisable to achieve some clarity about the fundamental assumptions on which one's investigation depends. Obviously, all scientific investigation is based on the faith that there is some lawfulness to be discovered in the phenomena under study. If it were not so, if the events one is observing were completely unpredictable and showed no discernible regularity, then any attempt at systematic investigation would be a waste of time.

In classical physical science this lawfulness is assumed to manifest itself in the form of clearly identifiable causes and effects whose relationship is such that any given cause or set of causes predictably produces specific effects. These effects in turn may act as causes for further effects, so that one ends up with a cause–effect chain. In this linear model any link in the chain always involves clearly identifiable causes and effects.

But modern physics also knows another model of the link between causes and effects. In the case of so-called servomechanisms, like a thermostat, the effect produced by certain determining conditions acts back on these conditions and alters them. Here the relationship between causes and effects is circular rather than linear. Such circular patterns involve the principle of *feedback*. In this case the link between two events is not based on the fact that one event acts as cause and the other event acts as effect, because each event is as much the cause as the effect of the other event. If one were to assign the status of "cause" to one of these events, and the status of "effect" to the other, one would miss the essential properties of the feedback mechanism.

Psychology has taken over the linear conception of cause–effect links from classical physical science and Experimental Social Psychology has followed suit. This has had disastrous consequences for the investigation of interpersonal communication because here, if anywhere, events are linked by feedback mechanisms rather than by linear cause–effect chains. In any ongoing interaction between two individuals the acts of one are both the cause and the effect of the acts of the other. During a discussion, for example, the statements of one individual not only have an effect on the statements of other individuals but are themselves affected by the statements of the latter. The same principle applies to nonverbal communication.

The bias in favor of linear cause–effect explanation and the neglect of circular patterns of influence has profoundly affected the questions that social psychological experiments in this area are usually designed to answer. In the majority of cases such experiments represent an attempt to establish relationships between measures taken before social interaction occurs and measures taken after it has had an opportunity of making its influence felt. Investigations of this type make no attempt to study the communication process as such but content themselves with "before and after" measures of the effects of social interaction.

In the case of correlational studies the predominance of the linear, one-way influence model has frequently resulted in a misinterpretation of empirical findings. Thus correlations between child and parent variables have often been interpreted in terms of the influence that parental behavior has on the children, while the reciprocal influence that children have on parental behavior has usually been neglected.

While stressing the principle of feedback in human interaction it is important to note that the circularity of interpersonal communication can be profoundly disturbed when it takes place in certain institutional settings that favor one-way influence processes. The most important of these settings is constituted by public and private bureaucracies where influence chiefly flows downward in the hierarchy and where the opportunities for counterinfluence are severely limited by institutional constraints. It is interesting to note that social psychological experiments reflect this type of social organization because they are based on a rigid distribution of experimenter and subject roles. The experimenter is in a position of power from where he attempts to control the influences that act on the subject, while the latter is merely expected to react to these influences. Because the experiment attempts to minimize the effectiveness of subject influences on the experimenter its findings are most likely to be applicable to other institutional settings that are characterized by similar constraints on the reciprocal flow of influence. These findings are usually not relevant to social settings that allow a relatively free unfolding of circular influence processes.

In the ideal bureaucratic institution it is only power or influence that flows from the top downwards while information flows in the reverse direction. This distinction alerts us to the existence of two components in human communication that can be separated by appropriate institutional constraints but that tend to occur together in the absence of such constraints. The one component involves a transmission of information, the other involves a transmission of commands or demands. When people communicate they not only report about this or that aspect of the world, they also issue explicit or implicit demands about how they expect one another to conduct themselves. For the social psychologist it is the latter component of human communication that is of primary interest because it is this component that plays the crucial role in the initiation, development, and dissolution of interpersonal relationships.

REFERENCES

Bell, R. Q. (1968). A reinterpretation of the direction of effects in studies of socialization. *Psychol. Rev.*, **75**, 81–95.

Bell, R. Q. (1971). Stimulus control of parent or caretaker behavior by offspring. *Developmental Psychol.*, **4**, 63–72.

Berlo, D. K. (1960). *The Process of Communication*. New York: Holt, Rinehart & Winston.

Caplan, N. (1968). Treatment intervention and reciprocal interaction effects. *J. Soc. Issues*, **24**, 63–88.

Charlesworth, R. and Hartup, W. W. (1967). Positive social reinforcement in the nursery school peer group. *Child Development*, **38**, 993–1002.

Danziger, K. (1975). Power and influence in parental interaction with adolescents. (Unpublished).

Gewirtz, J. L. and Gewirtz, H. B. (1965). Stimulus conditions, infant behaviors, and social learning in four Israeli child-rearing environments: A preliminary report illustrating differences in environment and behavior between the "only" and the "youngest" child. In B. M. Foss (Ed.), *Determinants of Infant Behavior*. Vol. 3. New York: Wiley.

Krippendorff, K. (1970). On generating data in communication research. *J. Communic.*, **20**, 241–269.

Milgram, S. (1963). Behavioral study of obedience. *J. abnorm. & soc. Psychol.*, **67**, 371–378.

Piaget, J. (1960). *The Psychology of Intelligence*. Paterson, N.J.: Littlefield, Adams.

Tilker, H. A. (1970). Socially responsible behavior as a function of observer responsibility and victim feedback. *J. Personal. & soc. Psychol.*, **14**, 95–100.

Wichman, H. (1970). Effects of isolation and communication on cooperation in a two-person game. *J. Personal. & soc. Psychol.*, **16**, 114–120.

Yarrow, M. R., Campbell, J. D., and Burton, R. V. (1968). *Child Rearing: An Enquiry into Research and Methods*. San Francisco: Jossey-Bass.

Yarrow, M. R., Waxler, C. Z., and Scott, P. M. (1971). Child effects on adult behavior. *Developmental Psychol.*, **5**, 300–311.

A System for Analyzing Rhetorical Codes in Conflict Situations

INTRODUCTION

In a previous chapter it was suggested that the understanding of interpersonal communication required their functional analysis. On one level this function involves no more than an exchange of information, but more frequently it is the social relationship between the participants that is at stake. Quite apart from their apparent overt content many verbal messages carry implied claims to define the relationship between the discussants in certain ways. Two types of cases must be distinguished here. In the first type there is essential agreement about how the relationship is to be defined. For example, one partner's messages may carry the strong implication that he or she is the authority and the other partner's contributions may indicate that he accepts this claim and is quite content to play a subordinate role. This kind of pattern is to be found in the successful social performances described by Goffman and in the correct use of address systems.

But social interactions do not always run off so smoothly. A certain presentation of the self may be challenged and ambiguities in the situation may cast doubt on the exact position each individual occupies in social space. In that case verbal maneuvers may have to be resorted to for balancing out rival claims.

In order to generate a widely applicable system of classification for *language in use* (what Charles Morris called "pragmatics"), functional principles must become primary. What this means is that we must base our classification of verbal utterances on the role that they play in the social interaction within which they occur.

The notion of function implies the identification of some hypothetical end state of a system. Anything that happens in the system can then be classified on the criterion of whether it brings this end state closer to realization or not. In a social psychological system such end states may be defined in three ways: by reference to the goals of a group, to the motives of individual group members, or to the interaction process itself.

The goals of a group have the advantage of easy manipulation. It is a relatively simple matter to impose certain tasks on a laboratory or work group from the outside. We then know at least some of the goals of the group because we have created them ourselves. The task structure therefore provides us with one possible basis for criteria to be used in classifying verbal interactions. For example, we might classify utterances in terms of their promotion of orientation to the task, directions toward task solutions, and so on. There are two major limitations of this type of functional classification: First, group tasks are extremely diverse, so that functional criteria based on tasks tend to generate a plethora of classificatory schemes, each being tailored to specific circumstances rather than being designed to generate a generally applicable scheme of verbal interaction. Second, human groups have a tendency to adopt, spontaneously, tasks other than those that we seek to impose on them. Typically, the goals of these tasks differ from those defined by the investigator when he assigned the original tasks. Very often, these self-generated tasks become more important to the group than those we have requested them to carry out, and they often remain obscure to the investigator. Task functions are therefore of limited usefulness in generating a truly comprehensive classification of verbal interaction.

The statements a person makes to another may also be classified in terms of their supposed function for the satisfaction of needs of individual group members such as dominance, affection, etc. This kind of functionalism may easily lead us back to the impasse of several competing lists of human motives, each as arbitrary as the lists of human instincts that flourished in an earlier age. Moreover, the difficulties of reliably coordinating hypothetical needs with specific kinds of statements are well-nigh insuperable. These difficulties are partly the result of an absence, in most practical instances, of independent measures of these needs, and partly due to the complex overdetermination of most utterances, so that there are few statements that can be unequivocally assigned to a particular motive and no other.

A third possibility for the functional classification of utterances arises out of the nature of human discourse itself or out of the interaction process. The basic question to be asked when someone makes a statement to another person is this: Why did he speak to that person instead of remaining silent? The fundamental observation to be made about human verbal interaction is that each of its participants alternates between two states: talk and silence. Thus the first question to be asked is what determines the transition from silence to talk?

The answer we give to this question is that the individual starts talking because he seeks to produce some effect on whoever he thinks is listening to him. Here we have the essence of the pragmatic aspect of language and the basis for our principle of classification. At the most general level, the different kinds of speech can be related to the different kinds of effects that people seek to produce in one another by means of words.

We should recall the ancient discovery that in addition to the structural principles to be used in classifying linguistic forms there were other, pragmatic principles that could produce a systematic description of language in use. This discovery was expressed in the time tested distinction between two separate disciplines, concerned with the systematic study of language: grammar and rhetoric. The latter involved the analysis of language in communication, and its emphasis on the techniques of persuasion points to the similarity between its concerns and those of large areas of contemporary social psychology.

So far, no one appears to have been able to improve much on Cicero's answer to the question of why men speak to one another. The functions of speech, said the ancient rhetoritician, were threefold: to teach, to please, and to move. Perhaps we should add to this a fourth, which is to be found in Aristotle's "Rhetoric," but which Roman pride preferred to overlook: to defend oneself.

These four basic functions of human speech, to teach, to please, to move, and to defend oneself, provide the initial framework for the classification of verbal utterances in the present coding scheme. Let us examine them briefly. Men talk to one another, first, in order to inform or to teach (*docere*). Here, the function of verbal communication is simply to convey *information*. The statement is purely objective containing no personal reference. But second, men also speak in order to express their evaluation of persons and events; the social function is one of winning approval by expressing the right choice, i.e. evaluating positively that which is, objectively or by common consent, good, right and true, and evaluating negatively that which is bad, wrong, and false. Statements of *evaluation* therefore provide us with a second broad functional category.

Third, men address others in order to move them to action of some kind. In other words, they make *demands* on them, although such demands may often be no stronger than a request for information. The attempt to instigate the other to an overt action is however clear even in the case of mild demands. Finally, individuals will use language to *justify* and defend themselves and their actions, and this provides us with our fourth broad functional category.

These four major functional categories constitute the basis for the present coding scheme. For each of these categories, there are various characteristic dimensions that provide the criteria on which further, subclassifications are then made. Demands, for example, can be clearly divisible in terms of strength or urgency. Thus we may distinguish a relatively mild form of demand, called a *request*, from a strong form called a command or *imperative*. Along the same line, indirect commands can be distinguished from direct commands.

Evaluations, also, may vary along several dimensions. They may, for example, vary along the dimension of strength, and this is coded partly in terms of the certainty with which they are expressed and partly in terms of the nature of their target or object of evaluation. Approval of a person as a whole, for instance, represents a stronger evaluation than approval of one of his responses or actions. Finally, evaluations may be either positive and favorable, or negative and unfavorable.

Justificatory statements, on the other hand, can be distinguished on the basis of their cognitive level. They may simply be repetitions of earlier statements that occurred earlier in a conversation. Or, they may take the form of concrete appeals, in which case the justification relies on characteristics of a situation or event, or they may rely on abstract arguments as justificatory remarks. Finally, all statements can be classified in terms of agency, i.e. the source from which they emanate and the target at which they are directed. In the present scheme, the coding of the source and target is described only for evaluation and justification, although in principle, the same analysis can be performed for statements in all four basic functional categories.

When the subclassification of the four major functional categories is made on the basis of the dimensions described above, twenty-nine coding categories are generated. The relationship between these categories is illustrated in the coding scheme shown below (Fig. 4). The coding of a given verbal unit involves the matching of that unit with a set of category definitions. The coder scans these category definitions and then decides on the appropriate classification. The order in which categories are

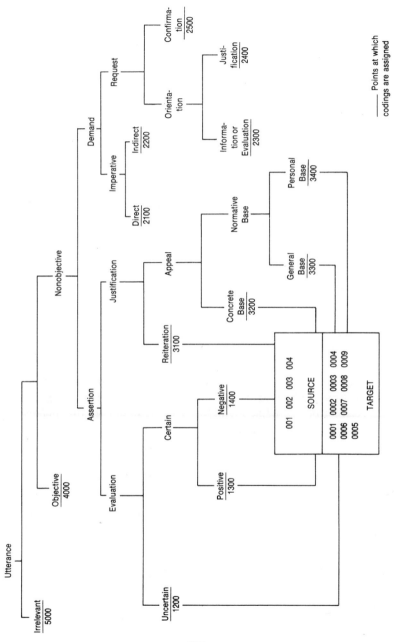

Points at which codings are assigned

197

scanned is predetermined by the procedure outlined in the coding manual. First, the coder must decide which of the four major functional categories best describes the verbal unit in question. Having selected one of these categories, the remainder of the coding process is reduced to a series of clearly identifiable binary decisions between subcategories describing the various dimensions of the four major functional categories.

This method of coding enormously simplifies the coder's task. It also makes it necessary to describe the characteristic features of each category more analytically than would otherwise have been the case. The result then is a series of very explicitly defined categories that can be applied by a coder with minimum training in coding procedures.

It is believed that coding in this way makes possible higher levels of inter-rater reliability* than would be obtained using alternative methods of coding. It is also possible, using this scheme, to pinpoint the idiosyncrasies of any particular coder during his training by comparing his decisions with those of experienced coders at each of the choice points.

The transformations of broad category descriptions into a structured sequence of specific decision rules yields a more unambiguous set of coding categories than that use in the past in similar coding systems. The hierarchical form of coding scheme employed here also increases the flexibility of the present system since further subclassifications can be added at the end of any branch without disturbing the system as a whole. Alternatively, coding may cease at any point before the end of a branch if the purpose of the research does not require any further subclassification. The present coding scheme is therefore adaptable to a large variety of research purposes, while maintaining a common core that makes possible the comparison of verbal interactions in very diverse social settings. For example, it has been possible not only to study verbal interaction in different kinds of discussion groups, but also to compare the nature of verbal interaction in such groups with that observed among parents and their children.

*The categories outlined above can be distinguished with fairly high reliability. The index of inter-coder agreement for nominal-scale judgments (Scott and Wertheimer, 1962) is 0.83 for protocols of English-speaking nine- and ten-year-old children and their mothers, and 0.82 for protocols of Italian-speaking nine- and ten-year-old children and their mothers. For each sample, two coders independently rated the protocols according to the present scheme.

USING THE CODING SCHEME

The scheme may be used to analyze a variety of psychological correlates of communication. So far, the scheme has been used successfully to analyze the discussions between mother and child as well as the discussions in groups consisting of four and five members. By means of the coding system presented here it is possible, for example, to specify the manner in which mother and child control each other's behavior. It is also possible to establish differential patterns of communication existing among mother–child pairs.

For the most part, all of the categories may be used to analyze most kinds of discussions. At times, however, it is possible to eliminate completely the analysis of the source and target used in statements labeled justification. For example, when the discussion involves decision making in an experimental task where the goal of the discussion is simply that of choosing one response, there is little information to be gained from specifying the source and target of a justification. When, however, the nature of the discussion is less action-oriented and involves theoretical arguments supporting a discussant's position on a particular issue, a valuable source of data may be found in the content of justification used. Here it is useful to specify the source and target of the justification. In this way it is possible to relate the nature of the justification used to various other variables such as the nature of the issue discussed, individual difference variables of the discussant, and patterns of dominance and control.

There are two basic tasks involved in using the present scheme. The first involves dividing the written protocols into units. The unit for analysis here is the *utterance*. The utterance is defined as a bit of speech by one person in a conversation. An utterance may be either an independent clause, a dependent clause occurring after an interruption, a single word, or a combination of words without a subject and predicate. An utterance should be a meaningful unit expressing a single idea. The conversation can be divided into utterances according to the rules set down in Part I of the coding scheme. The second task involves assigning each utterance to one of the categories described in Part II of the coding scheme. Each utterance is assigned a number consisting of four digits. The first digit indicates the general category to which the utterance belongs. The second digit shows the appropriate subcategory.

category. The third digit indicates the source of the utterance and the fourth digit, the target of the utterance, where applicable.

PART I

Instructions to Coders: Analyzing Conversations into Utterances

When people talk, they divide what they have to say into units. A unit of a conversation is an utterance. An utterance is a bit of speech by one person in a conversation. One person may make several utterances in a short period of time. You should classify a group of words into several utterances if it is apparent to you that one part of the group of words was part of a different meaningful unit, and accomplished a different purpose in the conversation than another part of a group of words.

Utterances are marked off:

> "How are you?"/
> "Fine."/
> "I bought a new car yesterday./ It was a beauty."/
> "Did you see her before she left?/ She was supposed to give me some money."/

1. *Clauses*

An utterance is an independent clause, standing by itself or occurring *along with* one or more dependent clauses.

1a. An *independent* clause can be distinguished from a dependent clause by the fact that when two independent clauses are connected, the second may be introduced by a coordinating conjunction or a conjunctive adverb such as: and, but, or, because, so that, for.

A *dependent* clause is a statement that is introduced by subordinating conjunctions or by pronouns such as: who, which, that, if, and when.

Utterances are marked off:

> "I chose this one/ because I liked it."/
> "But why did you choose that when it's wrong."/
> "This is the one that I think is right."/
> "You chose that one/ and I chose this."/
> "She sits/ and talks to him."/

1b. An utterance is an independent clause *occurring along* with a dependent clause even when a different utterance separates the independent from the dependent clause. In this case, the dependent clause must elaborate or explain the previously occurring independent clause.

Utterances are marked off:

M: "I chose this one."/
C: "Uhm"/
M: "When she showed them to me."/
("I chose this one when she showed them to me," is counted as one utterance.)
C: "His father told him to do his homework."/
M: "Uhm."/
C: "When he was finished bathing the dog."/
("His father told him to do his homework when he was finished bathing the dog," is one utterance.)

2. *False Starts*

A false start or a group of words that does not convey the speaker's meaning is not counted as an utterance.

Examples of false starts:

"Well, eh......I......"
"It's......uh......I think......"
"Let's see......uh......"

3. *Interruptions*

3a. If one independent clause is interrupted by another independent clause (either by the speaker or the listener), each is scored as a separate utterance.

Utterances are marked off:

"I thought you picked number three./ Number five looks better to me."/
"This one isn't right./ I picked that one."

3b. A dependent clause *itself* may be an utterance if it occurs after an interruption that is preceded by a nonutterance. In this case, only the dependent clause is scored as an utterance, although the speaker's meaning is conveyed through the nonutterance *occurring along* with the dependent clause.

Utterances are italicized:

> M: "Well ...... uh ...... this is ......"
> C: "What?"
> M: *"that I chose"*
> ("that I chose," is scored as an utterance.)
> C: " ...... it's ...... here."
> M: "Eh?"
> C: *"where his father read him a story."*
> ("where his father read him a story" is scored as an utterance.)

4. Repetitions

4a. An utterance may be repeated. If exactly the same utterance is repeated, verbatim, and it is said with the same intonation, it is not scored the second time provided that there are no utterances preceding its repetition.

Utterances are italicized:

> *"This is the right one ./* This is the right one."
> (The second time, the same utterance is said with the same intonation used the first time.)
> *"We chose this one./ We chose this one?"/*
> (Two utterances here since the second time it is said, a rising intonation is used.)

4b. If an utterance is repeated, the second time it occurs it is scored as a different utterance if one of the following conditions is present:

(a) One or more words are omitted the second time.
(b) One or more words are different the second time.
(c) The second time the utterance occurs, it is preceded by a different utterance.

Utterances are italicized:

> *"Number three looks good to me./ Number three looks good."/*
> *"That can't be right./ That one isn't right."*
> *"This one is right./ Number five looks good./ This one is right."/*

5. Single Words

An utterance may be a single word (or a combination of words) without a subject and predicate as long as the meaning is clear. You should classify single words (or a combination of words) as an utterance only if they seem to be used as full units of conversation by the speaker.

Examples of single words (or combination of words) that are utterances:

"What?"
"O.K."
"Uh-huh."
"Good."
"No."
"Want this one?"
"Have to decide now."

6. *Affirmation, Negation, and Confirmation*

6a. Affirmations and negations are utterances if they are single words or a combination of words.

Utterances are italicized:

"Yes."
"That's right."
"You're not right."
"No."

6b. Affirmations and negations are not counted as separate utterances if the speaker goes on to explain or amplify.

Utterances are italicized:

"Yes, I chose that one."
(This group of words is counted as one utterance.)
"No, that's not the right one."
(This group of words is counted as one utterance.)

6c. If, however, the affirmation or negation stands alone, i.e. if the group of words following the affirmation or negation does not amplify or explain the preceding word, it is counted as a separate utterance.

Utterances are italicized:

Q: "You chose that one, did you?"
A: *"Yes./ Let's look at the next story."*
(Two utterances are counted here.)
Q: "You didn't like that one?"
A: *"No./ Which one did you choose?"/*
(Two utterances are counted here.)

6d. Phrases like "isn't it," "I guess," "didn't you," etc. are confirmation requests that are often added onto a statement. These phrases are not considered separate utterances from the statement that they follow.

Utterances are italicized:

> *"This is the right one, isn't it?"*
> *"You chose this one, didn't you?"*
> *"This one would be good, I guess."*

PART II

Decide first whether the utterance is *relevant* or *irrelevant*.

From your knowledge of the experimental procedure, decide whether the utterance is *relevant* to the task as defined by the experimental instructions. Conversation about the experimenter or his assistant, or about the setting of the experiment is *not* relevant to the task defined. Similarly, talk about parts of the study other than the present task is not considered relevant, unless it is explicitly used to justify a response to the task in hand.

Often facts, opinions, or feelings not directly relevant to the task are brought into a conversation to justify some position of the speaker's that is related *to* the task. For instance, to justify a particular choice made, a parent may refer to a tradition of similar decisions in the family. Such a reference would be considered *relevant* to the task since it is used to justify a position of the parent vis-à-vis the task.

When the task is defined as the discussion of some social issue, or personal or moral dilemma, any utterance related to the issue should be regarded as relevant. Thus an evaluation of some agent involved in the issue would be regarded as relevant even if the basis of the evaluation is not related to the issue.

For example, in a discussion concerning civil rights, the statement:

> "Senator X has acne, and lisps."

would be considered as relevant.

To be relevant, an utterance must be related to some aspect of the task or issue. The coder is not required to make any judgment concerning the utility or value of the utterance relative to the completion of the task.

Irrelevant utterances most often occur where there is a clean break in the flow of conversation. They often occur as deliberate changes of topic or interruptions.

In summary, the persons whose utterances are being coded are expected to take the *role* of subjects. If their utterances are *consistent* with that role, they are *relevant*; if they are *inconsistent* with that role, they are *irrelevant*.

Examples of irrelevant utterances are italicized:

"What are we having for lunch to-day?"
"Why are you wearing that guck on your face?"
"When do we get out of here?"
"It's a nice day."
"We're playing ball after school."

Now decide whether the utterance you are coding is relevant or irrelevant.

If the utterance is irrelevant code it 5000. You have finished coding it. Now start coding the next utterance.

Now decide whether the utterance is *objective* or *nonobjective*.

A relevant utterance may be quite *objective* in character, conveying some neutral item of information about the external world and nothing else. The ideal case of such an utterance would be the statement of a physical law in response to a specific enquiry about it.

In the experimental situation certain kinds of objective utterances are encountered. For instance, reading part of the stimulus material aloud, and adding nothing, represents such a case. Also, describing the stimulus material without any attempt at interpretation or justification would be regarded as objective in this sense:

"These are plastic."
"A boy is talking."
"It's a tea towel."
"He is looking at her."
"The building cost fifty thousand to erect."
"A cease-fire was declared yesterday."

However, as soon as the description involves an interpretation or justification, e.g. "it might be," or "it looks like," it is no longer purely objective but tells us something about the speaker as well and it is *nonobjective*.

Quite commonly, an objective utterance will follow a request for information, and this is a useful contextual clue, but sometimes neutral information is volunteered without prior question. "Does Joan have the equipment?" "Yes she has it." Here, the answer to the question would fall into the objective category.

An objective utterance may sometimes be a statement recalling in a purely nonevaluative way something that happened or something that was said earlier. For example, the statement, "I chose that one" in response to the question "Which one did you choose?", would be scored as objective. Similarly, a repetition of a previous statement, without altering its meaning, is coded as "objective," provided it follows a request for such repetition.

An objective utterance should contain no expression of doubt or uncertainty, nor should it refer to a subjective state of the speaker. The utterance refers to an external fact, but of course the speaker must be in a position to know the fact.

Any description of objects in terms that imply an evaluation is nonobjective. Adjectives like "useful" or "pretty" would be in this category.

Now decide whether the utterance you are coding is objective or nonobjective.

If the utterance is objective assign to it a code of 4000. Now start coding the next utterance.

If the utterance is no objective decide whether it is a *demand* or an *assertion.*

A *demand* requires some response from the person spoken to. I can demand that you do something, ask that you do something, or demand or ask that you say something. All questions, commands, and other utterances that place requirements on those spoken to should be considered demands.

Examples of demands:

> "When are you coming home?"
> "Come home."
> "Would you come home please?"
> "Is this OK with you?"
> "Please make up your mind."
> "Put it there."
> "This one goes here."
> ".... don't you think?"
> "When did they do that?"

An *assertion* does not require a response of any kind from those spoken to. An assertion may be an expression of opinion, fact, or feeling on the part of the speaker. It may provide information to those spoken to, it may express the speaker's evaluation of the subject under discussion, the discussion itself, or those engaged in the conversation, including the speaker.

Examples of assertions:

"That's okay"
"I really think the boy's leaving the house."
"You're wrong."
"Yeah."
"If you do that I'll leave."
"I'm gonna choose this one."

If the utterance is a demand go to p. 210.

If the utterance is an assertion decide whether it is an *evaluation* or a *justification*.

An evaluation is any utterance that refers to a person's choice, his likes or dislikes, his expression of approval or disapproval, his preference, or any expression of uncertainty or indecision.

A justification is an utterance that attempts to justify any nonobjective response. The nonobjective response that is justified may be explicit or implicit.

Evaluations

(1) Evaluations are readily reduced to the form

SOURCE—EVALUATION—TARGET

The *source* is the person making the judgment or evaluation. The *target* is a person, object, situation, or action that is being evaluated.

(2) As implied above, the source of the evaluation is not necessarily the person making the utterance, although this will often be so.

(3) While evaluations always imply some scale of "goodness" or "rightness" on which the target is placed, the syntactical form in which they are expressed may vary. Thus evaluations may be expressed by use of pejorative nouns like "fools," "bastards," and "niggers." They may be expressed by verbs such as "like," "prefer," "choose," which establish positive or negative preference on the part of the source. Value-loaded adjectives and adverbs like "wrong," "beautiful," "efficiently," and "badly" may also express the evaluative relation between source and target. In addition, monomorphemic utterances like "right," "sure," "wrong," and "O.K.," often imply evaluation of the target.

Examples of evaluation:

"This is mine."
"Yours is number two."
"I like this one."
"That wasn't yours."
"I picked number three."
"I don't like yours."
"You chose that."
"Yes."
"Correct."
"No."
"I'm not so sure."
"I don't know."
"Maybe."
"Good."
"They hate the others."
"They are dirty."
"They didn't even . . . ."
"The swine!"
"That's a hard one."

Justifications

(1) A justification is an utterance that attempts to provide reasons that render an act or response more creditable or less discreditable. The act or response may have been emitted by the speaker, or by some other person.

Utterances that are introduced by connectives such as "but," "because," "so," "well," "if," or "therefore" are usually justifications.

Examples of justifications introduced by connectives:

"Because it is physically impossible."
"But she's too young."
"But that's what we always do."
"But she could not be doing that."
"Well she's wearing a hat."

On the other hand, the following utterances, introduced by connectives, would not be counted justifications:

"But you just said something different."
"If it rains it will be wet."

(2) The nonobjective response that is justified does not itself need to have been stated explicitly. For example, the statement:

"There aren't enough hospitals because there are too many people."

should be considered a justification of the lack of action by those responsible for providing hospitals.

(3) A justification may be an utterance expressing a preference, choice, or opinion that is introduced by a connective such as "but," "because," "so," "well," "if," or "therefore," etc.

Examples of justification:

"Because I need it."
"But I like it."
"Well I chose it."
"Because I wanted it."

(4) A justification may be an utterance expressing a preference, choice or opinion that is *not* introduced by a connective and that is preceded by a question. This type of justification frequently functions to justify a nonobjective response, i.e. an evaluation or a demand.

Examples of justification are italicized:

Q: "Why did you choose that?"
A: "*I like it.*"
Q: "Why the record?"
A: "*I like it.*"
Q: "Why did you pick number three?"
A: "*It's the right one.*"

(5) Often an utterance may serve two functions at the same time. It may serve as an evaluation as well as a justification. When this occurs it is necessary for the coder to use contextual evidence to decide which of the two functions is the primary one. For example,

"You chose that one *because you are so lazy.*"

may be a justification of the speaker's displeasure at the choice made. Similarly,

"The Government cannot do any more, since the Africans are too lazy to help themselves."

implies an evaluation of the Africans, but the main purpose of the statement implies justification of the Government's inaction.

Apply the following tests to every assertive utterance to decide on its classification as an *evaluation* or a *justification*:

1. Does it contain a word that clearly expresses an *evaluation*? If it does not, it cannot be an evaluation.
2. Does the context suggest that the speaker is simply expressing a preference, a rejection, or an uncertainty without justifying a nonobjective response? If so, it is probably an *evaluation*.
3. Is the utterance preceded by a connective? If it is, it is probably a *justification*.
4. Does the context suggest that the speaker is actually justifying a previous judgment or demand? If so, it is probably a *justification*.

Now decide whether the utterance you are coding is an evaluation or a justification.

If the utterance is a justification go to subcategories, p. 214.
If the utterance is an evaluation go to subcategories, p. 217.

Demands

Decide whether the utterance you are coding is an *imperative* or a *request*.

If one speaker orders or tells another what to do, the utterance is an *imperative*. An imperative can be phrased as a question. In such cases one must depend on context to determine whether a particular question is a request or an imperative.

Examples of imperatives:

"I hope you're satisfied now."
"Give me the pencil."
"Go over there."
"Let's finish up."
"I don't want to make up your mind."
"You must admit that . . .."

Utterances phrased as questions can sometimes be interpreted as imperatives. Such utterances are usually differentiated from requests by virtue of their omission of qualifiers such as "would you mind . . ." or "please." Examples of such utterances might be:

"Will you close that window?"
"Are you going to stop doing that?"

If one speaker asks another for information, opinion, or justification his utterance is a *request*. Requests are almost always in question form. Not all utterances in question form, however, can be best interpreted as requests. Be careful that you do not automatically decide an utterance is a request just because it is in question form. A question can in some contexts be considered an assertion, and in others an imperative.

Examples of requests:

"Are you ready to go?"
"Are you sure you're right?" (Under certain circumstances should be interpreted as an assertion, depending on context.)
"Which picture is the one you chose?"
"Have you decided yet?"
"Okay?"

Now decide whether the utterance you are coding is a request or an imperative.

If the utterance is an imperative continue straight on.

Go to p. 212 if the utterance is a request.

Now decide whether the utterance is a *direct imperative* or an *indirect imperative*.

A *direct imperative* unconditionally orders a person to do something. Direct imperatives are usually in the form of imperatives or questions.

Examples of direct imperatives:

"Give me that."
"Would you please turn it around."
"Choose that one."
"Don't do that."
"Let's hurry up."
"Please get on with it."
"Would you please hand me that one."
"You can't say that."

An *indirect imperative* either indirectly or conditionally orders a person to do something. For example, "Take that one" is a direct imperative. However, "If you feel you want that one, then take it" is an indirect imperative since the direction given is conditional on the listener's feelings. Indirect imperatives are frequently in the form of assertions. Although they may not consist of imperatives, the implication of these statements is an indirect imperative.

Examples of indirect imperatives:

"I don't want to make up your mind."
  (The implication is "make up your mind".)
"Well, I've done my part."
  (The implication is "do your part now".)
"I hope you're satisfied now."
  (The implication is "be satisfied".)
"If that what you said, take yours."
  (The directive is conditional on what the listener said.)
"If we have to take one, take mine."
  (The directive is conditional on what the speaker and listener have to do.)

Now decide whether the utterance you are coding is a direct or an indirect imperative. If it is a direct imperative assign a coding of 2100. If it is an indirect imperative assign a coding of 2200. You have finished coding this utterance.

Requests

Decide whether the utterance is a request for *confirmation* or a request for *orientation*.

An utterance is a request for *confirmation* if the speaker requests directly or indirectly, confirmation of a response that was previously made. A confirmation request must contain an explicit reference to a response that was previously made. Confirmation may be requested for a response that was made either by the speaker or the listener. A request for confirmation does not request justification for a response. There are two types of confirmation requests: One type is found purely in the form of a question, such as "Don't you think this is right?" and "Isn't this so?". Another type of confirmation request is found in utterances containing tag phrases such as "Is it?," "Doesn't it?," etc. These questions are confirmation requests as long as they contain tag phrases such as those mentioned above.

Examples of confirmation requests: In all of the following cases the whole utterance is scored as a confirmation request.

"Don't you think this is right?"
"You chose this one, didn't you."
"That's not the right answer, is it?"
"It's alright with you, isn't it?"
"I don't think I was wrong, do you?"

"I don't think I chose that one, you know?"
"This one, you know, could be right."

An utterance is a request for *orientation* if it is not a request specifically for confirmation. A request for orientation may inquire into the feelings of the listener, the nature of the task material or facts about the speaker, etc.

Examples of requests for orientation:

"Do you want that one?"
"How do you know?"
"What, that one?"
"Really?"
"What's this one for?"
"Is it any good?"
"What do you think of that?"
"Is it true?"
"Why did they do that?"

Now decide whether the utterance you are coding is a request for confirmation or a request for orientation.

If it is a request for confirmation assign a coding of 2500. You have finished coding this utterance. Go on to the next utterance. If it is a request for orientation go straight on.

Now decide whether the utterance you are coding is a request for *evaluation or information*, or a request for *justification* (reasons).

A *request for information or evaluation* is a request for either facts or evaluation about either the stimulus material or about a response made by either the listener or the speaker. A request for information or evaluation does *not* request justification or reasons for a response.

Examples of requests for information or evaluation:

"You want to take that one?"
"Which one do you think it is?"
"Could it be that one?"
"Do you see it my way?"
"What would you like?"
"You're satisfied?"
"Would you be happy?"
"What's this for?"
"Did you see that one?"
"How much did they spend?"
"Could they be doing any more than they are?"
"Is it true that . . .?"

A request for *justification* requests the listener to justify any nonobjective response or offers reasons for his response. Requests for justification frequently begin with interrogatives such as "why," "but," etc., and words such as "really." Often a request for justification must be inferred from the context.

Examples of requests for justification:

"Why did you let me take that?"
"Why did you change your mind?"
"But where are you going to play it?"
"But would everybody enjoy it?"
"Do you really think he wants to help?"
"Really?"
"How do you know?"
"Why not this one?"
"Won't you explain that?"
"How can you say that?"

The speaker may also be asked to justify the behavior or responses of others whom he has been defending, or is otherwise identified with, e.g. "Why then wait for (your friends) the Government to act on this issue?"

Now decide whether the utterance you are coding is a request for evaluation or information, or a request for justification.

If it is a request for evaluation or information assign a coding of 2300. If it is a request for justification assign a coding of 2400. You have finished coding this utterance. Go on to the next utterance.

Justification: subcategories

Decide whether the utterance you are coding is a *reiteration* or an *appeal*.

If the utterance is a *reiteration*, the speaker justifies thoughts, opinions, feelings, or actions merely by asserting or reasserting that the person justified has these thoughts, opinions, or feelings, or has already performed the act. For instance, if a child, asked to explain why he chooses one toy instead of another, asserts that he "likes" the toy chosen, or says that he thinks the toy is "nice" or "great," or says that he "wants" that toy more than the others, he has not said anything new, but has simply reiterated his choice. If on the other hand a reason is provided for the choice, and this reason is more specific than the simple reiteration of the original expression of preference, then a justification is being offered that goes beyond reiteration. In the example, if the child explains that he needs the toy for his collection, or says that anyone in his right senses would make the same choice, he is making an appeal that goes beyond reiteration of his initial choice.

Examples of reiteration are italicized:

"I chose it *because I like it*."
"I want it *because it's nice*."
"*But it's fun*."
"It's this one *because I chose it*."
"*But they've done it now*, so why complain?"

If the utterance is an *appeal*, the speaker justifies his thoughts, opinions, or feelings by something else besides mere reiteration of his preference. He may appeal to norms, his own feelings, common experience, or status differences between speaker and listener.

Examples of appeals are italicized:

"*That's what any self-respecting person would do*."
"*But he's too small to go there*."
"*That's the way we always do it*."
"*. . . . but you should wear a hat if you're going to church*."
"*It is natural to want to stay on top*."

Now decide whether the utterance you are coding is an appeal or a reiteration.

If the utterance is a reiteration code it 3100 and go to p. 219, "Source and Target".
Go straight on if the utterance is an appeal.

Now decide whether the utterance you are coding is *concrete* appeal or *normative* appeal.

A *concrete* appeal justifies a person's ideas or opinions by directing the listener's attention to the characteristics of the situation or nature of the material that the person is responding to. For example, an object's specific usefulness around the house may be used to justify the speaker's preference for that particular object.

Where description of the characteristics of an event, situation or object is offered as a justification for some response to that event, situation or object, this will usually be a concrete appeal.

Examples of concrete appeal are italicized:

"*. . . . look how he's holding it*."
"*. . . . see what he's doing*."
"*We can use it around the house*."

"But the kids will have fun playing with it."
"But we need it."
"He's holding her hand, though."
"They're outside."
"Well, that's what he said."
"Because it's made of leather."
"Our country isn't in such a financially good shape now."
"Digging ditches, you can make enough money to get through."

A *normative* appeal justifies the speaker's ideas or opinions by directing the listener's attention to norms or rules that are either based on the speaker's (listener's) personal characteristics, or are more general prescriptions.

Examples of normative appeals are italicized:

". . . . because that's the way we always do it."
". . . . but that's the way we are."
". . . . boys don't always help around the house."
"He should do that because his mother asked him."
"He's too big to be playing with that toy."

Now decide whether the utterance you are coding is concrete appeal or normative appeal.

If it is concrete appeal code it 3200 and go to p. 219, "Source and Target".

If it is normative appeal go straight on.

Now decide whether the utterance is a *general* normative appeal or *personal* normative appeal.

An appeal that is *general* normative justifies a speaker's ideas or opinions by directing the listener's attention to general precedents or norms of behavior that are based on characteristics such as age, sex, kinship, nationality, etc. Such status differences are not easily changed by efforts of those who possess them.

Examples of general normative appeal:

"But, fathers go to work every day."
"Little girls don't go shopping alone."
"Children shouldn't stay up so late."
"Mothers are supposed to help their children."
"One should not oppress the weak."
"But in a family that has triplets . . . ."
"The middle-class person always hears about bursaries."

An appeal that is *personal* normative justifies a speaker's ideas or opinions by directing the listener's attention to precedents or regularities of behavior that are based on the speaker's (listener's) personal experience.

Examples of personal normative appeal:

> "But we always do that on Sunday."
> "Daddy usually reads to you."
> "You always helped with spring cleaning."
> "We aren't like that though."
> "We usually try to help with your school work."

Now decide whether the utterance is general normative or personal normative appeal.

> If the utterance is general normative code it 3300 and go to p. 219, "Source and Target".
> If it is a personal normative appeal code it 3400 and go to p. 219, "Source and Target".

Evaluation: subcategories

Decide whether the utterance is a *certain evaluation* or an *uncertain evaluation.*

A *certain evaluation* is a statement that refers to a person's choice, his likes or dislikes, or his expression of approval or disapproval. Either positive or negative evaluation is always implied in a certain evaluation. Statements describing the self are evaluations. For example, "I am very good at this sort of thing" is a description of the self and is classed as an evaluation. Further, statements of the speaker's or of the listener's intentions are also classified as evaluation. For example, "I am going to do the dishes when I get home" is a statement of the speaker's intended action, and is classified as an evaluation. There is no uncertainty or indecision expressed in a certain evaluation.

Examples of certain evaluation:

> "This is mine."
> "Yours is wrong."
> "I like number two."
> "I picked number four."
> "You aren't right."
> "They are clever."

An *uncertain evaluation* is a statement in which the speaker expresses indecision or uncertainty about his (or the listener's) choice or his opinions. Uncertain evaluations may also express doubts about the correctness of an opinion or a response choice. Uncertain evaluations are usually statements about the speaker's (listener's) response in the decision-making process itself. Statements such as "I don't know" and "I'm not sure" are examples of uncertain evaluations since the speaker is expressing indecision about his choice.

Sometimes a statement of uncertainty indicates a negative evaluation. This is usually clear from the intonation. Such statements are, of course, classified as negative evaluation. For example, "Maybe you're right, but . . . ." is *not* classified as an uncertain evaluation since the implication of the statement is that the listener is probably wrong. However, the statement "It's just a guess" is an uncertain evaluation since the speaker is simply expressing uncertainty about the correctness of his response and he does not imply that he has failed to get the correct one.

Examples of uncertain evaluation:

"I don't know."
"Maybe."
"It's just a guess."
"Could be."
"You may be right."
(This is uncertain evaluation since the implication is *also* that you may be wrong.)
"Either one of us may be right."
"I think that may be so."

Now decide whether the utterance is certain evaluation or uncertain evaluation.

If the utterance is uncertain evaluation code it 1200 and to to p. 219, "Source and Target".
If the utterance is certain evaluation go straight on.

Now decide whether the utterance is *positive evaluation* or *negative evaluation*.

Positive evaluation is an evaluation that is favorable, pleasant, desirable, correct, or expresses the achievement of success. In an experimental situation the ability to come to an agreement might imply the achievement of success. Therefore, the utterance "looks like we both agree," for example, would be positive evaluation. Any utterance consisting of verbs such as "pick," "choose," "is," etc. underline the speaker's (listener's) choice and is therefore positive evaluation.

Examples of positive evaluation:

> "This is fun."
> "I like doing this."
> "I think you're right."
> "Yes."
> "Correct."
> "I picked this one."
> "You chose number two."
> "We agree on this one."
> "They made a good job of it."

Negative evaluation is an evaluation that is unfavorable, unpleasant, incorrect, or expresses failure. In an experimental situation the inability to come to an agreement may imply failure. For example, the utterance "Looks like we don't agree" is negative evaluation. There may be utterances that appear to express uncertainty but that by their intonation imply negative evaluation. For example, the utterance "You aren't always right, you know" implies that the listener is wrong and is therefore negative evaluation. Any utterance that suggests that the speaker (listener) was unable to choose the correct alternative is negative evaluation. For example, "I couldn't get this one" is negative evaluation of the speaker's own response.

Examples of negative evaluation:

> "I don't like this."
> "This is no fun."
> "You're wrong."
> "Stupid."
> "No."
> "You don't know what you're talking about."
> "Maybe you're right, but . . . ."
> "It is a frightening situation."
> "You think you're always right."
> "I don't know what you're talking about."
> "Mine is probably wrong."

Now decide whether the utterance you are coding is positive evaluation or negative evaluation.

If the utterance is a positive evaluation code it 1300 and continue straight on.

If it is a negative evaluation code it 1400 and continue straight on.

Source and Target

Now decide what are the *source* and *target* of the utterance. Both evaluations and justifications can be reduced to the form

SOURCE—EVALUATION—TARGET

OR

SOURCE—JUSTIFICATION—TARGET

The source is the person making the evaluation or justification. The target is the person/object/situation evaluated or justified.

Source: The source of the evaluation or justification may be in one of four categories,

"I," "WE," "YOU," "THEY."

"I"   This category should be coded when the source and the speaker are identical. Thus the statements:

"I like X."

"X is good."

are both examples of utterances in which the source is "I." In the second example the source is implicit in the statement. There is no need for the source to be named explicitly in the utterance.

"WE"   The source is coded as "WE" in two cases:

(a) Where the speaker is referring to the collective people at present in interaction, and including himself, e.g.

"*We* both like that one."

(b) Where the speaker is referring to the collectivity at present in interaction, including himself, *as well as* a wider group of which the present collectivity forms a subset, e.g.

"*We whites* fear the Negro."

"*We* wouldn't do a thing like that."

In the second example "WE" might implicitly refer to the set "decent law-abiding citizens," a subset of which is formed by the persons presently interacting.

"YOU"   The source is coded as "YOU" when the speaker is asserting that one (or more) member(s) of the collectivity at present in interaction has expressed or manifested some evaluation or justification, but does *not* include himself (the speaker) as having expressed the evaluation or justification. As in the second example given below, "YOU" may be expanded to include a larger set of people of whom one or more members of the present group form a subset.

"You like this one."

"You whites fear Negroes."

"THEY"   The source is coded as "THEY" when the person or group who, it is asserted, have expressed the evaluation or justification are *not* members of the presently interacting group. Two examples follow:

"*The Government* says it hasn't any money to build new universities."

"*Your father* is angry with you."

Note: Some confusion may arise in coding the source of the evaluation or justification, when a speaker refers to one of the members of the interacting group as "He," or mentions him by name to a third party. For example, a speaker may say "John, Paul has just said that he prefers the pink one." In this case Paul is clearly the source. Since Paul is in the presence of the speaker, the source should be coded as "You," in strict accordance with the rules.

If the source is
"I"   ADD   001 to the coding
"WE"   002 to the coding
"YOU"   003 to the coding
"THEY"   004 to the coding

Target: (a) If the target is a person, a group of persons, an object, a situation, or an event, it should be classified in one of four categories:

"I," "WE," YOU," "THEY/IT."

Examples illustrating each of the four categories follow:

"She loves me." (Target is "I.")

"We're a bright bunch." (Target is "WE.")

"This war is a tragedy." (Target is "THEY/IT.")

"He admires you." (Target is "YOU.")
"I choose this one." (Target is "THEY/IT.")
"You don't like them." (Target is "THEY/IT.")

(b) If the target is an action or action tendency (policy, intention), it is classified in terms of the person or persons to whom the action is attributed. Four categories are used, as before:

"I," "WE," "YOU," "THEY/IT."

Examples of actions in each of the four categories follow:

"Yours is correct." (Target is an action performed by "YOU.")
"I don't like the one you chose." (Target is an action performed by "YOU.")
"I still choose this one." (Target is an action performed by "I.")
M: "I think it's number four."
C: "Yes." (Target is an action performed by "YOU.")
M: "Do you approve of the government's policy?"
C: "Yes." (Target is an action performed by "THEY/IT.")

Now code the target:

If the target is
"I"   ADD   0001 to the coding
"WE"   0002 to the coding
"YOU"   0003 to the coding
"THEY/IT"   0004 to the coding

and

If the *target* is an action or action tendency attributed to
"I"   ADD   0006 to the coding
"WE"   0007 to the coding
"YOU"   0008 to the coding
"THEY/IT"   0009 to the coding

For certain purposes it may be important to distinguish between "THEY/IT" targets in general and "THEY/IT" targets constituted specifically by certain materials peculiar to the experimental task situation. In that case the code number 0005 may be used to refer to task-related materials.

APPLICATIONS OF THE CODING SCHEME

The development of coding schemes for the study of interpersonal communication has not been easy. Some investigators have simply sidestepped the whole issue by avoiding the direct analysis of ongoing interaction and either interviewing the participants *after* the interaction episode is all over, or else presenting subjects with hypothetical situations and asking them how they think they would deal with them. Needless to say, such indirect approaches add little to our knowledge of the actual process of interpersonal communication. At best they give us a measure of attitudes, and unfortunately such attitudes are so heavily influenced by wishful thinking, defensiveness, and social desirability that they may have little or nothing to do with what actually happens during the interaction. In any case the process of interpersonal communication and attitudes about that process belong to two entirely different psychological levels, and deductions from the one to the other lack either theoretical or practical foundation.

Various attempts have therefore been made to develop coding schemes that will enable us to analyze the interaction process as it occurs. Two kinds of coding schemes are to be found in the relevant research literature. In the one case the investigator is sharply focused on a particular interaction situation, and the categories of his coding scheme are carefully tailored to suit his special interests. Such interests might involve the analysis of mothers' communication with mental retardates (Kogan, Wimberger, and Bobbitt, 1969), interaction in the classroom (Amidon and Flanders, 1967), the antecedents of distractibility in children of a certain age range (Bee, 1967), power relationships in young children (Gellert, 1961), peer group sociability (Watson and Potter, 1962), etc. The number of interaction codes produced by this approach is potentially almost infinite. This is a pretty anarchic way of proceeding, for the different coding schemes tend not to be comparable with one another. It is obvious that this is not the way we are ever likely to arrive at generalizations about interpersonal communication that will have some validity for different interaction situations.

The second type of coding scheme developed in this context seeks to overcome the limitation of the first type by using rather broad, global categories that can be meaningfully employed in a great variety of situations. This can lead to the multiplication of such a large number of complex categories that the practical training of coders and the achievement of acceptable levels of reliability become major obstacles to the widespread applicability of the scheme (Moustakas, Sigel, and Schalock, 1956).

By far the most popular coding scheme in the analysis of social interaction has been Bales' Interaction Process Analysis (Bales, 1950). The IPA instrument involves twelve global categories, like "shows solidarity," "gives orientation," "shows tension release," etc. It is strong precisely where specifically focused coding schemes are weak, because it is readily applicable to a wide variety of situations. However, it suffers from severe limitations of its own.

The very global nature of the categories blurs too many vital distinctions and lumps together too many aspects of the interactive process that ought to remain distinct. For example, there is no attempt to distinguish between the contribution of different channels to the final categorization that is performed intuitively taking both verbal and various nonverbal components into account. This leads to characteristic reliability problems. Large differences in the frequency of various categories occur according to whether judgments of the same interaction episode are based only on typed protocols or whether the coder also uses a live recording of the interaction (Waxler and Mishler, 1966). Eliminating the latter eliminates paralinguistic cues, so that verbal content becomes the sole basis of judgment. Although IPA really becomes a different instrument when nonverbal cues are not available too many applications of the instrument have failed to make this vital distinction. Quite apart from the appearance of this ambiguity in the Bales system, attempts at developing a coding scheme that addresses itself specifically to modes of interaction of verbal and nonverbal channels have been quite rare. The coding scheme of Kogan and Wimberger (1966) represents a promising start in this direction.

Some other limitations of the Bales IPA technique have been the subject of revisions that have spawned derivative systems. For example, Leik (1963) noticed that the original twelve IPA categories were based on a mixture of instrumental and emotional dimensions. Accordingly, he cross-classified these dimensions and emerged with six categories that allow each act to be coded for both aspects.

Another source of dissatisfaction with the original Bales system stems from the fact that the classification of communicative acts is purely formal and leaves no room for judgments of intensity. This leads to the collection of very diverse acts in a single coding category. A category like "gives opinion," for instance, will contain everything from the mildest most hesitant statement to the most intense and emphatic claim. In an attempt to remedy this state of affairs Borgatta (1962) increased the number of coding categories to eighteen and redefined them so that they cut across the original twelve IPA categories.

Unfortunately, the increase in the number of categories does not make the coder's task any easier. The larger the list of categories the more difficult the coder's discrimination task becomes. However, this is true only if the coding categories are arranged linearly in a list, a practice that has been universally adopted in all extant coding schemes. The solution to this dilemma is to move from lists of juxtaposed categories to the kind of tree structure that was illustrated by the coding scheme presented in Fig. 4. In that case the coder has only a binary decision to make each time he arrives at a choice point. With such a structure the number of coding categories can be increased considerably without overloading the coder with more and more difficult decision problems. Moreover, the "tree" structure has a flexibility that is lacking in more conventional list structures. The addition of new categories does not disturb the existing arrangement of categories, and it can be performed at those points where the researcher's interests demand a greater subtlety of discrimination than the basic structure permits. This makes it possible to have the best of both worlds. The original tree structure provides a network of universal categories that makes possible the comparison of different research studies. At the same time, investigators with special interests can add new categories tailored to their particular purposes.

As an illustration of the use of the coding scheme of verbal exchange analysis some studies by E. R. Greenglass will be cited. The aim of these studies was the investigation of differences in mother–child communication patterns among first- and second-generation Italian immigrants and Canadians of Anglo-Saxon origin.

The main interest of these studies focused on patterns of parental control and on the matching of the verbal communication patterns of mother and child. Published work in this area converges in the claim that compared to North American parents, Italian parents are much stricter and authoritarian (Iacono, 1968; Pearlin and Kohn, 1966; Peterson and Migliorino, 1967). However, none of these claims is based on the direct analysis of actual interaction between parents and children. Even if these claims turn out to be correct they still require to be verified by direct observation. Moreover, there remains the question of how differences in parental power assertion express themselves in the style of interpersonal communication between parents and children.

The interest in the communication of parental control determined the choice of instigating conditions that would bring such communications into the open. Three tasks were selected that would potentially create conflicts between parents and children. How would parents deal with these conflicts? What patterns of control would they attempt to set up, and what attempts at counterinfluence by the children would they have to face?

In the first task, called the *object task*, mother and child were individually shown six objects (a teatowel, a potholder, a record, etc.) and asked to choose one to take home. Subsequently they were brought together and asked to come to a decision about which object they would actually take home.

In the *picture task* mother and child were separately shown eight photographs, each of which had four little stories attached to it. They then had to decide individually which story best fitted the photograph. They were then brought together, shown three pictures for which they had not chosen the same story, and asked to come to a joint decision about what was really the best story for each of the pictures.

In the *card task* mother and child were separately shown eight cards each of which showed three pictures that ostensibly told a story. They then had to choose the fourth picture that would complete the story. They were then brought together, shown three cards for which they had chosen different endings, and asked to agree on the picture that would constitute the one correct ending.

Comparative analysis of influence techniques used by Italian immigrant and Canadian mothers showed that the former were far more likely to make use of the "direct imperative" category, while the latter showed a distinct preference for the "justification" category (Greenglass, 1971a). The suggestion is that the Italian immigrant mother expects her child to follow her interpretations simply by virtue of her occupying the status of parent. On the other hand, the importance of "justifications" for Canadian mothers may derive from the fact that they had an average of ten years of formal schooling while the Italian mothers' formal schooling did not exceed four years. However, the combination of very limited formal education and transplantation to an alien environment renders Italian immigrant mothers quite dependent on their children who are much more at home in the new domicile. Hence we find that Italian mothers make relatively greater use of requests for orientation (Greenglass, 1971b). The overall effect of a communication pattern marked by direct imperatives and requests for orientation produces a pattern of close parent–child interdependence that does not have a counterpart in the nonimmigrant group. This may account for the fact that resistance to temptation in a cheating situation is significantly higher among immigrant Italian boys than among their Canadian age mates (Greenglass, 1972a).

Second-generation Italian mothers show communication patterns that deviate considerably from first-generation immigrants and approximate the native Canadian pattern rather more closely (Greenglass 1972b). These mothers tend to avoid the use of direct imperatives in favor of the indirect imperatives more characteristic of Canadian mothers. They also have less need to direct requests for orientation to their children, but their requests and provision of justification reach very high levels. In other words, they approximate the North American Canadian pattern rather closely and leave the first-generation immigrant pattern far behind.

These examples should serve to illustrate the scope of the scheme of verbal exchange analysis for the systematic comparative analysis of patterns of interpersonal communication. Needless to say, the potential applications of the scheme are not limited to the case of mother–child communications.

REFERENCES

Amidon, E. and Flanders, N. (1967). Interaction analysis as a feedback system. In E. J. Amidon and J. B. Hough (Eds.), *Interaction Analysis: Theory, Research and Application*. Reading, Mass.: Addison-Wesley.

Bales, R. F. (1950). *Interaction Process Analysis*. Cambridge, Mass.: Addison-Wesley.

Bee, H. L. (1967). Parent–child interaction and distractibility in 9-year-old children. *Merrill-Palmer Quart.*, **13**, 175–190.

Borgatta, E. F. (1962). A systematic study of interaction process scores, peer and self-assessments, personality and other variables. *Genet. psychol. Monogr.* **65**, 219–291.

Gellert, E. (1961). Stability and fluctuation in the power relationships of young children. *J. abnorm. & soc. Psychol.*, **62**, 8–15.

Greenglass, E. R. (1971a). A cross-cultural study of the child's communication with his mother. *Developmental Psychol.*, **5**, 494–499.

Greenglass, E. R. (1971b). A cross-cultural comparison of maternal communication. *Child Development*, **42**, 685–692.

Greenglass, E. R. (1972a). A cross-cultural study of the relationship between resistance to temptation and maternal communication. *Genet. psychol. Monogr.*, **86**, 119–139.

Greenglass, E. R. (1972b). A comparison of maternal communication style between immigrant Italian and second-generation Italian women living in Canada. *Journal of cross-cultural Psychol.*, **3**, 185–192.

Iacono, G. (1968). An affiliative society facing innovations. *J. soc. Issues*, **24**, 125–132.

Kogan, K. L. and Wimberger, H. C. (1966). An approach to defining mother–child interaction styles. *Percept. and motor Skills*, **23**, 1171–1177.

Kogan, K. L., Wimberger, H. C., and Bobbitt, R. A. (1969). Analysis of mother–child interaction in young mental retardates. *Child Development*, **40**, 799–812.

Leik, R. K. (1963). Instrumentality and emotionality in family interaction. *Sociometry*, **26**, 131–145.

Moustakas, C. E., Sigel, I. E., and Schalock, H. D. (1956). An objective method for the measurement and analysis of child–adult interaction. *Child Development*, **27**, 109–134.

Pearlin, L. I. and Kohn, M. L. (1966). Social class, occupation and parental values: A cross-national study. *Amer. Sociol. Rev.*, **31**, 466–479.

Peterson, D. R. and Migliorino, G. (1967). Pancultural factors of parental behavior in Sicily and the United States. *Child Development*, **38**, 967–991.

Watson, J. and Potter, R. J. (1962). An analytic unit for the study of interaction. *Hum. Relat.*, **15**, 245–263.

Waxler, N. E. and Mishler, E. G. (1966). Scoring and reliability problems in interaction process analysis: A methodological note. *Sociometry*, **29**, 28–40.

Wertheimer, M. and Scott, W. A. (1962). *Introduction to Psychological Research*. New York: Wiley.

Author Index

229

Subject Index

Address
  in interpersonal relations, 12, 16, 20, 79, 86, 129
  pronouns of, 45–47
  systems of, xvii, xviii, xx, 38–47, 54–55
Affect
  cultural influences on expression of, 170–172
  expression in families, 135–137
  reciprocal, 114
  verbalization of, 112–113, 115–116
Age relationship, 40, 41, 55
Alternation rules, 40
Attention
  claims, 96–97
  control, 129–130
  decentering of, 156
  demand for, 177
Attraction, 64
Audience, 31, 33, 34, 35
  effect on family interaction, 137
  See also Self-presentation; Social performance
Authority in institutions. *See* Bureaucratic institutions

Behavior modification. *See* Psychological control
Body contact, 61, 90
  cultural differences, 166

social class differences, 161
Body orientation, 62–63
Brainwashing, 8, 13
Bureaucratic institutions, 175–176, 181, 183, 191

Channels of communication, xvii, xx, 57, 58, 69, 84
  developmental difference in, 159
  interaction of, 65, 74–76, 78, 143–144
  social class differences in use of, 162–163
  See also Nonverbal signals
Coalition formation
  in families, 125, 129, 130
  in primates, 92–94, 98, 99
Coding, xviii, xix, xxi, 29, 40, 41, 53, 86
  elaborated and restricted, 162–164
  nonverbal messages, 57, 58, 62, 63, 71, 76–78
  scheme for analysis of utterances, xxi, 196–222
  See also Iconic signs; Representation
Communication competence, xvi, 152–157, 159
  and social class, 162–163, 172
Compliance, 8, 9, 11, 18
Confession, 8, 9, 12
Conflict, xx, xxi, 34, 193, 225–227
Cross-cultural data, xvii, 51, 164–172, 225–226

233